Monetary and Exchange Rate Systems

Monetary and Exchange Rate Systems

A Global View of Financial Crises

Edited by

Louis-Philippe Rochon

Assistant Professor of Economics, Laurentian University, Sudbury, Canada

and Sergio Rossi

Associate Professor of Economics, University of Fribourg, Switzerland

Edward Elgar
Cheltenham, UK • Northampton, MA, USA

Published by
Edward Elgar Publishing Limited
Glensanda House
Montpellier Parade
Cheltenham
Glos GL50 1UA
UK

Edward Elgar Publishing, Inc.
136 West Street
Suite 202
Northampton
Massachusetts 01060
USA

A catalogue record for this book
is available from the British Library

Library of Congress Cataloguing in Publication Data
Monetary and Exchange rate systems : a global view of financial crises / edited by
    Louis-Philippe Rochon and Sergio Rossi.
        p. cm.
    Includes bibliographical references and index.
    ISBN 1-84542-384-4
        1. Financial crises. 2. Foreign exchange rates. I. Rochon, Louis=Philippe.
    II. Rossi, Sergio, 1967-

    HB3722.M63 2006
332.4'5–dc22

                                                                                2005057708

ISBN-13: 978 1 84542 384 1
ISBN-10: 1 84542 384 4

Printed and bound in Great Britain by MPG Books Ltd, Bodmin, Cornwall

Contents

Figures

Tables

Contributors

Philip Arestis is University Director of Research, Cambridge Centre for Economics and Public Policy, Department of Land Economy, University of Cambridge, UK, and Professor of Economics at the Levy Economics Institute, New York, USA. He is also Visiting Professor, University of Leeds, UK, and School of Oriental and African Studies (SOAS), University of London, UK. His research interests are in the areas of macroeconomics, monetary economics, applied econometrics, political economy, and applied political economy. He has published as sole author or editor, as well as co-author and co-editor, a number of books, and has contributed in the form of invited chapters to numerous books, and produced research reports for research institutes. He has published widely in academic journals. His recent publications include papers in the *Journal of Money, Credit and Banking* (2001) and in *Economic Inquiry* (2004), and a book (with M. Baddeley and J. McCombie) entitled *The New Monetary Policy* (Palgrave, 2005).

Kok-Fay Chin is Lecturer in the Strategic Studies and International Relations Programme, Faculty of Social Sciences and Humanities, National University of Malaysia. His main research interests are on finance and development, international financial reform, financial globalisation and national security, and financial and monetary regionalism. He has recently co-authored *Malaysian 'Bail Outs'? Capital Controls, Restructuring and Recovery* (Singapore University Press, 2005). He is currently working on a country study on Malaysia's experience in managing external debt for the UNCTAD's project on 'Capacity building for debt sustainability in developing countries'.

Eugenia Correa is Professor of Economics at the Mexico National University, Mexico, where she teaches on finance and development. She has a PhD degree from the Mexico National University, and is a member of the Mexican Science Academy and of the National Research System. Her research interests are in the areas of macroeconomic financial policy and financial systems. She is the author of *Deregulation and Financial Crisis*

(Siglo XXI, 1998), and co-editor of *Banks in Mexico: Crisis and Future* (Miguel Angel Porrua, 2002, with Alicia Girón), *Contemporary Financial Economy* (Miguel Angel Porrua, 2004, four volumes, with Alicia Girón), and *Financial Consequences of the Globalization* (Miguel Angel Porrua, 2005, with Alicia Girón). She has also published a number of articles on financial issues in the *Review Comercio Exterior, Información Comercial Española* and *Revue internationale des sciences sociales*.

Paul Davidson is Emeritus Professor of Economics at the University of Tennessee, US, and Visiting Scholar in the Bernard Schwartz Center for Economic Policy Analysis at the New School for Social Research, New York. His main research interests are in the area of international finance and economic growth. He has published a considerable number of articles and books, the latest of which is entitled *Financial Markets, Money and the Real World* (Edward Elgar, 2002). He has also contributed several chapters in edited books, among which recently: 'Uncertainty and monetary policy', in P. Mooslechner et al. (eds), *Economic Policy Making under Uncertainty* (Edward Elgar, 2004); 'The effect of ending hostilities on output and employment', in *Encyclopedia of Life Support Systems* (UNESCO, 2004).

Jesús Ferreiro is Reader in Economics at the University of the Basque Country in Bilbao (Spain). He has a PhD degree from the University of the Basque Country. His research interests are in the areas of macroeconomic policy, incomes policy, labour market, and foreign direct investments. His most recent publications about these topics include papers in journals like *International Review of Applied Economics* (2001), *International Papers in Political Economy* (2001), *Problemas del Desarrollo* (2001), *Revista del Ministerio de Trabajo y Asuntos Sociales* (2003, 2004), *Ekonomiaz* (2004), and *Journal of Post Keynesian Economics* (2004), among others. He is also the co-editor of the book *Financial Developments in National and International Markets*, published by Palgrave Macmillan (2005).

Claude Gnos is Associate Professor of Economics at the University of Burgundy in Dijon, France, and Director of the *Centre d'Études Monétaires et Financières* therein. He is the author of *L'euro* (Éditions Management et Société, 1998) and *Les grands auteurs en économie* (Éditions Management et Société, 2000), and co-editor (with L.-P. Rochon) of *Post Keynesian Principles of Economic Policy* (Edward Elgar, forthcoming) and *The Keynesian Multiplier* (Routledge, forthcoming). He has also published a number of articles on monetary economics and on the history of economic thought in edited books and in refereed journals such as *Économie Appliquée*, *International Journal of Political Economy*, *Journal of Post Keynesian Economics*, and the *Review of Political Economy*.

Carmen Gómez is Lecturer in Economics at the University of the Basque Country in Bilbao (Spain). She has a PhD degree from the University of the Basque Country. Her research interests are in the areas of foreign direct investments and labour market. She is the author of several papers and chapters of books on these subjects. Her most recent publications about these topics include papers in journals like *Boletín Economico de ICE* (2003, 2004), *Relaciones Internacionales* (2003), *Problemas del Desarrollo* (2004), *Revista del Ministerio de Trabajo y Asuntos Sociales* (2004), and *Ekonomiaz* (2004). She has also co-authored a chapter in the book *Financial Developments in National and International Markets*, published by Palgrave Macmillan (2005).

Jesper Jespersen is Professor of Economics in the Faculty of Social Sciences at Roskilde University, Denmark. He has a PhD degree from the European University Institute, Florence, Italy. His main research interests are related to macroeconomic theory and methodology, history of economic thought, and environmental economics. He has published many books as author and editor, and also contributed chapters in edited books. Among his recent publications are: 'The Maastricht Treaty: unemployment, competitiveness and distribution', in S.C. Dow and J. Hillard (eds), *Keynes, Uncertainty and the Global Economy* (Edward Elgar, 2002); 'Why do macroeconomists disagree on the consequences of the euro?', in P. Arestis et al. (eds), *Money, Macroeconomics and Keynes* (Routledge, 2002); 'The Stability Pact: a macroeconomic straitjacket!', in J. Ljungberg (ed.), *The Price of the Euro* (Palgrave Macmillan, 2004).

Jean-François Ponsot is Assistant Professor of Economics at Université Pierre Mendès-France, in Grenoble, France. At the time of writing his contribution to this book, he was Assistant Professor of Economics at Laurentian University, Canada. He has also spent four months as a Research Fellow at the central bank in Ecuador in 2004. His research interests include the political economy of monetary regimes – more particularly currency boards and dollarization – in a historical perspective, and Keynes's thought. He has recently published a number of articles related to these issues in the *History of Political Economy, International Journal of Political Economy, Revue d'économie financière*, and *Techniques financières et développement*.

Louis-Philippe Rochon is Assistant Professor of Economics at Laurentian University, Canada. He has written more than 50 articles on endogenous money and its historical roots, post-Keynesian economics, the monetary circuit, and macroeconomics. He is also the author or editor of 14 books (including some currently in production), among which: *Money, Credit and Production: An Alternative Post-Keynesian Approach* (Edward Elgar, 1999), *Credit, Interest Rates and the Open Economy: Essays on Horizontalism* (Edward Elgar, 2001, co-edited with Matias Vernengo), *Théories monétaires post keynésiennes* (Economica, 2003, co-edited with Pierre Piégay), *Modern Theories of Money: The Nature and Role of Money in Capitalist Economies* (Edward Elgar, 2003, co-edited with Sergio Rossi), *Dollarization: Lessons from Europe and the Americas* (Routledge, 2003, co-edited with Mario Seccareccia), *Post Keynesian Principles of Economic Policy* (Edward Elgar, forthcoming, co-edited with Claude Gnos). His recent research focuses on inflation targeting, the New Consensus, and central banking. He is currently working on a book with Sergio Rossi on the endogeneity of money and its historical roots.

Sergio Rossi is Associate Professor of Economics at the University of Fribourg, Switzerland. He is also Senior Lecturer in Economics at the University of Lugano, Switzerland, and a member of the Research Laboratory of Monetary Economics at the Centre for Banking Studies, Lugano, Switzerland. He has a DPhil degree from the University of Fribourg, Switzerland, and a PhD degree from the University of London (University College). His recent publications include: *Money and Inflation: A New Macroeconomic Analysis* (Edward Elgar, 2001, reprinted 2003), *Modern Theories of Money: The Nature and Role of Money in Capitalist Economies* (Edward Elgar, 2003, co-edited with Louis-Philippe Rochon), *Money and Payments in Theory and Practice* (Routledge, forthcoming). He has also published several articles on monetary and public sector economics in the *International Journal of Political Economy, International Review of Applied Economics, Journal of Asian Economics, Journal of Post Keynesian Economics, Public Choice, Review of Political Economy, Studi Economici,* and in the *Swiss Journal of Economics and Statistics.*

Andrea Terzi is a Professor of Economics at Franklin College Switzerland, and also teaches Monetary Economics at the Università Cattolica del Sacro Cuore, Milan, Italy. His current research interests include international financial instability, deficit spending and interest rates, and the relationship between stock market prices and interest rates. He is the author of *La moneta* (il Mulino, 2002), and of several articles among which: 'Is a transactions tax an effective means to stabilize the foreign exchange market?' (*Banca Nazionale del Lavoro Quarterly Review*, 2003), 'Animal spirits' (*International Encyclopedia of Political Economy*, Routledge, 1999), and 'Financial market behavior: rational, irrational, or conventionally consistent?', in P. Davidson and J.A. Kregel (eds), *Full Employment and Price Stability in a Global Economy* (Edward Elgar, 1999).

Domenica Tropeano is Researcher in the Department of Economics at the University of Macerata, Italy, where she teaches a course on monetary and financial markets. She has a PhD degree from the European University Institute, Florence, Italy. She has published a number of papers in the areas of monetary economics and history of economic thought. Her present research interests concern liberalization policies in emerging economies, particularly financial liberalization, on which she has published a book (Carocci, 2001) and an article in *Economia Politica* (forthcoming). She is presently working within a research group funded by the Italian Ministry of the University on 'Globalization, income distribution, and growth'.

Gregorio Vidal is Professor of Economics at the Metropolitan University–Mexico City, Mexico. He has a PhD degree from the Mexico National University, and is a member of the Mexican Science Academy and of the National Research System. His research interests are in the areas of macroeconomic policy, enterprises and entrepreneurs, and foreign direct investments. He has published a number of papers on these subjects in refereed international journals and several chapters in edited books. He is the author of *Privatizations, fusions and acquisitions: The largest corporations in Latin America* (Anthropos, 2001), 'Main results of the privatizations of basic services in Latin America' (*Claves de la Economía Mundial*, 2004), 'Foreign direct investment and outsourcing in developing countries: Mexico' (*Review Economiaz*, 2005).

L. Randall Wray is Professor of Economics at the University of Missouri–Kansas City (UMKC) as well as Research Director at the Center for Full Employment and Price Stability, at UMKC, and Senior Scholar at the Levy Economics Institute of Bard College, New York. He has a PhD degree from Washington University in St. Louis. His research interests are in monetary theory and policy, macroeconomics, financial instability, and employment policy. He is the author of *Money and Credit in Capitalist Economies* (Edward Elgar, 1990) and *Understanding Modern Money: The Key to Full*

Employment and Price Stability (Edward Elgar, 1998). He is the editor of *Credit and State Theories of Money* (Edward Elgar, 2004) and co-editor of *Contemporary Post Keynesian Analysis* (Edward Elgar, 2005). He is also the author of numerous scholarly articles in edited books and academic journals, including the *Cambridge Journal of Economics, Eastern Economic Journal, Economic and Labour Relations Review, Economie Appliquée, Journal of Economic Issues, Journal of Post Keynesian Economics*, and the *Review of Political Economy*.

Acknowledgements

The editors would like to thank all the contributors to this book. They also wish to express their gratitude to Edward Elgar and all his collaborators in Camberley and Cheltenham for their enthusiastic and professional support during the development of the book. Finally, they also are grateful to Dante Caprara for his excellent research assistance and to Denise Converso–Grangier for her tireless efforts in preparing the whole typescript in camera-ready form.

L.-P.R.
S.R.

Introduction

Louis-Philippe Rochon and Sergio Rossi

The financial crises that occurred since the early 1990s have gathered public and the specialists' attention. Unprecedented capital flow reversals, contagion reaching distant countries, as well as the size, the geographic extension, and the social costs of the crises have surprised the international community. The questions concerning the causes of these crises, the best ways of dealing with them, the possible externality effects of financial turmoil, and finally some new proposals for reforming the current international monetary and financial architecture have mobilized politicians, and stimulated academic debate.

The major characteristics of the recent financial crises can be summarized in five points:

1. the source of the crisis was to be found in emerging market economies;
2. the dimension of the crisis was widespread;
3. the capital engaged was mainly short-term, foreign, and private;
4. reversals in the capital account were extremely rapid; and
5. the virulence of these crises was eventually much more intense than one could have expected.

Further, contrary to the crises that occurred in the 1980s, in the 1990s many of the economies affected by a crisis were considered as good pupils, or even as star performers.

Most of the financial crises that came about since the early 1990s can be described as multiple (or 'twin') crises, with some of the banking, currency, or debt crisis characteristics dominating at some particular stage of the crisis. The typical sequence (observed most clearly during the East Asian crisis) was that of a currency collapse, provoking or simply revealing banking system problems, and eventually leading to serious disturbances in domestic credit flows and to an important contraction of capital formation.

In light of these recent financial crises, many economists have questioned the wisdom of unfettered capital movements. Indeed, since the push for deregulation and liberalized markets in the 1980s and 1990s, particularly the push for increased and intensified capital flows, as is embedded also in the Washington Consensus, the distribution of economic benefits has been at best unbalanced, with emerging countries still struggling to attain sustained levels of economic growth. The international financial system has had to adapt to the increasing role of private capital flows. This process was evident in the shift towards flexible exchange rates among the major currencies some 30 years ago, rightly or wrongly, and it continues today, as we absorb and react to the lessons of the emerging country crises of the last decade. The evolving system poses several challenges.

In the realm of exchange rate arrangements, flexible rates have proven as destabilizing as the regimes that they sought to replace. Free (dirty) float or intermediate regimes such as a crawling peg are likely to provoke financial instability, particularly in emerging or transition economies undergoing rapid liberalization of capital flows vis-à-vis the rest of the world. In most of these countries this contrasts with a limited ability of the banking sector to manage financial flows. Further, in general the banking system of these countries lacks experience in creditworthiness assessment, which may lead banks to over-lend to potentially default borrowers, with an ensuing risk of financial turmoil and breakdown. Also, transition economies often suffer from their central bank's poor management of banking supervision, in so far as it does not meet international standards on accounting, capital adequacy, insolvency, effective prudential supervision, and avoidance of moral hazard problems. Currency boards and dollarization have also not proven to be as successful as they once promised (Rochon and Rossi, 2003a). In fact, fixed exchange rates, hard pegs, and currency boards entail the risk of inflexibility, and may result in costs for a country if it is likely to face asymmetric shocks in respect of the currency area to which its currency is anchored. In this respect, it appears that capital controls have somehow been successful, although largely discredited. Argentina is a case in point.

Monetary and exchange rate strategies are notably also a matter of concern for countries seeking to build, or to participate in, a regional monetary union. The recent EU enlargement to the South-East is a case in point. In the setting up of their monetary relations with the euro area, new EU countries need to consider the exchange rate strategy that better suits their development needs as transition economies, but also that allows them to converge in nominal as well as real terms, to integrate the euro-area economy without putting at stake financial stability and socio-economic cohesion across borders (Rossi, 2004).

The various projects of regional economic integration in Asia, or in parts of it, deserve also the attention of monetary macroeconomists. For instance, a regional monetary arrangement for the member countries of the Association of South-East Asian Nations (ASEAN) does not seem to be possible along the path that indeed led to the European single currency: political as well as economic divergences – more intensive than within the European Union (EU) – point to the necessity to search for alternative strategies for Asian monetary integration than the making of the euro. In particular, rapid liberalization of capital flows in emerging market economies might prove to be incompatible with exchange rate stability, not to say with exchange rate fixity and adoption of a single currency.

As regards the management of financial crisis over the last 15 years or so, several points can be noted. First, the amount of international commitments and disbursements was unprecedented. Looking at the support programmes of the International Monetary Fund (IMF), the financial aid exceeded 400 per cent of a country's quota, reaching in some cases more than 2000 per cent (it reached 1939 per cent in South Korea in 1997, and 2548 per cent in Turkey in 2002). Secondly, in several cases the lending process involved not only the IMF but also a number of multilateral and bilateral ('second line defence') agreements that represented up to four times the amount of IMF's credit lines. Even with this significant aid, however, the socio-economic costs of the crisis could not be avoided. These costs mostly occurred in terms of output losses (owing to misallocation and under-utilisation of resources), which aggravated the rates of unemployment in the countries hit by the crisis.

Now, as the IMF and World Bank are making liberalization a component for successful aid from the international community, we need to ask whether the world as a whole is heading increasingly towards instability as well as destabilization. In this respect, a deeper and more comprehensive reform of the international financial and monetary system ought to be a priority. If this is the case, how should this reform proceed and what should it look like? *The Meltzer Report* that the US Congress solicited at the end of 1998 might be a first step towards a thorough reconsideration of the role of the institutions set up in Bretton Woods in 1944 (see Meltzer, 2000).

First and foremost, the role of the IMF in financial crisis situations should be reconsidered afresh. As an IMF official put it, the Fund was 'surprised by the speed and virulence [of the financial crises in Asia, and] had not kept up with the rapid developments in international capital markets' (Dawson, 2002, Internet). Secondly, since the end of the Bretton Woods era the IMF has been intruding more and more into the traditional area of intervention of the World Bank, which gave rise to institutional overlapping and mismatch. Thirdly, as Kenen (2002) notes, the IMF has been forcing countries to pursue orthodox policies under conditions that would have required unorthodox solutions.

Now, at the institutional level, solutions might consist in establishing:

a) an international lender of last resort on a different basis than what Meltzer (2000) suggests, namely, as a central bank of national central banks, or at least in the form of a supranational settlement institution for international transactions (Rossi, 2005);[1]
b) an international regulator agency with sanction powers;
c) an international deposit insurance; or
d) a standing committee for global financial regulation.

The present situation and new potential threats resulting from the most recent financial crises may also encourage efforts in order to supplement the current international, post-Bretton Woods 'non-system' (unable to cope efficiently with increased volatility and instability of exchange rates and financial flows) with a more coherent international financial architecture involving substantial changes in the realm of exchange rate and capital account regimes (Davidson, 2002).

This book is intended as a contribution to the current debate in this area. It brings together a number of well-known scholars from different horizons and with different approaches to the subject matter, who offer their views on the causes and consequences of financial crises. It also intends to provide some original solutions on how to restructure the financial system, national as well as international, and on how to avoid these crises in the future.

THE CONTRIBUTIONS

The book is divided into two parts.

The first part is devoted to the analysis of both financial liberalization and financial crises episodes. Chapter 1, written by Andrea Terzi, addresses the problem of international payments in an environment of diverse currencies in a world economy that is not truly globalized. As Terzi notes, this is a problem that, to date, has not yet been considered enough in debate on financial crises. One has indeed a more comprehensive view, and understanding, of the latter crises if one puts the international settlement issues in the right perspective. First of all, Terzi reviews how economists have answered the main question of what causes international financial crises and what can be done in order to prevent them from happening. He then explores some of the questions raised by the existence of a hierarchy of currencies in the current world economy.

His analysis leads him to conclude that there are only a limited number of options left if we want to prevent financial crises from happening again. In order of effectiveness (from the bottom to the top) there is: dollarization (on condition that the United States indeed agrees on taking responsibility for the world monetary matters); currency blocs; supranational currencies or a single world currency (on condition that countries can politically cooperate in their co-management of monetary matters); and the 'bancor' solution proposed by Keynes in the 1940s (on condition that the political willingness of countries overcomes the resistance of the existing, yet precarious, regime).

In the second chapter, Jean-François Ponsot explores dollarization and the hegemonic status of the dollar in the existing international monetary regime, which has been strongly questioned recently owing to depreciation of the US currency in foreign exchange markets and the growing twin deficits of the US economy. According to Ponsot, despite these obvious signs of weakness the US dollar retains its power, and is still the leading international currency. He explains the superiority of the US dollar given its continued use by the general government sector, and as a primary currency for financing and investment on global capital markets, not to mention that the dollar is still the leading currency in international trade in the private sector. In this context, Ponsot views the rise of dollarization as the most revealing sign of the actual power of the US dollar. This leads him to explore the United States' attitude towards dollarization, and to conclude that the United States will likely adopt a less passive attitude when the euro overcomes the US dollar's supremacy as an international currency.

The third chapter, contributed by Eugenia Correa and Gregorio Vidal, is a detailed survey of those reforms in banking and financial systems that Latin American countries have been experiencing over the last 30 years. All these events have deeply changed markets and institutions, as well as monetary and fiscal policies in Latin America. The authors show that, in spite of these deep transformations, the obstacles to financing the economic development of that region have not been surmounted. On the contrary, gross capital formation in Latin America has either fallen or stagnated, and the number of firms issuing equity on the stock markets has decreased rather than increased. In fact, the financial reforms in Latin America have not helped finance the expansion of investment and productive capacity. Today, local and central governments, firms, and households are suffering from overindebtedness. Correa and Vidal argue that financial bankruptcies, debt moratoria, and economic crises are the direct result of deregulated financial markets in developing countries.

Chapter 4, written by Kok-Fay Chin, explores the Asian financial crises of the 1990s and elaborates on the various attempts to provide monetary and financial cooperation in East Asia since then. Monetary cooperation ranges from steps to enhance regional financial surveillance and policy dialogue or swap arrangements, to more intensive forms of monetary regionalism such as exchange rate coordination (including regional basket pegs or a regionally-harmonized exchange rate band), to full monetary integration incorporating a single currency and a common monetary policy. Financial cooperation can be subsumed under the policy measures facilitating cross-border financial flows by removing frictions and obstacles. It ranges from the creation of a regional bond fund to more intensive cooperation, such as multilateral agreements on regional financial standards and prudential measures, cross-trading of some financial instruments in various national markets, as well as facilitating intra-regional payments and settlements. Chin shows that each of these different forms of cooperation carries its own calculus of potential costs and benefits. He notably points out that how monetary and financial cooperation will take place ultimately also depends on the prevailing regional and global political-economy factors, which impinge on the degree of cooperation.

The contribution of Domenica Tropeano, in Chapter 5, asks if financial liberalization reduces the cost of capital and leads to an increase in both firms output and productivity as neoclassical theory argues. In order to explain why empirical evidence contradicts most propositions of the neoclassical theory about the effects of financial liberalization, she reviews different approaches of the transmission channel from financial liberalization to the distribution of income. She argues that the increase in investment and saving, and in output growth, resulting from improved efficiency does not often materialize in the real world. Although there is a broad consensus on the mostly disappointing results of financial liberalization policies, no agreement exists so far on the possible explanations of these failures. From a post-Keynesian perspective, Tropeano is able to show that financial liberalization worsens the distribution of income. She notably points out that the increase in savings, as a result of financial liberalization, creates a lack of effective demand, excess capacity, and falling profits.

Chapter 6, written by Louis-Philippe Rochon, explores and discusses the reasons for the failure of the Washington Consensus, in both its original and 'augmented' forms. The approach based on this consensus considers notably fiscal discipline, financial liberalization, deregulation, and privatization as the 'prêt-à-porter' macroeconomic policy for any market-based economy around the world and at any time. The underlying argument here is that in the age of globalization, the only possible solution to avoiding a crisis is to open goods and financial markets, including the domestic banking and financial systems, to market-friendly policies. In his analysis, Rochon focuses on two specific issues: the need to guarantee long-term financing of domestic investment, and the role of foreign direct investment and capital controls in developing economies. Noting that in several developing countries the domestic banking system is largely within the hands of foreign interests, Rochon points out that in a number of developing and emerging economies the increased presence of foreign banks contributes to generating financial instability, and also leads to the disruption of local credit markets. As a matter of fact, foreign banks are inclined to lend only to the more profitable industries and borrowers, leaving the more risky borrowers to local banks. Further, Rochon also points out that there is a need to regulate international capital flows, to avoid the depressive effects that these movements of financial capital can have on the economies of developing countries, particularly in the case of capital outflows when the central bank raises the policy controlled rate of interest in order to prevent the exchange rate of the local currency from depreciating. As Rochon observes, however, the detailed structure of the new international financial architecture that should avoid these negative effects remains to be clarified.

The second part moves from financial instability to macroeconomic performance, and aims indeed at clarifying and elaborating on a number of different solutions to avoid both currency turmoil and financial crises in the future. Chapter 7, written by Claude Gnos, opens this part and explains the setting within which the following contributions will consider one or the other issue that this setting raises. As Gnos points out, the structural reform of the international monetary system that Keynes sketched out at the Bretton Woods Conference in 1944 was rejected by conference delegates, because, in monetary macroeconomics probably more than elsewhere, escaping from habitual modes of thought seems to be very difficult today as it was in the past. In Gnos's view, it is this sort of difficulty that still besets proposals for reform of the international settlement system that consider the bookkeeping nature of modern money as their analytical starting point. Indeed, although money has been dematerialized and its linkage to any physical yardstick has been abandoned (at least since the early 1970s), most economists as well as the general public still think of it as a thing that is somehow comparable to real goods and assets. In this regard, they believe, as do a host of national and international authorities, that the unrestricted operation of markets is able to provide solutions to any economic problem that might arise, in the financial and monetary sphere as well as in the realm of production and exchange.

In Chapter 8, Philip Arestis, Jesús Ferreiro and Carmen Gómez focus extensively on free international capital mobility. They take the view that untrammelled international capital mobility does not free up capital flows in such a way as to encourage large-scale lending from rich and developed countries to poor, developing countries. Their basic argument is that lifting capital controls does not help the world's poor; it actually hurts them. Their argument is based on the international financial experience of the world from 1960 to 2004. This period may be conveniently split into two sub-periods: 1960–85 and 1985–2004. The former period may be characterized as one where capital controls were in place, while the latter period has been one of lifting controls. Three reasons were suggested for removing capital controls: the resulting capital flows would directly boost production and productivity in developing countries; developing countries' firms and populations would enjoy the benefits that were expected to flow from technical advances and from learning-by-doing in using them; and capital account liberalization will help reduce corruption and improve the quality of government in developing countries. In fact, exactly the opposite occurred over the period 1985–2004: developed countries have not invested in developing countries, with the latter often investing in developed countries. As a result, financial capital has flown in the opposite way that it had been expected. This increased substantially the vulnerability of developing countries with free capital mobility to financial crises. Arestis, Ferreiro and Gómez conclude by emphasizing the role of capital controls in financial crises, and suggest that they are necessary both in terms of preventing these crises and in terms of mitigating them.

The discussion of liberalization versus regulation of international capital flows is also the focus of Chapter 9, contributed by Paul Davidson. This chapter shows that how one interprets financial market activity and chooses a policy stance regarding either liberalization or regulation of financial markets depends on the underlying economic theory that one explicitly, or implicitly, uses in order to explain the role of financial markets in a monetary economy of production. In this respect, there are two major alternative theories: (1) the neoclassical efficient market theory, and (2) Keynes's liquidity preference theory. Each theory produces a different set of policy prescriptions: while the former theory suggests liberalization is a desirable social objective, the latter theory suggests the need for an understandable, publically known set of rules and regulations. By showing that, in the real world, financial markets do not necessarily produce an efficient allocation of capital resources, Davidson can argue that there is an important role for some degree of international capital flow regulation for the global economy of the twenty-first century. In light of Keynes's liquidity preference analysis, Davidson gives some suggestions for reforming the international payments mechanism, particularly under the aegis of an international clearing union that provides for capital controls.

Chapter 10, written by Sergio Rossi, critically expands on the Keynes–Davidson plan. It focuses on the need for a structural monetary reform of the international payment system along the lines that Keynes put forward at the Bretton Woods Conference, which, once refined, ought to avoid the occurrence of further currency crises and their negative effects on the real economy. Rossi also aims to show that the alleged inconsistency between full international capital mobility, monetary policy autonomy, and stable – although not fixed – exchange rates could eventually be disposed of, if the Keynes–Davidson scheme for a new world monetary order is developed considering the financial issues in concert with the monetary ones. Considering the performance of, and the challenges for, the contemporary international economy, with respect to monetary as well as financial instability, Rossi elaborates on a proposal showing in particular how a structurally-improved international monetary architecture could be set up to avoid the disruptive effects that currency crises can have on our economic systems. He notably illustrates the main benefits of the proposed architecture, and discusses some of the objections that might be raised against it.

The eleventh chapter is written by L. Randall Wray and considers the issue of the choice of an exchange rate regime, between free float and fixity. Wray sets out the different views on money, national as well as international, that have been put to the fore in the history of monetary thought. He contrasts the traditional view of money with what he dubs the neo-chartalist view. In the traditional, orthodox view, money is considered primarily as a means of payment that facilitates the circulation of goods either domestically or internationally. In the neo-chartalist view, money is seen first and foremost as a unit of account. Wray then analyses the implications for the international financial system that result from these different views on money, stressing in particular the pros and cons of flexible and fixed exchange rate arrangements in light of the different standpoints on money's role. He assimilates the fixed rate view with the Keynes–Davidson scheme, and argues that this view puts too important a weight on flexible exchange rate regimes to explain instability and financial crises. On these grounds, he puts to the fore an alternative plan, which is based on a synthesis of the endogenous money–exogenous interest rate approach plus the state money–chartalist approach.[2] In his view, the best of the practically feasible alternatives is a floating exchange rate regime with a sovereign-issued currency and independent fiscal and monetary policy. This allows a nation to exogenously set its overnight rate as desired, and to pursue fiscal policy directed toward achieving full employment.

In the last chapter of this book, Jesper Jesperen analyses existing exchange rate regimes with respect to the May 2004 enlargement of the EU. Jespersen first provides a brief overview of two distinct and competing macroeconomic theories, namely, the so-called new consensus macroeconomics (which is a merger of neoclassical and new-Keynesian equilibrium economics), and post-Keynesian macroeconomics. He then evaluates all the different monetary and exchange rate arrangements and balance-of-payments constraints within the EU from a post-Keynesian stance, before discussing how the exchange rate arrangements existing today within the EU fit the overall growth strategy of its new member countries. His conclusion is that these new member countries should be allowed to follow an individually-adapted exchange rate strategy, which should allow for the differences among these countries and the fragile structures of their transition economies.

NOTES

1. The concept of a lender of last resort can be traced back to Bagehot (1873), who noted all the requirements for such an institution to avoid bank runs and crisis in a closed economy. These requirements implied that: a) short-term loans should be granted to all banks in trouble, but only if these banks are creditworthy; b) these loans are collateralized; c) the relevant interest rate has to be fixed above market rates, to limit moral hazard risks. See Goodhart and Illing (2002) for elaboration.
2. See Rochon and Rossi (2003b).

REFERENCES

Bagehot, W. (1873), *Lombard Street: A Description of the Money Market*, London: Henry S. King & Co, third edition.

Davidson, P. (2002), *Financial Markets, Money and the Real World*, Cheltenham, UK and Northampton, MA, USA: Edward Elgar.

Dawson, T.C. (2002), 'The IMF's role in Asia: part of the problem or part of the solution?', paper prepared for remarks at the Institute of Policy Studies and Singapore Management University Forum, Singapore, 10 July, available at http://www.imf.org/external/np/speeches/2002/071002.htm.

Goodhart, C.A.E. and G. Illing (2002), *Financial Crises, Contagion, and the Lender of Last Resort: A Reader*, Oxford: Oxford University Press.

Kenen, P.B. (2002), 'Currencies, crises and crashes', *Eastern Economic Journal*, **28** (1), 1–12.

Meltzer A.H. (2000), *The Meltzer Report*, Washington, DC: House of Representatives, available at http://www.house.gov/jec/imf/meltzer.pdf.

Rochon, L.-P. and S. Rossi (2003a), 'Dollarization out, euroization in', *International Journal of Political Economy*, **33** (1), 21–41.

Rochon, L.-P. and S. Rossi (2003b), 'Introduction', in L.-P. Rochon and S. Rossi (eds), *Modern Theories of Money: The Nature and Role of Money in Capitalist Economies*, Cheltenham, UK and Northampton, MA, USA: Edward Elgar, xx–lvi.

Rossi, S. (2004), 'Monetary integration strategies and perspectives of new EU

countries', *International Review of Applied Economics*, **18** (4), 443–69.
Rossi, S. (2005), 'The Bretton Woods institutions sixty years later: a "glocal" reform proposal', in P. Arestis, J. Ferreiro and F. Serrano (eds), *Financial Developments in National and International Markets*, Basingstoke: Palgrave Macmillan, 56–76.

PART ONE

Financial Liberalization and Financial Crises

1. International Financial Instability in a World of Currencies Hierarchy

Andrea Terzi

INTRODUCTION

Financial instability is a long-known characteristic of market economies, but an intermittent subject of economists' empirical and theoretical investigation. In the three decades following the Second World War, the relative tranquillity of financial markets seemed to validate the view that financial crises are rare episodes. Consequently, research in this field was given lower priority. Minsky (1975, p. 16) was well aware of how, at any given time, current developments concur in shaping the dominant paradigm, when he wrote:

> Economics and other sciences whose data are generated by history are not like the experimental natural sciences with respect to anomalous observations.... In economics if history over a thirty-year period does not cast up observations with at least a family resemblance to a financial panic or a deep depression, then arguments to the effect that these anomalies are myths, or that what happened can be explained by measurement errors, human (policy) errors, or transitory institutional flaws which have since been corrected, may be put forth and gain acceptance.

The post-World War II period was also the time when the long-run money neutrality paradigm was shared by both Keynesians and monetarists: in good, classical tradition, the belief was that monetary affairs are a reflection of underlying, real phenomena, and that money matters only in the short run. Notable exceptions were seen, however, in the works of Harrod and Kaldor, the critique to money neutrality by Davidson (1972), the contributions to financial instability by Minsky – drawing from both Keynes and Fisher – and by Kindleberger (1978) – himself deeply influenced by Minsky.

After a period during which research on the problem of financial crises was never a top agenda item, the 1990s have witnessed a remarkable surge of interest in this field. The compelling factor behind this resurgence has been the more frequent occurrence of episodes of financial turbulence at the domestic as well as at the international levels: in the past 30 years, financial crises have become a major source of disruption in the growth path of several countries and of the world economy as a whole. Hence, what had been a distinctive concern of a minority of researchers became a primary concern for a broader group of economists, who approached the problem from a variety of angles. Not surprisingly, their efforts have produced an array of competing policy recommendations.

This chapter contends that this debate has not yet fully explored one of these angles, that is to say, the problem raised by international payments in an environment of diverse currencies in a world economy that, as Arestis et al. (2005) put it, is not truly globalized. Once this dimension of the problem is put into full perspective, one has a better view of the quality of the standing proposals.

This chapter has two main sections and a short conclusion. The following section reviews how economists have answered the questions: what causes international financial crises, and what can be done to prevent them from happening again? The third section explores the questions raised by the existence of a currency hierarchy in the world economy and its impact on international settlements. The aim here is to provide a criterion by which one could recognize the effective power of the different proposals. It is suggested that only a limited set of effective, though conditional, actions can stabilize international finance, including dollarization, the creation of a single world currency, or a major international reform of international settlements along the lines of Keynes's 'bancor' proposal.

DIVERSE VIEWS AND A GLUT OF PROPOSALS

The accumulation of empirical evidence offered by major financial crises in the 1990s was the primary catalyst behind the renewed efforts to understand the causes and cures of international financial instability. The sequence of episodes is too well-known not to sound like a nursery rhyme by now: the European Exchange Rate Mechanism (ERM) crisis, the Tequila crisis, the East Asian crisis, the Russia–Long Term Capital Management crisis, the Brazilian crisis, and so on. This succession of events was responsible for a flourishing of articles on the subject, whose main aim was to investigate whether these episodes epitomized an increasing financial fragility in the global economy (a new growing problem in international finance and something that economists were not ready to explain, assess, and counter).

It would seem that the words of Minsky were vindicated: the illusion that financial crises are rare episodes that can be explained as exceptional events caused by errors or transitory flaws had, at least for a while, gone. Indeed, the frequency, the size, the geographic extension, and the social costs of financial crises in the last quarter-century have made the topic a global policy issue.

Most of the efforts in this strand of research went in two directions. One aimed to empirically explore the seriousness of the problem and to show how current instability compares with historical experience, although the causes of the recent resurgence of financial instability are still debated. The other attempted to model financial crises, and proved to be more problematic, as models often seem much more powerful in explaining the last crisis rather than the next.

After a little taxonomy, this section reviews the major empirical findings and theoretical points on this topic, and concludes with a critical review of policy recommendations.

A Little Taxonomy on Crises

This section offers the necessary clarification of the meanings of a variety of terms normally used in the debate on financial crises.

Though defined somewhat differently and sometimes loosely in the literature, a working definition of '(systemic) *financial crisis*' should designate a state of affairs where a drop in the value of assets and/or a rise in the value of liabilities cause a serious impairment of the balance sheets (and thus on the net worth) of a sufficient number of economic units, severe enough to induce negative repercussions on aggregate real activity. A crisis is systemic when it causes distress to a variety of economic units, independently of their initial financial strength or of their 'share of responsibility' (their being 'innocent' or 'guilty') in causing the crisis.

By contrast, a financial crisis in the balance sheet of a *single* economic unit (not big enough to spread its effects significantly) remains contained and is resolved locally, without becoming 'systemic'. This latter case is not of our interest here, and every subsequent reference to 'crisis' should be understood as referring to a 'systemic' crisis.

There is, however, a special case of one single defaulted entity that may have systemic repercussions, and this is the case of the sovereign state. This is referred to as a *sovereign debt crisis*, when government-backed debt obligations are defaulted or rescheduled. The financial strain caused by a sovereign debt crisis depends on its relative size and how it impacts other economic entities' net worth, and thus it may or may not cause a financial crisis.

A *financial market crisis*, a case of asset deflation, is a collapse of the market price of financial assets. This clearly afflicts the balance sheet of economic units, and it threatens to impair the net worth of firms and banks. The latter suffer from the direct impact on their assets, from the loss in the value of collateral, and from the impairment in their clients' balance sheets.

A subset of the notion of financial crisis is a *banking crisis*, when the normal functioning of banks as liquidity providers is hindered by a financial crisis of the banks. Not only is this a common configuration of a financial crisis, it is also unquestionably the worst. Because their balance sheets are strained, banks become illiquid, and if things are not quickly corrected they become insolvent, and the blow on real activity can be substantial. One can indeed argue that a banking crisis is likely to spread to non-financial firms, as the latter lose their normal access to credit. But crisis can also originate within the non-financial sector, in which case the impact will depend on whether the banking system can resolve the balance sheet difficulties of firms, or rather will catch the contagion instead. It may then be convenient to refer to banking crises when the balance sheet strain originates in the banking sector, and to financial crises when it originates in the non-bank sector.

A *currency crisis* is a collapse in the foreign value of the domestic currency unit. This raises those liabilities in the balance sheets that are denominated in units of the appreciating foreign currency, and afflicts the balance sheet of exposed economic units. Whether this generates a financial or banking crisis depends on the impact of the currency drop. Again, banks may be affected directly or, through their clients' exposure, indirectly.

Though a currency crisis may show up as a dramatic drop in the exchange rate, it often comes in the form of a breakdown of a unilaterally pegged exchange rate arrangement and as an outcome of a *balance-of-payments crisis*. This is a loss of the government's (or central bank's) ability to enforce a given parity so that the peg must be abandoned. It normally follows a quick reduction of international reserves facing an international flow imbalance. The latter may result either from a current account imbalance or from a large request of redemption of domestic currency for internationally accepted reserves. Again, whether a currency crisis causes a financial crisis depends on its impact on economic units' net worth.

Finally, an *international financial crisis* is one that involves effects in more than one country, either because of an 'international spillover' effect (on foreign balance sheets), or because of an 'international contagion' effect, whereby a confidence crisis spreads abroad.

Financial Instability on the Rise

Was there something new in the financial instability of the 1990s? Did some critical combination of events and circumstances set the fire? A primary task of empirical and historical research was to assess the seriousness and the extent of the problem. The results quickly delivered a change in perspective: as Goldstein and Turner (1996, p. 5) candidly admit, there 'is a natural inclination to think of financial crises as rare events. Yet banking crises have become increasingly common – especially in the developing world.' Empirical research of course needs an operational, not just a conceptual definition of crisis, and thus detection and classification of crises requires some judgment and may not be precise. This notwithstanding, the notion that financial crises have become more frequent in the last 30 years became widely recognized.

In fact, a character of financial instability was identified in the increased general occurrence of banking crises. Since 1996, Caprio and Klingebiel have maintained a database on banking crises, operationally defined as 'much or all of bank capital being exhausted'. In their 2003 update, they count 117 systemic banking crises in 93 countries during the last quarter of a century. The context of each crisis is different: while some remain local, others have an international character. Beim (2001) classified 96 crises (in the period 1976–99) listed in Caprio and Klingebiel's database, and found that over half of the crises had been triggered by war, a transition to communism, a major political change, and another deep political confidence crisis; over one-fourth had been triggered by pressure from the International Monetary Fund (IMF) or the World Bank regarding loans, conditions, reforms, and other recommendations; and the remaining 21 episodes had been triggered by financial market or currency crises. This latter list included Argentina (1980, 1989, 1995), Brazil (1990), Chile (1976, 1981), Finland (1991), Indonesia (1997), Israel (1983), Korea (1997), Malaysia (1997), Mexico (1982, 1995), Nigeria (1992), Norway (1987), Philippines (1998), Russia (1998), Sweden (1991), Thailand (1986, 1997), and Uruguay (1981). Most of these events had international ramifications, and nine were combinations of banking and currency crises.

Dual currency and banking woes is a phenomenon that Kaminsky and Reinhart (1999) had dubbed the 'twin crises', that is, 'episodes in which the beginning of a banking crisis is followed by a balance-of-payments crisis within 48 months'. Using a sample of 20 small open economies with some form of exchange rate pegging, these authors found that although there was evidence of only a slight increase in the frequency of balance-of-payments crises, the number of banking crises per year more than quadrupled in the 1980–95 period as compared to the 1970–79 period, and almost all had occurred simultaneously with currency crises.

This suggests an interaction between a crisis of confidence in the official parity of a currency and a crisis of confidence in its banking system, in the form of both a fragility of the banking system to currency turbulence, as well as a fragility of the currency parity to banking troubles. But how 'new' was this combination of events and what was the increase in its frequency? Extending to a broader historical perspective that spans 120 years, Bordo and Eichengreen (1999, p. 43) conclude that:

> If one thing is distinctive [about our period], it is the coincidence of banking and currency crises – the twin-crisis problem – and the severity of the associated effects. This is more evidence, if more is needed, of the importance of preventing and containing this particularly virulent strain of the virus.

And in another co-authored study, Bordo et al. (2001, p. 72) ask:

> What, then, was different about the last quarter of the twentieth century? The obvious answer is the greater frequency of crises. After 1973 crisis frequency has been double that of the Bretton Woods and the classical gold standard periods and matched only by the crisis-ridden 1920s and 1930s. History thus confirms that there is something different and disturbing about our age.

Although no single virus of recent financial epidemics could be isolated, a variety of hypotheses were made on what may have triggered such an increased occurrence of events. One set of explanations point to financial liberalization and free capital mobility. For example, Bordo and Eichengreen (1999, p. 43) claim that:

> Under Bretton Woods, banking crises were essentially non-existent, and the effects of currency crises were mild. This is more evidence, as if Chinese and Malaysia policy makers needed it, that strict controls on domestic and international financial transactions can suppress the symptoms of financial instability. Whether there are costs, in terms of slower growth than would have obtained otherwise, is, of course, the question of the day. The speed of growth in this period provides no obvious support for those who would emphasise the negative side effects.

Another set of explanations point to the process of financial liberalization taking place too rapidly in emerging countries with weak institutional environments. For example, Demirgüç-Kunt and Detragiache (1998, p. 7) find evidence that financial liberalization tends to have a particularly significant impact on the probability of a banking crisis in those countries where 'the rule of law is weak, corruption is widespread, the bureaucracy is inefficient, and contract enforcement mechanisms are ineffective'.

These and other interpretations will be further considered below in conjunction with theoretical models of financial instability.

Overlapping Generations of Models

Up until the 1980s, and with the notable exceptions stressed above, the consensus was that both currency and banking crises, though in different ways, reveal serious imbalances in economic 'fundamentals'. Currency crises were considered to be the outcome of international payments crises caused by poor macroeconomic management. When governments do not hold on to good old classical economic principles (such as when they pursue a persistent, inflationary budget deficit), it becomes intolerably expensive for a country to defend a foreign exchange parity. If the exchange rate is free to adjust, the foreign value of the domestic currency will immediately reflect the deteriorated macroeconomic environment; but if, instead, an official parity is maintained through pegging, this parity will be maintained beyond what is economically justified and sooner or later will become untenable. When either domestic or foreign investors, aware of fundamental imbalances, also become aware of the ongoing drain of reserves, a portfolio reallocation will ensue away from the pegged currency at risk of realignment until the official parity must be abandoned.

Banking crises, in their turn, were considered to be the outcome of an adverse macroeconomic operating environment: bad macroeconomic fundamentals cause a rise in non-performing loans that undermine banks' capital and, unless the economy recovers in a timely way, this will ultimately generate a widespread banking crisis.

In the wake of the then ongoing process of financial liberalization the consensus approach carried an optimistic message: avoiding financial crises requires no specific caution in proceeding with liberalization. It requires that governments learn sound macroeconomic principles. If this is the case, only unpredictable (and presumably rare) macroeconomic shocks will cause a crisis. The question of how to avoid financial instability then shifted to the question of what are the best macroeconomic policies, and the answer could of course be found within classical principles. This approach has long influenced the attitude of the IMF, which has always stressed macroeconomic adjustment as the best way to prevent, or manage, financial crises.

With the currency crises of the pound sterling (and the ERM) in 1992 and the Mexican peso in 1994, this confidence in the fundamental stability of the existing world monetary arrangements was partially shattered. It was generally recognized that in both cases crisis had been triggered by tremendous speculative activity that could hardly be viewed as the inevitable consequence of well-known fundamental imbalances in either Mexico or the United Kingdom. Neither the crisis in Mexico nor that in the United Kingdom clearly fell into the 'first generation' family of models, and if the pound crisis could alternatively be rationalized within the broader context of the crisis in the ERM, Mexico came to be considered as 'different', and it became commonplace to characterize the peso collapse as the first crisis of the twenty-first century.

Hence, 'second generation' models brought into the picture the role of self-fulfilling expectations, that is to say, the possibility of financial panic in a multiple equilibria model. In this new perspective, even countries with solid 'fundamentals' may be subject to a currency crisis: one only needs a 'sunspot' that functions as the triggering event of devaluation fears, and/or bank default fears, to draw down a currency and/or a banking system.

Although the triggering event may change case by case, a general form of it is understood to be a situation where some difficulties arise in the macroeconomic management of a country: an occurrence that may happen in well-managed countries also. If the medium-term sustainability of a country's macroeconomic policies is being questioned, and policy inconsistencies create the possibility that policy makers will revise their policy priorities to pursue some other, perhaps more popular, objective, then the loss of confidence in the government's future ability to implement good macroeconomic policies may erode confidence in the banking sector as well as in the official parity until it creates self-fulfilling speculation.

The message had therefore changed, and the new view was that good macroeconomic management may not be sufficient to maintain financial stability: pegging arrangements are structurally and inherently weak, because they are subject to self-fulfilling expectations. Currency stability was not only challenged by inflationary follies but also by the fact that good policy decisions aimed at safeguarding external equilibrium may look inconsistent with domestic objectives and affect government popularity. Also, pegging arrangements were seen as a particular form of moral hazard, inducing traders to undertake riskier activities than under floating exchange rates. The conclusion was that financial crises can strike at any time, and a search for a new international system was in order.

This is when the 'two-corner solution' view of exchange rate arrangements developed. If unilateral, 'soft' pegging arrangements are too fragile there remain two 'corner regimes' that are viable: a 'hard' peg such as a currency board, or a free float.[1] Following this 'bipolar view', a number of countries have moved away from 'soft pegs' to either floating arrangements, or to 'hard' pegs such as currency boards, dollarization, and currency unions.

This 'second generation' family of models, however, would quickly become obsolete as the Asian crisis struck. Not only were these countries in good macroeconomic shape and considered good pupils of the IMF policy recommendations, but also it was hard to identify a macroeconomic trigger of self-fulfilling expectations. Yet, the Asian crisis unfolded in a typically contagion effect, with a combination of currency and banking crises.

The occurrence of this type of crisis brought back explanations based on a boom-and-bust cyclical pattern, where credit expansion generates a rise in risk-taking activities and thus becomes the premise for financial crisis, along Minsky–Kindleberger lines. The debated question thus became what triggers the boom and the bust. For some authors, like Kregel (2000), the Asian crisis was not a simple balance-of-payments crisis, but rather a debt-deflation crisis, and the IMF policies that assumed it was a balance-of-payments crisis made the problem worse. Kregel (2000, p. 27) also stresses his belief that capital reversals had been triggered not by random, irrational reactions to peculiar circumstances, but rather were the natural results of the workings of the system and thus '"systemic" to the current configuration of the international financial system and . . . that will certainly recur, no matter what prophylactics are put in place to dampen them. Preventing financial crises will therefore require systemic changes, not simply improvements in the operation of the existing system'.

In a similar credit cycle perspective, but pointing at different triggers, other authors stressed that credit expansion and financial overheating become problematic when the quality of loans declines, as monitoring borrowers becomes more difficult. This poses the question of the problematic combination of 'macroeconomic and financial policies [that] combine with financial deregulation to create an unsustainable lending boom' (Eichengreen and Arteta, 2000, p. 29).

This consideration of national policies as being responsible for generating boom-and-bust cycles opened the way to a new family of ('third generation') models. It was in many ways a return to the past: a real fundamental imbalance still explains financial crises. The difference, however, was that while in the first generation models crises were caused by a fundamental macroeconomic imbalance, in third generation models they were caused by a microeconomic bank mismanagement, encouraged by the lack of adequate institutions. The success of financial liberalization was then understood to be subject to the condition of parallel progress in institutional conditions. The capital flows to Asian countries had clashed with backward financial systems, bad functioning banking systems, and an inefficient regulatory system. Information asymmetries, biased incentives, bad loans, and corruption created an enormous moral hazard problem: banks and financial institutions 'felt protected', and this led to the creation of excessive risks.

This situation continued to worsen the financial side of these countries. In his two-phase interpretation of banking crises, Beim (2001) maintains that the Asian crises outbreak followed a long, silent build-up of capital flows into fast-growing economies, with banks making bad profligate loans domestically, encouraged by the safety net of deposit insurance and of the IMF. As long as the banks remained liquid, banking distress could persist for a prolonged period. When the worsening situation was finally recognized, capital flows reversed when some 'funder' of the system started to withdraw its support: causes may act slowly, but triggers act quickly.

This meant that financial liberalization could only proceed safely if good macroeconomic policies were complemented by adequate institutional design. Countries that have only recently joined the industrialized world should therefore carefully move along their 'learning curve', avoiding financial liberalization that can occur prematurely under weak supervisory frameworks, poor transparency, and poor accounting and auditing practices.

Institutional weakness is one example of a disadvantage that may afflict emerging countries. In a similar vein, but arriving at very different conclusions, the 'original sin hypothesis' explores the vulnerability of emerging countries that cannot borrow from abroad in their domestic currency. Eichengreen and Hausmann (1999, p. 330) describe:

> a situation in which the domestic currency cannot be used to borrow abroad or to borrow long term, even domestically. In the presence of this incompleteness, financial fragility is unavoidable because all domestic investments will have either a currency mismatch (projects that generate pesos will be financed with dollars) or a maturity mismatch (long-term projects will be financed with short-term loans).

In this view, the problematic position of emerging countries does not depend on a lack of prudence or on institutional weakness. Rather, the country is exposed to crises because it finds it impossible to match the maturity structure of its assets and liabilities. Regardless of the exchange rate regime, the country is at a disadvantage: 'If the government allows the currency to depreciate, the currency mismatch will cause bankruptcies. If, instead, it defends the peg by selling reserves and hiking interest rates, it will precipitate defaults on short-term domestic debts' (Eichengreen and Hausmann, 1999, p. 331). Considering that it takes time for a country to abolish 'original sin', a faster solution is to eliminate the exchange rate through the substitution of the domestic currency with the dollar, or some other original sin-free currency.

A Summary of Public Policy Proposals

How can global financial instability be reduced? How many crises must the world undergo before a better method to contain them can be found? The variety of theoretical models and empirical investigations that have flourished offers a wide spectrum of public policy recommendations. A summary of the range of proposals is now warranted. The reader will notice that public policy proposals differ in their preference for market as opposed to public sector solutions, as well as in the relative weight given to national as opposed to international arrangements.

An intervention limited to the broad institutional environment within which financial markets and institutions operate is advocated by proposals that stress the need for countries to improve financial sector supervision and fight corruption and 'cronyism' by strengthening property rights. To play the game of financial globalization safely, they could, if necessary, be subject to supranational surveillance. This solution is consistent with the belief that the instability of the 1990s was the unfortunate result of emerging countries initiated to financial liberalization with backward national financial structures.

Amendments of greater significance are advocated by proposals that call for a radical reassessment of the existing risk protections apparatus. Based on the notion that risk protection systems generate moral hazard, such proposals call for national reforms aimed at reducing existing deposit protection. The principle of relying on market discipline should, in some proposals, be extended to international practices, by limiting the scope for major central banks or international institutions to rescue troubled financial institutions. Other proposed schemes, however, call instead for an 'international lender of last resort' that could prevent financial contagion of one (guilty) country to spread to the (innocent) rest of the world. The moral hazard implication of bailout expectations makes this device problematic, and its creation is often viewed as being part of a broader system of cooperative crisis management with access to a contingent provision of emergency lending, not an automatic mechanism.

An older type of approach stresses the role of national macroeconomic policies to maintain sustainable standards. Based on the notion that an international commitment limits the room for 'time inconsistency', a more effective approach is considered today as being a system of supranational surveillance of nations' macroeconomic, exchange rate, and balance-of payments policies. In this respect, classical macroeconomic policy prescriptions provide the most popular standards: a combination of public-sector budget rules, inflation targeting, and floating exchange rates.

On a different track are those policy prescriptions based on the notion that the problem of international financial instability is not transitory and thus requires a higher order of intervention in international finance. One of these prescriptions recommends that national policies enforce capital controls. Although this is an often-debated question, very few of those who favour this provision believe this is a sufficient device.

The dollarization approach needs no capital controls, and its advocates do not regard a reduction of moral hazard as a sufficient condition for stabilizing international finance. There are two distinct arguments for dollarization: there is the notion that dollarization is a more efficient way to strengthen national policy commitments, and there is also the notion that adoption of a 'strong' currency is the way for emerging countries to access international capital markets. The debate on 'original sin' has also suggested an alternative approach that aims at establishing supranational currencies, and claims that a condition for a more stable international financial environment is a drastic reduction of the number of currencies being used.[2]

A different way to address the problem of international payments in a world of diverse currencies, which counters both the dollarization solution and the creation of currency blocks, is tackled by a set of proposals that build on Keynes's plan presented at the Bretton Woods conference in 1944. This set includes Davidson's (1991) design of an international clearing unit, and D'Arista's (2005) proposal for a multilateral international payments system, managed by an international clearing agency.

There are, as suggested, different perspectives that distinguish these proposals from one another, but a major divide in this discussion is probably that between the objective of creating the conditions for an orderly functioning of financial, banking and currency markets, and the objective of considering monetary institutions in need of a significant upgrading in the face of financial globalization.

INTERNATIONAL MONEYNESS, CURRENCY HIERARCHY, AND INTERNATIONAL SETTLEMENTS

It is common to define money as a universally accepted means of payment, and thus the asset with the highest degree of liquidity. This definition, however, must refer to a single currency area where all contracts fall under a single state jurisdiction enforcing the use of a single legal tender. In a world where different currencies exist, this definition may not apply to each of the existing currencies when not every single currency is 'universally' accepted. Economic historians provide evidence that in the history of the world economy currencies have typically differed in terms of their breadth of acceptance. This is easily observed today as well, when the probability that the US dollar is accepted as a means of payment far from US borders is much higher than the probability of acceptance of the Thai baht or the Ethiopian birr or the Costa Rican colon far from national borders. In a multi-currency world, the statement that money is universally accepted is either loose or outright incorrect.

That currencies do not circulate as 'equal' suggests that there exists a hierarchy of currencies in terms of their degree of 'moneyness'.[3] This is hardly a new concept: economic historians and political economists[4] have long made use of the notion of a core–periphery structure of the world economy, while economists have long recognized the quality of 'key currencies' that function as vehicles of payments across borders, and other ('soft') currencies that are less, or not at all, accepted in international transactions. With few exceptions, however, this remains a missing element in debates on international financial crises.

The problem of the existence of different currencies and banking systems is how to settle international payments. Consider a world of 'currency islands', where traders in each country insist (either by law or by habit) in denominating contracts exclusively in their own currency, and in only accepting their own currency as a means of contractual settlement (that is, nobody is willing to hold foreign currency, and the degree of moneyness of every currency abroad is zero). No basis for international payments exists: no capital flows are possible across borders, and trade is only possible on the basis of a bilateral agreement in the form of an international barter.

By contrast, a multi-currency world is a world where traders in each country are free to decide how to denominate debts and prices, and whether to accept currencies other than their own as means of contractual settlement. Here, each trader's willingness to accept any currency depends on the range of goods, services, and assets (including debt obligations) that each currency can purchase. Hence, any given currency has a higher or lower degree of moneyness, depending on how extensively it is used as a unit of contractual debt in international transactions, how extensively it is accepted as a means of payment in lieu of the unit specified in the contract, and how extensively it is chosen as a store of value or as the unit of denomination of assets held. In sum, international moneyness depends on the access that a currency guarantees to goods, services, real and financial assets abroad, and it is higher, the greater is the international use of a currency.

How can international settlements be made possible in a world of currency islands? And what constraints are imposed by international settlements in a multi-currency world? These questions can be approached along three fundamental basic configurations. Of course, reality may be the result of a combination of more than one.[5]

An International asset Guarantee (IG) system   Although they denominate debts and prices exclusively in their own currency, traders in each country are willing to accept a commonly agreed international asset as a means to discharge international debts. Cross-border payments are made possible by either of two settlement techniques. In one, traders in each country obtain the foreign currency required to carry on foreign trade from their central bank, which obtains the foreign currency from the foreign central bank in exchange for an international asset. In the other, traders in each country are willing to accept the foreign currency as a means of contractual settlement as long as they can quickly obtain domestic currency from their own banking system, while their central bank clears any foreign currency holdings by obtaining an international asset from the foreign central bank.

In an IG system, international settlements are made possible by a conventional recognition of an international asset as a means to settle international debts. Currencies are granted international moneyness on the basis of international reserves: as long as they can be converted in the international asset, currencies are 'convertible' and thus accepted in foreign trade, as well as in the assets market.

A logical consequence is that countries' imports (not exports) are constrained by their reserves in the international asset. When a country lacks the international asset, acceptance of its currency drops. Countries' reserves, when accumulating in some countries and fading out in others, create asymmetry in countries' ability to settle international payments, and this builds the threat that some currencies may suddenly lose their international moneyness. A hierarchy of (convertible) currencies is thus established.

International financial instability in an IG system occurs as a result of a shortage of international reserves: a disruption of international trade credit creates financial strains on economic units' balance sheets. In addition, if capital flows develop in an IG system, balance-of-payments problems and an expected shortage of a country's reserves can quickly set off financial market, banking, and currency crises, as a result of the speculative nature of financial markets.

A Multi-currency Capital-flow-based (MC) system Although they denominate debts and prices exclusively in their own currency, traders in each country are willing to accept (and hold) foreign currency as a means to discharge international debts. They are willing to accept the foreign currency as a means of contractual settlement because they are willing to invest any excess holdings that are not spent towards goods and services into foreign-currency denominated assets. Hence, in this system financial markets and capital flows are the source of mutual acceptance and provide the ground for international payments.

In an MC system, international acceptance of currencies is not based on reserves of an international asset guarantee: it is based on capital and money markets that make a well-organized currency market possible. Inevitably, however, differences in size, organization, and depth of financial markets create a hierarchy of currencies. This is inherent in any international system with free capital flows. In the language of Keynes's (1936) *General Theory*, currencies differ in terms of their liquidity premium, with the higher-hierarchy currencies carrying a premium (l) higher than lower-hierarchy currencies.

Countries in an MC system will feel a different constraint depending on their position in the articulated financial hierarchy, and international financial instability occurs as a result of increasing difficulties of the low-hierarchy ('soft') currency countries to honour cross-border public or private debt obligations, as well as the speculative nature of financial markets. It may also originate from the banking system facing a demand of conversion of bank money denominated in the foreign currency: a banking system with foreign currency-denominated liabilities (that is, bank money issued by banks not belonging to the banking system of the currency-issuing country) faces a greater risk, because its own central bank cannot address international liquidity problems that may arise in the normal conduct of business.

A Key Currency (KC) system Traders in each country denominate debts and prices in their own currency, as well as in what they consider the key world currency. Although traders in the key-currency country do not accept foreign currencies as means of contractual settlement, traders in every other country do, and are willing to hold the key foreign currency. This gives one of the currencies an international money status, while the other currencies remain for strictly domestic use, to wit, their degree of international moneyness is zero. Under these conditions, trade can be carried out in terms of the currency accepted across borders, functioning as the international money. Goods, services, and assets, however, can only be exchanged under the condition that they must be denominated in the currency with international money status.

In a KC system, all countries but one are constrained in their ability to purchase foreign products by their holdings of foreign currency. Country holdings, on their turn, depend on exports proceeds, as well as on its capacity to borrow. The latter, however, is impaired by the fact that assets can only be denominated in the foreign currency, so any borrowing requires a further effort to dispose of foreign currency to pay interest. Hence, all countries but one are squeezed between two corner options: that of autarchy and that of consistently generating a trade surplus. Whether the latter is a feasible option depends on whether the key currency country is willing to flow its own currency into the rest of the world against imports (or the sale of assets). Financial instability occurs as a result of this asymmetry between currencies, and specifically of the increasing difficulties of governments and residents of all countries but one to honour public or private debt obligations in the key currency.

There is a financial fragility in each of the three configurations above, produced by some kind of asymmetry. In the IG system, it is the disparity of holdings of international reserves that may spoil the international moneyness of some currencies. In the MC system, it is the hierarchy of currencies and financial systems that lends itself to international instability. And in the KC system, it is the complete dependence of all countries (but one) on their disposal of a currency they can neither issue nor borrow without limits.

The current world system is a combination of the MC and the KC configurations: it is a capital-flow-based system with sizeable capital, money, and currency markets, where one currency (perhaps along with a very limited set of currencies) plays a key role as an international means of payment. Other currencies have a limited international moneyness, and a number of currencies have a near-zero degree of international moneyness. Thus, one can attempt to assess the validity of standing public policy proposals for stabilizing international finance in light of the conceptual framework developed above.

This suggests, first, that any provision uniquely aimed at creating well-functioning financial, banking, and currency markets in the current system, although welcome for its contribution to operational efficiency, does not address the fundamental problems of financial instability. Secondly, it suggests that any provision that aims at bringing all countries to the same playing field by improving national institutions through some form of coordinated surveillance fails to address the fundamental question of either currency or international reserve asymmetry. Thirdly, it further supports the recent reformulations of Keynes's original 'bancor' proposal as not only feasible, but as the only so far known viable alternative to either the *status quo* or world dollarization. For the latter to be effective, it should combine the KC configuration with a commitment by the United States (accepted by the rest of the world) to serve as lender of last resort of the world economy.

Fourthly, it suggests that the surge of crises in the 1990s may have been made possible, as explored in this and in the previous section, by the increase in capital flows in emerging, lower-hierarchy currency countries, in the absence of truly international reserves and common settlements rules. The reason for the greater stability of the Bretton Woods system, apart from the greater political tranquillity of those times, should be found in the adoption of an international asset combined with limited capital flows. A system where currencies are protected by capital controls and multilaterally agreed pegs makes currency diversity a less prominent feature than it is today.

CONCLUDING REMARKS

The international economy is a world of currencies of diverse quality. It is best to accept these differences as inherent in a world system than trying to hide them under the label of 'policy commitment': forcing all countries to follow the same policy and regulation rules will not resolve the problem of international payments, unless countries become politically willing to create, or accept, a single world currency.

As Keynes firmly contended, the monetary side of a global economy is not a neutral factor. In fact, it may be the problems posed by the different international moneyness that makes currencies unequal that should be considered as one of the fundamental factors behind any model of financial instability.

Viewed in this light, the options for the future international monetary system seem limited and include (a) dollarization – on condition that the United States agrees to take responsibility for the world monetary matters, (b) currency blocs, supranational currencies, or a single world money – on condition that countries can politically cooperate in their co-management of monetary matters, and (c) the 'bancor' solution – on condition that the political willingness of countries overcomes the resistance of the existing, yet precarious system.

NOTES

1. Although bank money is also an example of a 'soft' pegging arrangement with respect to central bank money, this debate has not included recommendations to move towards either a free float or a hard peg for bank money. Hence, we do not analyse them here.
2. An extreme form of dollarization is the establishment of a single world currency, a proposal that has flashed at times since at least the sixteenth century.
3. The term 'moneyness', being referred to a characteristic of money and not of all assets, is here preferred to that of 'liquidity'. This type of hierarchy may be related to, but should not be confused with, (a) the pyramidal structure of domestic money including (from the top down) central bank money, bank money, and other near-monies, and (b) the difference between 'complete' and 'partial' monies, where the latter only play the function of unit of account, not of means of payment (Hicks, 1967).
4. One may look at the works of Carlo Maria Cipolla, Marcello De Cecco, and, for an attempt to define hierarchy levels in today's world economy, Cohen (1998).
5. Notice that configurations abstract from exchange rate arrangements.

REFERENCES

Arestis, P., S. Basu and S. Mallick (2005), 'Financial globalization: the need for a single currency and a global central bank', *Journal of Post Keynesian Economics*, **27** (3), 507–31.

Beim, D.O. (2001), 'What triggers a systemic banking crisis?', *The Chazen Web Journal of International Business*, Columbia Business School, available at http://www2.gsb.columbia.edu/chazenjournal/.

Bordo, M.D. and B. Eichengreen (1999), 'Is our current international economic environment unusually crisis prone?', in D. Gruen and L. Gower (eds), *Capital Flows and the International Financial System*, Sydney: Reserve Bank of Australia, 18–74.

Bordo, M.D., B. Eichengreen, D. Klingebiel and M.S. Martinez-Peria (2001), 'Is the crisis problem growing more severe?', *Economic Policy*, **16** (32), 51–82.

Caprio, G. and D. Klingebiel (2003), 'Episodes of systemic and borderline financial crises', World Bank database, January.

Cohen, B.J. (1998), *The Geography of Money*, Ithaca: Cornell University Press.

D'Arista, J. (2005), 'The role of the international monetary system in financialization', in G.A. Epstein (ed.), *Financialization and the World Economy*, Cheltenham, UK and Northampton, MA, USA: Edward Elgar, 220–39.

Davidson, P. (1972), *Money and the Real World*, London: Macmillan.

Davidson, P. (1991), 'What international payments scheme would Keynes have suggested for the twenty-first century?', in P. Davidson and J.A. Kregel (eds),

Economic Problems of the 1990s: Europe, the Developing Countries and the United States, Aldershot, UK and Brookfield, USA: Edward Elgar, 85–104.

Demirgüç-Kunt, A. and E. Detragiache (1998), 'Financial liberalization and financial fragility', *International Monetary Fund Working Paper*, no. 98/83.

Eichengreen, B. and C. Arteta (2000), 'Banking crises in emerging markets: presumptions and evidence', *Center for International and Development Economics Research Working Paper*, no. C00-115.

Eichengreen, B. and R. Hausmann (1999), 'Exchange rates and financial fragility', *Federal Reserve Bank of Kansas City Proceedings*, August, 329–68.

Goldstein, M. and P. Turner (1996), 'Banking crises in emerging economies: origins and policy options', *Bank for International Settlements Economic Paper*, no. 46.

Hicks, J. (1967), *Critical Essays in Monetary Theory*, Oxford: Clarendon Press.

Kaminsky, G. and C. Reinhart (1999), 'The twin crises: the causes of banking and balance-of-payments problems', *American Economic Review*, **89** (3), 473–500.

Keynes, J.M. (1936), *The General Theory of Employment, Interest, and Money*, London: Macmillan.

Kindleberger, C.P. (1978), *Manias, Panics, and Crashes: A History of Financial Crises*, London: Macmillan.

Kregel, J.A. (2000), 'Diagnostics before remedies in formulating new strategies for dealing with instability', in J.J. Teunissen (ed.), *The Management of Global Financial Markets*, The Hague: FONDAD, 27–37.

Minsky, H.P. (1975), *John Maynard Keynes*, London: Macmillan.

2. Dollarization and the Hegemonic Status of the US Dollar

Jean-François Ponsot

INTRODUCTION

The hegemonic status of the US dollar on the international scene has been strongly questioned recently. If this view is correct, then the era of the dollar as the leading international currency would be over, after more than 60 years of ultimate supremacy. Indeed, some claim that its epoch is already over, like that of the sterling pound after the mid twentieth century. In fact, two arguments are put forth to support this point of view. The first is the more recent strong depreciation of the dollar against its two rival currencies on the international scene. Indeed, between the beginning of 2002 and early 2005, the dollar depreciated 35 per cent against the euro, and 25 per cent against the yen, coinciding with the increase of the balance of payments deficit of the United States. Its net external debt increased from 8.5 per cent of GDP at the end of 1999, to 26.3 per cent of GDP at the end of 2004. In fact, the external debt of the United States is the second argument put forth by those who claim that the US dollar is nearing its end as a world currency. The United States has had a current account deficit since 1982 (excluding 1991). Today, however, this deficit would have reached such an 'intolerable' level that it would involve both a loss of confidence in the US currency and its inevitable downfall (Schmidt, 2005).

The objective of this chapter is to show that despite some obvious signs of weakness, the US dollar retains its power and is still by far the leading international currency. The chapter is structured as follows. In the next section we consider the superiority of the US dollar given its continued use by the official (public) sector. The third section considers closely the use of the dollar as a primary currency for financing and investment on global capital markets. In the fourth section we look at the use of the dollar as the leading currency in international trade in the private sector. In this context, the rise of dollarization is interpreted as the most revealing sign of the actual power of the US dollar. In the fifth section we explore therefore the United States' attitude towards dollarization. The last section examines an important conclusion of this analysis. Indeed, we believe that the United States will adopt a less passive attitude as the euro overcomes the US dollar's supremacy as international currency. Finally, we also explore, though only briefly, the role that China will play in the future of the US dollar as dominant currency.

INTERNATIONAL REFERENCE CURRENCY OF THE PUBLIC AUTHORITIES

The US dollar remains the international currency of choice in its use by the public sector as anchor currency for the exchange rate of the local currency, as a reserve currency, and as an intervention currency on foreign exchange markets. It is evident that these three functions jointly reinforce each other (Portes and Rey, 1997). If a country decides to peg its own currency to the US dollar, the local central bank will maintain its reserves of US dollars and will intervene in the foreign exchange market with that currency.

Anchor Currency

Since the 1970s, fixed exchange rate systems have lost their popularity. In 2004, there were only 48 countries out of 181 that pegged their currency, from which 24 were pegged to the US dollar and 24 to the euro. However, these numbers must be interpreted with some caution. In fact, many countries unofficially peg their currency. In 2003, 48 currencies were unofficially pegged to the US dollar, while 36 were unofficially pegged to the euro.

The US dollar remains the currency of choice as the *de facto* anchor currency. The decision to peg one currency is usually motivated by a strong commercial and financial integration with the country to which the chosen currency belongs. This is the case with those countries that have pegged their currencies to the euro. Among this grouping are the countries that either have just joined or are planning to join the European Union (EU), as well as 14 countries within the so-called *Communauté Financière Africaine* (CFA), to wit, the currency bloc in Africa that uses the CFA franc. On the other hand, some countries have decided to peg their currency to the US dollar even though the United States may not be their principal commercial and financial partner. The most remarkable examples of this are the cases of Argentina and

Lithuania. In the first case, recall that from 1991 to 2002 Argentina maintained a currency board pegged to the US dollar in order to 'import' the stability and credibility of the latter currency. With respect to the second case, after its gain of independence from Russia, in 1994 Lithuania also adopted a currency board pegged to the US dollar, even though its potential economic integration zone is the EU.[1] Today, more than half of developing economies still have their currency pegged to the US dollar. These examples show that the US dollar remains the currency of choice as anchor currency.

Official Reserves and Intervention on Foreign Exchange Markets

Many factors force a country's government and its central bank to choose a reserve currency. The first factor concerns the necessity to intervene on the foreign exchange markets in order to manage the country's exchange rate. These actions are influenced by the anchor currency chosen. Two additional factors are the payment of imports and the settlement of the external debt. These primarily concern emerging and developing countries. The invoicing currency as well as the currency in which the external debt is denominated will have an impact on the composition of official reserves.

The share of the US dollar in official reserves accumulated by public authorities was 76.1 per cent in 1976, and 64.1 per cent in 2003. Contrary to what is often believed, the introduction of the euro did not bring on a significant change in the composition of official portfolios (Table 2.1).

Table 2.1. Official reserves: currency shares as a percentage of total identified holdings (end-of-year values)

Currency	1976	1981	1990	1996	1999	2000	2001	2002	2003
US dollar	76.1	59.2	50.1	60.2	65.9	66.6	66.9	63.5	64.1
euro	–	–	–	*20.3	*19.6	16.3	16.7	19.3	19.7
yen	–	3.9	8.1	6.0	5.5	6.2	5.5	5.3	4.7

* Currencies replaced by the euro.

Sources: International Monetary Fund (2004) and European Central Bank (2001, 2002, 2003, 2005).

The US dollar makes up almost two thirds of central banks' reserves world-wide. Initial declarations by China, Hong Kong, and other countries about the diversification of their portfolios have not yet been put into practice. The most spectacular case since 2002 has been the diversification by the Russian central bank. The share of euros in its reserves went from 10 per cent to 25 per cent of the total of its reserves (85 billion dollars), to the expense of the dollar. This event has gained much attention. Yet, at the same time, another much more favourable occurrence took place for the US dollar. Since May 2004, Saudi Arabia has abandoned its reserves diversification policy (valued at 200 billion dollars), considering that the euro has not yet obtained the rank of the dollar as a major reserve currency.[2]

More recently, the central bank of South Korea – which has the world's fourth largest US dollar reserves after Japan, China, and Taiwan – denied that it planned to shed its US dollar assets after media speculation it was about to do so sent the US currency plunging worldwide.

The effect of the reserves accumulated by central banks is important for the future of the dollar as a leading international currency. It is estimated that central banks contribute to 75 per cent of the financing of the external deficit of the United States. The major actors are located in Asia. The share of financing of the external deficit of the United States by the accumulation of dollars in Asian central banks' reserves is estimated at 64 per cent (Aglietta and Rzepkowski, 2004).

INTERNATIONAL FINANCING AND INVESTMENT CURRENCY

Despite the arrival of the euro, the US dollar retains its status as a leading currency in the eyes of non-US private and public operators in capital markets.

Bond Issues and External Debt

There is no doubt that the German mark, between 1980 and 1990, and then the euro, have increased their shares as currencies used to borrow funds on the international bonds markets. The year 1999 seemed to be important for the internationalization of the euro. That year, the issue of international debt and bonds in euros surpassed those in dollars (44.6 per cent of the total, compared to 42.5 per cent). But the excitement was only temporary. It was soon realized that the strength of the euro had only increased in Europe – 75 per cent of the issuers of international bonds in euros were euro-area residents – and the data collected from 1999 contained statistical biases that overestimated the issue of debts and bonds in euros (Bourguinat, 2001, p.

29). Despite significant issues of euros in Canada, Brazil, South Africa, and Argentina, the US dollar quickly regained its lead. In 2004, the share of the euro in international bond issues fell to 38.2 per cent, while that of the dollar rose to 47.1 per cent.

This strengthening of the US dollar as an international financing currency is particularly evident in emerging economies and in developing countries, which still favour the issue of government bonds in US dollars, to the expense of bond issued in their own currencies or in another currency. If we consider emerging economies only, however, the use of the euro tends to grow. It would probably reach a share of almost 20 per cent of new issues from emerging economies on international bond markets. Nevertheless, this process is slowed down by the fact that the major debtors among emerging economies are Latin American countries. The large share of creditors in the United States, and the necessity to refinance earlier debts in US dollars incite the continued use of this currency instead of the euro. Taking into account these practices and the inertia created, the external debt remains related to the US dollar, and this belief will not change anytime soon. Between 1990 and 2000, the share of the US dollar in the composition of long-term debt of emerging and developing countries went from 41.2 per cent to 56.0 per cent, while the share of the euro – or its related currencies – fell from 14.3 per cent to 9.3 per cent.

A Deep and Liquid Market

Why does the euro have so much trouble getting onto international capital markets? Despite enormous changes in European financial systems with the creation of the euro area, European financial and monetary markets remain highly segmented, poorly integrated, small in size, and not very liquid, compared to US financial and monetary markets. In the euro area, private bonds markets, the regulatory divergence, and different market practices are still large while the number of participants remains small. In public bonds markets, the segmentation is even more evident: there is still no convergence between the characteristics of the different national public bonds markets within the euro area. The United States has fared much better. The US Treasury is the unique issuer of state loans – contrary to the euro area, within which each country can issue national public bonds. The Federal Reserve intervenes daily to assure market liquidity while the European Central Bank intervenes only once a week in order to regulate the liquidity of the European markets. The size, integration, depth, and liquidity of US markets remain high, and this explains the undeniable success of the US dollar.

International Currency and Balance of Payments

Another handicap of the euro with respect to the US dollar is the fact that the European single currency must impose itself as international currency, while the US dollar has long been recognized as a leading currency. For the euro to be able to impose itself as an instrument of international liquidity, it would still be required that there exists a guarantee to this offer of liquidity. This would require that the net liabilities of the euro area toward the rest of the world be regularly increasing, which means a deficit in the euro-area balance of payments. How can the euro area demand its partners to make more use of the euro if it maintains a surplus position? The problem is that the present situation does not seem ready to change, and it is difficult to imagine that it can change without a precise agreement with the primary issuer of international liquidities, namely, the United States. It is therefore obvious that as long as the euro remains the currency of a surplus zone, it will be difficult to rival against the US dollar as a major international instrument of liquidity. In this light, let us recall that as businesses expand internationally, so too does the need for international liquidity. After the Second World War, this need was fulfilled by the US currency. It will probably continue to be fulfilled by the US dollar because the current account deficit of the United States is the main source of international liquidity. As noted by Frank (2003, p. 253), '[t]he U.S. current account deficit should be understood not as evidence of American weakness but as evidence of the degree to which the world economy continues to be organized around the United States'.

THE DOMINANT INTERNATIONAL CURRENCY OF PRIVATE TRANSACTIONS

The hegemonic status of the US dollar in the operations of private agents does not only concern the financing and investment opportunities on capital markets. Operators also favour the US dollar as an invoicing currency for international trade, and as a vehicle currency on the foreign exchange market.

Invoicing and International Trade Payments

Among the different economic functions attributed to money, the most important role is that of unit of account. Once one has the habit of counting and measuring transactions with a standard measure, it is difficult to change that. A change in the unit of account leads to the loss of a point of reference among economic agents. For example, many Europeans continue to convert prices posted in euros into their previous national currencies. This also goes for international units of measure. It was not until the 1960s that the dollar overtook the British pound as a primary invoicing and settlement currency in international trade, while the decline in the British currency had begun during the 1930s.[3] On these conditions, data on the share of the US dollar within private international transactions do not seem to help to measure the strength of the dollar. Nevertheless, let us present them here.

In 2004, the US dollar was still used as the invoicing currency of choice in more than half of the world's exports (Table 2.2). Its share decreased little since 1980. In 2004, the euro was used in one fourth of the world's exports. The problem is that we take into account the internal trade of the euro area in this calculation. So, we should pin down the breakthrough of the euro as an international trade currency.

Table 2.2. Invoicing currencies in international trade

Currency	Share in world exports (%)		Coefficient of internationalization	
	1980	2004	1980	2004
US dollar	56.0	52.0	4.5	3.8
euro	–	24.8	–	1.1
German mark	13.6	–	1.4	–
pound sterling	6.5	4.9	1.1	1.1
yen	2.1	5.2	0.3	0.6

Sources: Author's calculations from Henry (2004) and European Central Bank (2005).

The coefficient of internationalization for any given currency is calculated by the ratio of the share of exports expressed in this currency to the share of the issuing country in the total of world exports. Again, the euro is far from being an international invoicing currency. The euro share as an invoicing currency in international trade is not larger than what can be justified. Meanwhile, the dollar is used 3.8 times more than what can be justified for the United States in international trade.

Valuation Currency of Raw Materials

The superiority of the US dollar in international transactions is due to the fact that prices of raw materials are denominated in this currency and determined partly on stock markets situated in the United States and in the United Kingdom. Moreover, the British pound is the only other currency used for these types of transactions. To date, the EU continues to settle its purchases of natural gas from Norway, Algeria, and Russia, as well as its purchases of phosphates from Morocco, in US dollars. The case of crude oil shows how the euro is not ready to compete against the US dollar on this strategic market. The Secretary General of the Organization of Petrol Exporting Countries (OPEC) – which produces more than half of the world's oil and holds two thirds of reserves – explains that the prices of the OPEC's crude oil are calculated from a complex formula based on reference crude oils like the Brent, the West Texas Intermediate, and the Dubai, which are themselves expressed in US dollars. Furthermore, the US dollar is at the centre of a complex world system of contracts and sales coverage, which have no reason to change (Yarjani, 2002). The only factor that could act in favour of the euro would be the adoption of the European single currency by Norway and by the United Kingdom, the two largest European producers of Brent. The weakness of the euro, however, does not only concern raw materials. Turkey, who intends to join the EU before too long, has recently reinforced some of its trade in US dollars, including with EU members.

Vehicle Currency

A currency is used as vehicle currency when it is less expensive to use it as an intermediary in the exchange of two currencies as opposed to the direct exchange between the two currencies. In 2001, the US dollar was used in 90 per cent of all transactions on the foreign exchange markets, as much as in 1989. The euro participated in 38 per cent of the transactions, the yen in 23 per cent of them, and the British pound in 13 per cent of them. The US dollar's supremacy was even more pronounced on the futures market (with a share of 95 per cent on currency exchanges). In 2003, six of the nine pairs of the most exchanged currencies involved the US dollar (Table 2.3).

Table 2.3. Chief pairs of currencies exchanged on foreign exchange markets in 2003

Pairs of exchanged currencies	Amount in billions of dollars	Share (%)
US dollar – euro	354	30
US dollar – yen	231	20
US dollar – pound sterling	125	11
US dollar – Swiss franc	57	5
US dollar – Canadian dollar	50	4
US dollar – Australian dollar	47	4
euro – yen	30	3
euro – pound sterling	24	2
euro – Swiss franc	12	1

Source: Author's calculations from Bank for International Settlements (2004).

DOLLARIZATION: THE APOGEE OF THE US DOLLAR

The Substitution of Domestic Currencies for the US Dollar

Dollarization is the process of replacing a domestic currency with a foreign currency. This process may be spontaneous and results from an arbitrage of private agents who prefer to use a strong foreign currency instead of the weak domestic currency. This is referred to as *de facto* dollarization. The majority of emerging and developing economies are confronted with the penetration of a foreign currency in their own domestic monetary and financial system. The phenomena was further emphasized from the 1980s, as more and more of these economies were engaged in the globalization process and were faced with monetary and financial instability (hyperinflation, currency crises, and so on). This process can also be institutionalized by the authorities of the country – this is dubbed official dollarization.[4] The objective is then to import monetary stability by adopting a strong foreign currency. This eliminates the need to build up credibility of a domestic currency, since it disappears to be replaced by a stronger currency. This was the strategy adopted by Ecuador in 2000, followed by El Salvador and Guatemala.[5]

The euro is also concerned by the process of official dollarization (see Rochon and Rossi, 2003). Kosovo and Montenegro are not independent territories, but the euro is the legal tender therein. This phenomenon of 'euroization' remains marginal with respect to dollarization. The fact that the term 'dollarization' is used to qualify this phenomenon indicates well that the dollar remains the currency of choice. This is confirmed by the fact that East Timor, a new country created in 2002, has chosen the US dollar as its unique official currency, while logic would dictate that the Australian dollar would be the currency of choice.

Benign Neglect

The official adoption of the US dollar in Ecuador, the likelihood of its extension to other Latin American economies, or even projects of monetary unions in the heart of the North-American Free Trade Area (NAFTA) – see the union of the Americas (Western hemisphere) – are as much events that have obliged US authorities to unveil their position towards dollarization. In principle, three attitudes are possible (Cohen, 2004): (1) active discouragement of countries tempted by dollarization, (2) passive neutrality ('benign neglect' policy), or (3) active encouragement in favour of dollarization. Washington favours the second attitude.[6] It is possible to think that this attitude will persist as long as the pre-eminence of the dollar on the international scene is preserved. Only the eventual questioning of the supremacy of the dollar could incite the United States to modify its current plans.

The attitude of the United States results from the stand of the US Treasury, the Federal Reserve, and the State Department. This attitude depends on the economic, political, and geopolitical advantages and drawbacks of dollarization. Let us first have a look at the economic implications of dollarization.

Advantages

The economic advantages expected from dollarization concern four distinct levels. First, dollarization reinforces the 'exuberant privilege' from which the United States already benefits by making its own currency accepted in US foreign transactions, in contradiction with the principle that 'no one can pay with one's own debt'. The United States thus does not have to bear the adjustment costs. Secondly, full dollarization preserves the remuneration of the dollar reserves accumulated by central banks of non-dollarized economies, in the form of US Treasury bonds for example. The third purely economic advantage resides in the decrease of transaction costs that would imply the elimination of foreign exchange risks. This would imply a fourth more general advantage: an environment more stable and favourable to the development of US trade and investment.[7]

The United States can also catch two (geo)political interests with dollarization. By exercising, alone, the monetary power affiliated with the dollar, the United States implicitly establishes a hierarchical relation with the dollarized economies. According to Cohen (2004), through dollarization the United States acquired a potential powerful instrument of influence. The relationship with a dollarized country is clearly hierarchical – implying a link between domination and dependence – and this ascendancy inevitably signifies a vulnerability for the dollarized country (Cohen, 2004). The example of sanctions taken in 1988 against Panama and their consequences on the domestic economy – a decrease in GDP of 18.6 per cent – show the spread and efficiency of sanctions.[8]

The second (geo)political interest relates to the prestige that dollarization can bring to the United States. The currency exerts a symbolic role, from which issuers do not generally deprive themselves. The use of the US dollar implies the reinforcement of the influence of the US dollar and what this currency represents across a daily modelling of beliefs and perceptions of each of us.

Inconveniences

Taking into account the potential advantages, the costs of dollarization for the United States seem laughable. In particular, the transfer of a part of 'seigniorage revenues' to dollarized economies proposed by Senator Mack and Robert Barro can be assimilated to a form of a subsidy to encourage dollarization. The primary economic inconveniences come mostly from the potential consequences on US monetary policy by a circulation continuously enlarged of the US dollar as foreign currency. Do the supply of and demand for the US dollar in dollarized economies – which are not controlled by the Federal Reserve – risk affecting the overall liquidity of the dollar and by this influence US monetary policy decisions? Furthermore, what would happen if one or more dollarized economies decided to reintroduce their own currencies? Would 'de-dollarization' not provoke a brutal depreciation of the US dollar on foreign exchange markets? The risks associated with the extension of dollarization relate to the loss of control of monetary power. We are thus confronted with the questions of monetary sovereignty and the (geo)political nature of its implications posed by dollarization.

CAN THE EURO CHALLENGE THE US DOLLAR?

Asymmetric Monetary Union

If US authorities maintain, for the time being, a non-cooperative strategy with respect to dollarization, this is firstly because this attitude allows the benefits of (geo)political advantages to be obtained without directly engaging US responsibility in the monetary and financial affairs of dollarized economies. Contrary to all treaties of monetary integration or currency union, official unilateral dollarization does not imply any formal engagement on the part of the United States. In particular, the Federal Reserve is not forced to take up immediately the role of lender of last resort next to the banks of dollarized economies. Dollarization is a form of asymmetric monetary union in which the issuer has monopoly over monetary power.

We can question ourselves about the durability of the passive attitude on the part of the United States for at least three reasons. First, can the US authorities really remain indifferent toward the monetary and financial situations of dollarized economies? For example, what would be the United States' reaction towards a severe and brutal liquidity crisis in a dollarized economy – a hypothesis that is largely plausible given the supposed absence of domestic lenders of last resort? Would they content themselves with remaining stationary when faced with a crisis that can affect US banks? Like any other central bank confronted with the rise of systemic risk, would the Federal Reserve act as a lender of last resort?

Subsequently, it is suitable to take into consideration the impact of the size-effect of the dollarized economy. The position of the benign-neglect country with respect to economies of reduced size, like that of Ecuador or El Salvador, proves to be very convenient for the United States. But would it be so if dollarization were to reach more important economies like that of Mexico?

Finally, and most importantly, the US position cannot be separated from the evolution of the euro on the international scene. If the euro were to compete against the US dollar as international currency, there is no doubt that the US strategy would be more aggressive. It is significant that the favourable positions of the US authorities towards dollarization progress as monetary union in Europe becomes more and more concrete.

The Currency War

For the moment, European authorities officially do not make an important case for the rise of the international role of the euro. Euroization is not officially part of the preoccupations of the European Central Bank (ECB). According to the President of the ECB, the internationalization of the euro is not a politically driven process.[9] The official euroization of Kosovo and Montenegro – as well as its possible extension to the Balkans – is the logical consequence of the 'markization' of the region. Many elements assist in the questioning of this apparent European lack of concern towards the international status of the euro. One of the principal arguments in favour of the creation of a European single currency was to have a currency capable of competing against the US dollar. Does the evolution of the euro/dollar exchange rate represent a symbol of the 'strength' or the 'weakness' of the euro? Finally, can we consider the ECB's decision to issue 200-euro and 500-euro bank notes as a willingness to compete against the green 100-dollar bill – which is the main reserve bill in the world?[10] The hegemonic urges are therefore not absent from the ECB decision. Once again, the (geo)political considerations have enclosed purely economic motivations. Euroization is an option among others to fight against the hegemonic status of the US dollar. If this situation accelerated, it is with no doubt that the United States would not content itself to the technical and logistical assistance it now offers in the case of official dollarization of peripheral economies. The recent project aimed at making Ecuador's central bank a branch ('oficina')[11] of the Federal Reserve, destined to feed with US dollars the Andean countries, is revealing of the new US attitude encouraging the use of the US dollar in this region.

CONCLUSION

The US dollar remains without a doubt the international currency of choice. If we consider the decline of the dollar, this process is very slow. It would take many decades to occur – as was the case for the British pound in the twentieth century.[12] The strong appreciation of the euro against the dollar will not be sufficient to make the euro the future leading international currency. In fact, at the time of writing, the euro has already lost some ground against the dollar. The power of the euro as an international currency is far from being made, and the United States will no doubt come up with strategies destined to defend – more or less artificially – the dollar's supremacy as soon as the euro starts to eclipse the dollar. It is evident that the economic policies followed by the US government and the Federal Reserve will determine the economic situation in the United States, and the leadership of the dollar on the international scene.

Another important factor to consider is the attitude and economic strength of China. For the time being, China is content with pegging the yuan to the US dollar (8.277 yuans for one US dollar), which was established in the spring of 1995, and accumulating colossal reserves in US dollars. Chinese authorities, however, have announced in 2004 that they might peg the yuan to a basket of currencies[13] – without specifying which currencies they would consider in the basket. Now seems to be the ideal moment to abandon the peg (Rzepkowski, 2004). Expectations of a lasting increase in interest rates in the United States would indeed contribute to limit an eventual overreaction of the exchange rate (an appreciation of the yuan).[14] Whatever happens, it seems that the fate of the supremacy of the US dollar, or its decline, rests in the hands of the Sea of China. History seems to repeat itself. Indeed, we remember that it was in Hong Kong that the decline of the British pound was completed in 1967.[15]

ACKNOWLEDGEMENTS

This chapter was written while the author was Assistant Professor of Economics at Laurentian University, Canada. The author would like to thank Louis-Philippe Rochon, Ted Schmidt, and Eric Tymoigne for their fruitful comments on an earlier version of this work, which was presented at the 2005 Eastern Economic Association conference in New York, 4–6 March. Remaining errors are the responsibility of the author.

NOTES

1. In 2002, Lithuania abandoned the US dollar and chose the euro as anchor currency. This was a condition that needed to be satisfied in order for the country to join the EU.
2. This statement is from the sub-governor of the Saudi Arabian central bank (Henry, 2004, p. 96).
3. Some go further, situating the decline of the sterling at the end of the First World War.
4. See Ponsot (2003) for a more detailed presentation of dollarization regimes.
5. By contrast to Ecuador, both El Salvador and Guatemala have kept their own currencies. The latter two countries are therefore economies with a parallel currency (the US dollar).
6. This is more particularly the case in Iraq. Official and complete dollarization regimes and currency board systems have been imagined for Iraq by the US Treasury Department. These plans were abandoned. In January 2004, a new dinar has been created to substitute that of the Saddam era.

7. We refer here to the conclusions that the Joint Economic Committee presented to the US Congress in 1999–2000 (Joint Economic Committee, 2000).
8. The Panama crisis – a dollarized country since 1904 – broke out in 1988, following the US desire to overthrow General Noriega, who was accused of corruption and of favourable drug trafficking practices.
9. 'The ECB sees the internationalization of its currency beyond the borders of the euro area as a market-driven process' (Trichet, 2004, website).
10. Taking into account the preferences of foreigners and of underground economies to use higher denomination banknotes, the decision of the ECB to issue such notes constitutes an aggressive movement aiming at monopolizing a large part of the demand for strong currencies coming from developing countries (Rogoff, 1998, p. 264).
11. Another 'branch' project of this type has been imagined for the new central bank of Iraq. The latter central bank serves as a relay between the Federal Reserve and the Middle East.
12. As noted by Frankel (1995, p. 9), '[t]here is little likelihood that some other currency will supplant the dollar as the world's premier reserve currency by 2020. One national currency or another must occupy the number-one position, and there is simply no plausible alternative'.
13. 'We do not think that a fixed system is good. We think that a floating system is good' (Shuqing, 2004, website).
14. The flexibility of the Chinese currency, however, could have a destabilizing effect on the Chinese financial system and, by ricochet, on the world economy. In fact, we consider that more than half of credits granted by Chinese banks are bad debt. The stability of the Chinese banking system is insured in large by the limited convertibility of the yuan, which prevents depositors from choosing another reserve currency. Now, the necessary condition for the flexibility of the yuan would be the abolition of capital controls and the possibility for local investors to invest in other countries. Flexibility of the yuan exchange rate would therefore release important retrievals of capital deposited in Chinese banks. However, this argument is not defended by everybody. For a contradiction to it, see Eichengreen (2004).
15. For a description of this often forgotten event, see Schenk (2004).

REFERENCES

Aglietta, M. and B. Rzepkowski (2004), 'Les banques centrales asiatiques et le dollar', *La lettre du CEPII*, no. 230.
Bank for International Settlements (2004), *Quarterly Review*, Basel: Bank for International Settlements, December.
Bourguinat, H. (2001), *L'euro au défi du dollar. Essai sur la monnaie universelle*, Paris: Economica.
Cohen, B.J. (2004), *The Future of Money*, Princeton: Princeton University Press.
Eichengreen, B. (2004), 'Chinese currency controversies', University of California, Berkeley, mimeograph.
European Central Bank (2001), *Review of the International Role of the Euro*, Frankfurt am Main: European Central Bank, September.
European Central Bank (2002), *Review of the International Role of the Euro*, Frankfurt am Main: European Central Bank, December.
European Central Bank (2003), *Review of the International Role of the Euro*, Frankfurt am Main: European Central Bank, December.
European Central Bank (2005), *Review of the International Role of the Euro*, Frankfurt am Main: European Central Bank, January.

Frank, E. (2003), 'The surprising resilience of the U.S. dollar', *Review of Radical Political Economy*, **35** (3), 248–54.

Frankel, J. (1995), 'Still the lingua franca: the exaggerated death of the dollar', *Foreign Affairs,* **74** (4), 9–16.

Henry, G.M. (2004), *Dollar, la monnaie internationale*, Levallois–Perret: Studyrama.

International Monetary Fund (2004), *Annual Report*, Washington, DC: International Monetary Fund.

Joint Economic Committee (2000), 'Dollarization: a guide to the international monetary stability act', staff report, Washington, DC: Joint Economic Committee.

Ponsot, J.-F. (2003), 'The obsession of credibility: a historical perspective on full dollarization and currency boards', *International Journal of Political Economy*, **33** (1), 83–99.

Portes, R. and H. Rey (1997), 'The emergence of the euro as an international currency', *Centre for Economic Policy Research Discussion Paper*, no. 1741.

Rochon, L.-P. and S. Rossi (2003), 'Dollarization out, euroization in', *International Journal of Political Economy*, **33** (1), 21–41.

Rogoff, K. (1998), 'Blessing or curse? Foreign and underground demand for euro notes', in D. Begg, J. von Hagen, C. Wyplosz and K.F. Zimmerman (eds), *EMU: Prospects and Challenges for the Euro*, Oxford: Basil Blackwell, 261–300.

Rzepkowski, B. (2004), 'Spéculations sur le yuan', *La lettre du CEPII*, no. 234.

Schenk, C.R. (2004), 'The empire strikes back: Hong Kong and the decline of sterling in the 1960s', *Economic History Review*, **57** (3), 551–80.

Schmidt, T. (2005), 'The rise and fall of the dollar empire: the political economy of the dollar as international reserve currency', paper presented at the Eastern Economic Association 2005 conference, New York, 4–6 March.

Shuqing, G. (2004), 'Interview', *Financial Times*, 23 April.

Trichet, J.-C. (2004), 'The international role of the euro', speech delivered at the Schierensee Gespräche, 14 May.

Yarjani, J. (2002), 'The choice of currency for the denomination of the oil bill', speech delivered at a conference on 'The International Role of the Euro', 14 April, Oviedo, Spain.

3. Reform and Structural Change in Latin America: Financial Systems and Instability

Eugenia Correa and Gregorio Vidal

INTRODUCTION

The continuing financial reforms in Latin American countries (LAc) have deeply changed markets and institutions, as well as monetary and fiscal policies in Latin American financial systems over the last 30 years. In spite of these deep transformations, however, the obstacles to financing the economic development of LAc have not been surmounted. On the contrary, gross capital formation has either fallen or stagnated, and the number of firms issuing equity on the stock markets has decreased rather than increased. Moreover, the external debt of most LAc is still growing, although it is being repaid. The governments' tax revenue is stagnant or falling in spite of successive increases in the value-added tax rate, and the local and central governments' debt is growing because of growing financial costs burdening public spending, including the successive costs of rescues and bank flotation. Finally, real interest rates remain above the growth rate of firms' cash flow, especially small and medium businesses that are outside the credit market.

To wit, recent financial reforms in Latin America have not helped finance the expansion of investment and productive capacity. On the contrary, the last few years have seen local and central governments, firms, and households suffering from overindebtedness. It would appear therefore that financial bankruptcies, moratoria, and economic crises are the direct result of deregulated financial markets in developing countries.

These reforms were initially demanded by the World Bank (WB) and the International Monetary Fund (IMF), based on some neoclassical concepts about insufficient savings, overregulation and disloyal competition of state companies and banks, high and inflationary public sector deficits, and the requirements of financing an inefficient and unproductive public sector. Today, the analysis and policy prescriptions of these institutions remain the same. The IMF and the WB insist on laying the blame for the successive and frequent financial crises – as well as for the slow growth, the high levels of unemployment, and poverty – on the lack of structural reforms. Ironically, both institutions also recognize that the existing reforms have gone beyond all expectations.

The level of interference in public policy design, not only in every aspect of government actions, but also in the decision-making and entrepreneurial process of local enterprises, is evident and, in fact, is now considered natural and necessary (see Kuczynski and Williamson, 2003). From the point of view of the WB and the IMF, it appears that the cross supervision between the IMF and the WB orchestrated for more than two decades has been fruitful, turning short-term economic adjustment into permanent economic and political intervention (International Monetary Fund, 2004b, p. 16).

The economic authority exerted by the IMF and the WB is not subject to elections, and one government after the other, with perhaps the recent remarkable exception of Argentina, continue putting all local interests under their will. The domestic consensus around the Washington Consensus and the different generations of economic reforms have passed through diverse ways and key actors in LAc, but the main role has been played by the financial markets' major operators, that is, transnational corporations, dealers, investment banks, central banks and treasury authorities, and rating agencies.

The IMF has been consistently worried about fiscal deficits. In the last few years, without explicitly claiming that the treasury has to be, as the central bank, an independent authority, the IMF has strongly suggested that fiscal policies must be carried out to the extent of the tax revenues raised by the government. This implies that it is possible to have a political discussion on government expenditures, irrespectively of the level of public deficit or debt, because these levels are fixed by the IMF. Indeed, one can argue that the same argument has been made with respect to monetary policy. The purpose is the same, namely, to make fiscal policy efficient, credible, and transparent (International Monetary Fund, 2004a).

In some LAc, rules-based fiscal policy has been especially restrictive. It parallels the government's abdication of money creation, proclaiming the independence of the central bank and abandoning the central bank's main function of financing the general government sector. The abdication of the money creation capacity by the government was apparent by the successive rounds of dollarization and currency boards imposed on many LAc, which have disarticulated the fundamental function of the central bank as a fiscal agent for the government. All these measures, in addition to the decreasing capacity of the governments to raise tax revenues, are seriously injuring one of the fundamental pillars of government power: money creation.

In the next section we analyse the successive stages of financial reforms in LAc, considering the main trends and the relationships between the debt inflows and the processes of financial liberalization. We will argue that the financial reforms were executed following the main business trends of the largest creditors of and portfolio investors within LAc. In the third section we describe the links between foreign direct investment (FDI) and the various privatization processes. We will analyse the large market position of some transnational corporations in core economic sectors, and the displacement of the domestic private and public firms as well as their main consequences over the economic performance in the long term. In the fourth section we consider the current trend in foreign control of the domestic banking sector by global financial corporations and their consolidation in domestic markets. This remains largely unexplored by post-Keynesian authors (see, however, Gnos and Rochon, 2004–5). We will argue that these changes in financial structures make possible a new relationship between the foreign corporations and the financing of their activities. In the fifth section we analyse the financial constraints due to the increasing pressure on LAc to record net capital transfers towards creditors and investors (FDI returns and debt interests). This growing capital outflows for developing LAc harms their domestic saving and investment capacities, especially in local currencies, and creates a trend of economic stagnation. The last section briefly concludes.

ECONOMIC REFORMS AND FINANCIAL FLOWS

Economic reforms in Latin America began in the 1970s and were driven by the deregulation and liberalization of capital account transactions, although these reforms took place mainly in the 1980s, when the idea of encouraging development projects sustained by domestic markets was put aside. The export-led growth model was winning consensus in various LAc, largely as a result of the increasing service burden of the external debt as well as of the decreasing export capacity needed to fund these payments. There were many changes in international financial markets, and the credit cycle of the 1970s was the main force driving financial and economic reforms. The first reforms were directed to increasing the payment capacity for external commitments. Later, however, reforms went toward a deeper reconfiguration of economic and institutional structures, opening the economy to commercial imports (thus displacing domestic production), FDI and portfolio allocations, cross-border privatizations and acquisitions, debt securitization, and financial innovation.

During the 1970s, LAc were net receptors of syndicate loans coming from transnational banks. The quick growth of credit arising from domestic banks in developed countries, as well as the international credit from these markets, resulted in loan flows of close to 200 billion dollars in LAc, between 1970 and 1981 (Girón, 1995). The LAc's foreign debt doubled in only four years (1978–81) as a result of Volcker's interest rate increase aimed at slowing or halting inflation in the United States, which provoked a recession in the first half of the 1980s. In short, banks stopped principal refunding and interest capitalization, and, as a result, a debt crisis erupted. This was the end of the first credit bubble after the collapse of the dollar–gold parity regime (Correa, 1992).

For Latin American domestic financial systems, lending from large international banks to LAc meant that those banks that were doing business inside Latin America, including local domestic banks, had to face new conditions of financial competition. For instance, during the 1970s, Latin American banks routinely lent to Latin American governments in order to compete and participate in the syndicated credit system existing in the region. When the 'debt crisis' eventually occurred after eight years of rapid expansion in international credit, the main LAc had to introduce IMF stabilization programmes, which dictated a necessary contraction of income, public spending, and domestic profits in order to generate the required fiscal surplus to meet debt service payments. In addition, such policies required that the solvency of banks' creditors was not threatened.

The large domestic banks were not subject to competition in a market that little by little was being made more open and global. During the 1980s, the capital inflows were not voluntary, but occurred because of loans refinancing. Those LAc that recorded positive resource transfers during some years in the 1970s returned to negative resource transfers in the 1980s. The net transfer of resources is equal to total net capital inflows minus net payments of interests and profits (Economic Commission for Latin America and the Caribbean, 2005). As a result of the reforms and the crises in the 1970s and 1980s, we can reach the following three conclusions:

1. When a devaluation of local currencies occurred, many banks with highly dollarized balance sheets, and currency mismatches, were forced into technical bankruptcies (in particular, in Argentina, Chile, Colombia,

Mexico, Peru, and Uruguay).
2. There were important changes in the regulation of interest rates, government domestic debt securitization, and new relationships between local interest rates and international market rates. The issuing of public bonds during the 1980s affected monetary policy as well as interest rates regulation (in particular, in Argentina, Bolivia, Brazil, Chile, Mexico, Peru, Uruguay, and Venezuela).
3. The privatization processes in a number of different economic sectors during this period occurred in parallel with the growth in debt swapping by firms' assets or foreign investment, with a discount factor owing to the reduction in the market value of the debt (especially in Argentina, Brazil, Chile, and Mexico).

In the 1990s, financial market deregulation in the United States modified capital inflows and outflows in the LAc, with the inevitable result that these countries re-emerged as capital-importing countries. The new capital inflows came from the new expansion and market positioning strategies of institutional investors (Correa, 1998), who turned to high-yielding government bonds in Argentina, Brazil, and Mexico, denominated in local currency. They also turned their attention to the debt of local firms in Argentina, Brazil, Chile, Mexico, and Venezuela. This trend reached its first peak in 1994, when the Federal Reserve again reverted to increasing interest rates.

The returns from capital inflows in the second half of the 1990s were due to a new large wave of privatization processes. Indeed, FDI annual inflows increased from 30 billion dollars to 107 billion dollars between 1995 and 1999. Financial services for FDI privatizations and acquisitions were granted by an increasing presence of foreign financial firms and commercial banks, as well as investment banks and insurance companies. Because of the wave of financial bankruptcies during the 1990s, some global financial corporations were taking positions within the largest Latin American economies. Nevertheless, in the first five years of the new millennium, the largest Latin American economies have become again capital exporters.

PRIVATIZATIONS, FDI, MERGERS AND ACQUISITIONS

As Table 3.1 shows, LAc have a very small position in the world with respect to population, production, trade, and financial assets. In spite of the important growth in FDI, trade, and capital flows, Latin American economies still have a relatively small worldwide position, even lower than that achieved during the 1990s. Latin American financial markets have a relatively marginal position in the worldwide financial markets, but they have been the destination of transnational corporations and global banks' expansion.

Table 3.1. Latin America in the world, 2003 (as a % of the total world)

Item	Percentage
Population	8.3
Extreme poverty (2002)	6.7
Gross domestic product	4.8
Exports (2002)	4.5
Official reserves (minus gold stock)	6.2
Stock market capitalization	1.9
Public and private sector securities	1.6
Banks' assets	1.9
Foreign direct investment	9.9

Sources: World Bank (*World Development Indicators* database, April 2003) and International Monetary Fund (*Global Financial Stability Report*, September 2003).

The recent growth of FDI is associated with the global trends in mergers and acquisitions between large corporations. This is a process by means of which corporations consolidate globally their operations, close plants and reduce the number of their employees, and at the same time expand their position in the markets. In fact, FDI has been expanding the productive capacities of those sectors in which corporations outsource some parts of the productive process. This is the new form in which large corporations are growing, especially in sectors such as telecommunications, thereby entering markets once reserved to the governments (Vidal, 2001).

The largest increase in FDI was recorded in the 1990s. Most of the inflows came from the United States and the European Union (EU). Altogether these countries represented more than 70 per cent of total FDI between 1999 and 2002. A large part of the FDI flows were used in mergers and cross-border acquisitions. One component of these purchases was state companies, particularly in the telecommunications sector, but also in other basic public services, like electrical energy, potable water, and sewage systems (Vidal, 2001). In LAc, the most important foreign capital acquisitions of state-owned banks and financial companies were made mainly by large banks from the

United States or the EU.

The FDI made by firms with headquarters in the United States and the EU between 1995 and 2002 was aimed principally toward the acquisition of domestic companies around the world (76 per cent of FDI from the United States, and 84 per cent of FDI from the EU). By contrast, a significant part of FDI inflows to most of the developing countries was directed towards the purchase of pre-existent companies.

For the three largest Latin American economies (Argentina, Brazil, and Mexico), the period of largest privatizations and FDI inflows occurred between 1995 and 2002. Consider the following data:

1. Brazilian FDI inflows were 163.4 billion dollars, 72 per cent of which were directed to purchase local companies, notably the acquisition of the telephone network (Telebras); but also to buy electricity companies, banks, and some railroads.
2. Mexican FDI inflows were 113.2 billion dollars, more than 55 per cent of which were directed to the purchase of companies, in particular banks and other financial institutions, and to participate as partners in the main telephone company. A great part of these firms were first privatized with domestic capital, and later were sold to foreign investors.
3. Argentinean FDI inflows were 68.8 billion dollars, 96 per cent of which were directed to acquire assets, including the petroleum and gas firm Yacimientos Petrolíferos Fiscales, along with the telephone, aviation, and electrical energy companies.

The acquisition of privatized companies on behalf of transnational corporations was a phenomenon characteristic of the 1990s, and several of the largest worldwide operations were made in LAc. Table 3.2 lists the transactions that are amongst the hundred largest cross-border privatizations. Latin American acquisitions by this set of transnational corporations have two main characteristics: first, several firms that have bought Latin American assets have only recently initiated this type of operations abroad; secondly, the amount of resources involved is considerable, and the firms' expansion towards LAc has become fundamental to their competitive and market position strategies.

To wit, for the largest Latin American economies the most important FDI inflows were registered during the 1990s, and their main goal was to acquire domestic firms. A small group of transnational corporations was fortified in public services, telephone, and IT industries.

Table 3.2. Main cross-border privatization processes in Latin America, 1987–2003

Target firm	Country	Year	Foreign firm	Acquisition amount (billions of dollars)
YPF S.A.	Argentina	1999	Repsol, Spain (84%)	13.2
Aeropuertos Argentinos	Argentina	1998	Empresas, USA	5.1
TELESP (a part of Telebras)	Brazil	1998	Telefonica, Spain (56.6%); Iberdrola Inv, Spain (7%) and Telecom Portugal (23%)	5.0
Banco do Estado de Brasil São Paulo (BANESPA)	Brazil	2000	Banco Santender Central, Spain (100%)	3.6
Telefónica del Perú	Peru	2000	Telefónica, Spain (56.7%)	3.2
Telesp Celular	Brazil	1998	Telecom Portugal (100%)	3.1
Embratel (a part of Telebras)	Brazil	1998	MCI (100%)	2.3
YPF S.A.	Argentina	1999	Repsol, Spain (14.9%)	2.0
Entel Perú	Peru	1994	Telefonica, Spain (100%)	2.0
Telefónica de Argentina	Argentina	1990	Telefonica, Spain (10%); Citibank, USA (20%) Other foreign banks (37%)	2.0
Telecom Argentina	Argentina	1990	Telecom Italy (32.5%); France Télécom (32.5%)	1.8
Telecentro Sul (a part of Telebras)	Brazil	1998	Techold Part, Italy (19%)	1.8
COELBA	Brazil	1997	Iberdrola, Spain (39%)	1.8
Elektro	Brazil	1998	Enron, USA (100%)	1.7

Table 3.2. Main cross-border privatization processes in Latin America, 1987–2003 (continued)

Target firm	Country	Year	Foreign firm	Acquisition amount (billions of dollars)
Light SE	Brazil	1996	AES, USA (20.3%); Houston, USA (20.3%); EDF, France (20.3%); BNDES, Brazil (16.4%)	1.7
Electricidad de Caracas	Venezuela	2000	AES Corp. (81.3%)	1.7
Telmex	Mexico	1990	Carso, Mexico; Southwestern Bell, USA and France Télécom (20.4% 'AA')	1.7
Cia de Electricidade do Estado da Bahia	Brazil	1997	Iberdrola (39%)	1.6
Reserva de Gas Camisea	Peru	2000	Pluspetrol Energy, Argentina; Hunt Oil Co., USA, and SK Co., Korea	1.6
Ferrocarril Pacifico Norte (Hoy Ferromex)	Mexico	1997	Union Pacific USA (26%)	1.4
Cia Centro Oeste	Brazil	1997	AES Corp.	1.4
COELCE	Brazil	1998	Endesa, Spain (37.5%), and CERJ, Brazil (36.5%)	1.3
Aerolíneas Argentina	Argentina	1990	Iberia Airlines, Spain (69.4%)	1.3
Empresa Bandeirante de Energia	Brazil	1998	Eletricidade de Portugal (56%)	1.2
Telesudeste Celular	Brazil	1998	Telefonica	1.2
Companhia de Geracào de Energia Elétrica de Paranapanema	Brazil	1999	Duke Energy Corp, USA (100%)	1.1

Table 3.2. Main cross-border privatization processes in Latin America, 1987–2003 (continued)

Target firm	Country	Year	Foreign firm	Acquisition amount (billions of dollars)
Comgas	Brazil	1999	British Gas (70%), and Shell (26%), UK	1.1
Cemig (Minas Gerais)	Brazil	1997	Southern Electric, USA	1.1
Companhia Energética de Pernambuco (CELPE)	Brazil	2000	Iberdrola, Spain (79%)	1.1
Cia Riograndense de Telecomun	Brazil	1998	Telefonica (Spain) and associates (83%)	1.0
Aseguradora Hidalgo	Mexico	2002	Metropolitan Life Insurance, USA (100%)	1.0
Companhia de Eletricidade do Estado de Rio de Janeiro	Brazil	1996	Eletricidade de Portugal (30%); Electricidad de Panama (30%)	1.0

Sources: Economic Commission for Latin America and the Caribbean (2000), *La inversión extranjera en América Latina y el Caribe*, Santiago de Chile: Economic Commission for Latin America and the Caribbean; Vidal (2001); Economic Commission for Latin America and the Caribbean (2002), *La inversión extranjera en América Latina y el Caribe*, Santiago de Chile: Economic Commission for Latin America and the Caribbean; UNCTAD (2002), *World Investment Report*, Geneva: United Nations, p. 134; Banco Nacional de Desenvolvimento Economico e Social (2005), *Privatizações no Brasil 1990–2004*, Rio de Janeiro: Banco Nacional de Desenvolvimento Economico e Social.

The main consequences of this expansion of transnational corporations due to trade liberalization and privatization in the LAc are as follows:

1. A displacement of local firms (especially small and medium-sized firms) and of domestic networks. An increase of the monopoly degree.
2. A dynamic economic growth in those sectors that are controlled by foreign companies and/or produce for exports.
3. A reduction of formal employment and an increase of non-formal employment. Flexibility in labour markets. A stagnation of or a reduction in real wages.

4. An increase in the prices of public sector services, thus reducing the access of the poor population.
5. Growing net resources outflows to allow for the payment of profits. Since they are produced in domestic markets but are neither spent nor invested in them, these outflows of profits lead to both investment and employment stagnation.

Also, corporations from the United States and the EU acquired banks and other (non-bank) financial institutions, an issue to which we now turn.

FINANCIAL CRISES AND FOREIGN BANKS

Despite the fact that the Latin American financial system is characterized by a predominant banking sector and strong state support, it faced important weaknesses and went into repeated crises owing to several factors. These factors include new foreign financial competition inside Latin American markets that came with liberalization and deregulation, trade opening that led to confrontation between economic structures with different prices and yields, and the insistence on balanced budgets that led to increasing reduction of public expenditures. These elements contributed to successive episodes of banking crises of diverse magnitude (Correa, 2003).

The first wave of Latin American banking crises occurred in the 1980s in Argentina, Chile, Mexico, Peru, and Uruguay, and resulted from the process of financial liberalization and the debt crisis. This first wave had its origin in a number of factors:

1. A change in the monetary policy of the Federal Reserve that led to rapid increases in interest rates.
2. An abrupt stop in the North American banks' balance sheet expansion, created by difficulties in refinancing external liabilities for the largest indebted LAc.
3. A devaluation of local currencies, which led to a partial dollarization, thereby creating a currency mismatch.
4. For many Latin American domestic banks, the temporary impossibility to continue participating in the business of the internationalization of domestic capital and wealth.
5. Governments and domestic banks did not have increased loan access to the private credit markets, and specifically to the banks in the United States.

From that moment, it became evident that in developing countries the ongoing liberalization processes, even without a greater trade and current account liberalization, required a lender of last resort (LOLR) in dollars (possibly the Federal Reserve, the United States' Treasury, the IMF, or some set of transnational private banks). With the parallel circulation of the local currency and the US dollar in many Latin American financial systems, along with financial liberalization and deregulation, a LOLR in dollars became an imperative for these countries.

In fact, the second wave of Latin American banking crises in the 1990s hit Argentina, Brazil, Mexico, and Uruguay. It contributed to massive banking failures and a variety of government support. Asian, African, and East European countries also had banking crises in those years. This second wave had its origins in the capital inflows and outflows that in their ascent phase produced a domestic credit boom, dollarization, and an exchange rate overvaluation. In their descent phase, however, they led to overindebtedness, currency devaluation and mismatch, and possibly to a new round of pesofication. Once the local banks were financially sound thanks to the fiscal support given by the government at the expense of taxpayers, they were sold to global financial corporations.

In conditions of trade and financial openness, the smaller availability of capital inflows increased the pressure on the economy, because the financial costs associated with these capital inflows increased considerably (that is, capital outflows, FDI returns and dividends, and debt interests). During the 1990s, the larger Latin American economies had moments of high dollarization and, later on, expensive pesofication processes, of which a recent example is Argentina, where the debt moratorium and its succesful renegotiation of cuts in its debt principal allowed the reversal of five years of deep recession (1997–2002).

The successive local and international financial crises in Mexico, South Asia, Russia, and for the Long Term Capital Management fund in the last half of the 1990s unleashed a new round of competition between the most important international financial corporations. Worldwide financial consolidation in 1998–99 allowed financial corporations to manage and to internalize, at least partly, the high risk levels and the associated costs due to this financial stress.

In addition, the expansion of financial corporations towards markets with some growth potential, such as those in East Europe, Latin America, and to a lesser extent in Asia, advanced in the search of size and global competitiveness, taking overseas market positions. This analysis could explain the increased presence of foreign banks' in the last five years (1999–

2004), in countries such as Argentina, Chile, Colombia, the Czech Republic, Hungary, Mexico, Peru, Poland, Venezuela, and to a lesser extent in Brazil, Korea, Malaysia, and Thailand.

Citibank, BBVA, BSCH, HSBC, ABN–AMRO, and Scotiabank are some of the financial corporations that occupied a central position in the financial system through the acquisition of domestic banks, mainly private banks. Other large financial corporations represented a smaller market share, creating new banks and following the corporate bank service model.

In contrast to a number of developed countries – such as those in Europe, the United States, and Japan – where foreign banks do not hold an important market position, in Bolivia, Brazil, Chile, Colombia, Costa Rica, El Salvador, Mexico, Paraguay, Peru, and Venezuela foreign banks have had an increasing presence since 1994 (see Gnos and Rochon, 2004–05, for an analysis of this phenomenon). Their presence and participation became important and unchanging in Aruba, Bahamas, Panama, and Uruguay, whereas it remains relatively small, but stable, in Cuba, Ecuador, Guatemala, and Nicaragua. Moreover, state banks hold an important portion of the market in Brazil and Argentina, and in all LAc they still represent 20 per cent of the market.

Among foreign banks, Spanish financial organizations, and in particular BBVA and BSCH, found in LAc a favourable environment to consolidate their internationalization efforts, obtaining a size and global competitiveness corresponding to the new conglomeration conditions opened during the late 1990s in the global financial market. Their presence in Latin America allowed them to operate at a global level. It also allowed them to promote their resources and technological and management capacities, as well as risk diversification and internalization. In addition, it further allowed the expansion in Latin America of large Spanish companies like Telefónica, Repsol, and Iberdrola.

In several developing economies, the domestic banking crisis largely encouraged the penetration of foreign banks, which took control over the domestic banking system in developing LAc. In Central Europe, this foreign control was 8 per cent in 1994, and rose to over 56 per cent in 1999. In Latin America, excluding Brazil and Mexico, foreign control rose from 13 per cent to 45 per cent in those years. This change in the ownership was not limited to deposit banks, but also included insurance firms, investment banks, and other financial firms.

In the first half of the 1990s, the foreign banks' participation in Latin American assets was rather minimal. Generally speaking, this participation represented a very small component of their balance sheet, and had even been regulated and restricted. In addition, the large Latin American economies had an important state bank sector as well as development banks, owing to the regulation put into practice in the years immediately after the economic depression of the 1930s. These banks were particularly active in financing long-term investment and infrastructure. They were also important in their support and intermediation of foreign loans to governments and public agencies. With the financial reforms of the 1980s they have been privatized, reduced, or closed.

Figure 3.1 shows foreign bank penetration for a number of LAc. Note that in the early 1990s foreign banks were important largely only in Chile. Yet, by 1994, foreign banks held 18 per cent of total assets in Argentina, and 16 per cent in Chile. In Brazil, Colombia, and Peru this proportion was less than 10 per cent, and in Mexico less than 1 per cent. Since then, however, foreign bank expansion in LAc underwent a very particular trajectory in each country.

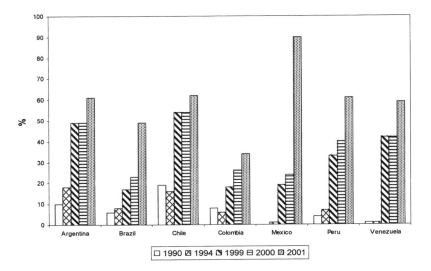

Source: Economic Commission for Latin America and the Caribbean (2002), *La inversión extranjera en América Latina y el Caribe*, Santiago de Chile: Economic Commission for Latin America and the Caribbean, p. 118. These figures do not include the participation of the banks owned by the state.

Figure 3.1. Latin American foreign banks' assets, 1990–2001 (as a % of total assets)

In Mexico, for instance, the first privatization process took place between 1990 and 1992, but it was exclusively for domestic capital participation, as a strategy to strengthen some domestic corporations in order to create a new worldwide insertion for the Mexican economy and to face global competition (Vidal, 2002). In Brazil, the first stage of the privatization programme consisted in selling some large industrial firms, in order to support the growth of domestic corporations. Yet, the sale of state banks to foreign partnerships was not considered pertinent (see Banco Nacional de Desenvolvimento Economico e Social, 1997, 1998; Vidal, 2001). It was the second wave of privatization, in the second half of the 1990s, which was particularly important, since it did not distinguish between domestic and foreign capital.

In other LAc, privatization followed FDI, but in the banking and financial services sectors foreign capital participation did not increase significantly. Within the North American Free Trade Area, Mexico maintained temporary restrictions against foreign capital participation in financial services (Armendáriz and Mijangos, 1995).

Nevertheless, in the second half of the 1990s a remarkable and dramatic change took place. In 1999, foreign bank assets in domestic markets stood at 49 per cent in Argentina, 54 per cent in Peru, and increased considerably in Brazil and Mexico. In 2001, foreign banks dominated the banking industry in Argentina, Chile, Mexico, Peru, and Venezuela. In response to the financial crises, Latin American governments carried out new reforms and adopted an explicit policy to attract foreign banks (Economic Commission for Latin America and the Caribbean, 2003).

In the early 2000s, operations to manage and control all capital branches were made. The expansion of foreign global financial corporations created important changes in the financial reform strategies (Correa, 2003). As a result, many reforms that were undertaken since then can be explained by the new market position of global banks that are expanding and consolidating their Latin American position. Among the largest 25 banks in LAc, a good number of them have foreign investment, or have become foreign bank subsidiaries, as shown in Table 3.3. The exceptions are the largest Brazilian banks. Nonetheless, the Spanish BBVA and BSCH banks have had the largest expansion in the region (Vilariño, 2001). They have the largest branches with investments of nearly 13 billion dollars controlling 30 banks in ten countries with assets higher than 153 billion dollars, or almost 10 per cent of Latin American bank assets. They also participate in the pension funds management of almost 45 per cent of total funds (Mathieson and Roldós, 2001).

Table 3.3. Top-25 banks' main shareholders in Latin American countries, 2004

Position	Bank	Host country	Assets (billion dollars)	Shareholders	Participation (%)
1	Banco do Brasil	Brazil	73,181	National Treasury	71.80
				Previ	13.70
				BNDES	5.80
				Foreign capital	1.00
				Pension funds	1.20
				Local investors	4.80
				Local enterprises	1.70
2	Bradesco	Brazil	56,728	Cidage de Deus (Brazil)	24.45
				BES	3.24
				Crédit Agricole	3.26
				Deutsche Bank	0.43
				Sanwa Bank	1.28
				Bradesco Foundation	9.51
				BBVA (Spain)	4.44
3	Caixa Econômica Federal CEF	Brazil	53.652	Brazilian government	100.00
4	BBVA Bancomer	Mexico	43,803	BBVA-Spain	99.55
5	Banco Itaú	Brazil	39,510	Investinetmos Itaú S.A.	47.70
				Local investors	52.30
6	Banamex Citibank	Mexico	38,511	Citigroup (USA)	99.50
7	Unibanco	Brazil	25,722	Grupo Moreira Salles (E. Johnston)	29.54
				Caixa General de Depositos	12.42
				Commerzbank	11.44
				Dai-Ichi Kangy Bank	2.71
				Float PN/Unit	6.92
				Float GDS	32.29
				Float ON	3.58

Table 3.3. Top-25 banks' main shareholders in Latin American countries, 2004 (continued)

Position	Bank	Host country	Assets (billion dollars)	Shareholders	Participation (%)
8	Santander Serfín	Mexico	23,648	Santander Central Hispano (Spain)	71.10
				Bank of America (USA)	24.90
9	Santander Banespa	Brazil	22,042	Santander Central Hispano (Spain)	98.00
10	ABN–Amro Bank	Brazil	19,295	ABN AMRO BANK N.V. (Canada)	50.69
				ABN AMRO BRASIL	45.86
11	Banorte	Mexico	18,194	Gónzalez Barrera and Family	41.14
				Gruma Group	10.95
				JPMChaseBank (Investment Fund)	n.a.
				Darby Overseas Investment, Ltd	n.a.
12	Santander Santiago	Chile	17,895	Santander Central Hispano (Spain)	84.00
13	HSBC (before Bital)	Mexico	15,970	Hong Kong Shangai Bank (UK)	100.00
14	Banco de Chile	Chile	15,141	Private local capital	n.a.
15	Banco de la Nación Argentina	Argentina	13,451	Argentinean government	100.00
16	Banco del Estado de Chile	Chile	12,517	Chilean government	100.00
17	Banco Safra	Brazil	11,919	Family Safra	n.a.
18	Votorantim	Brazil	11,225	Votorantim Finanzas	99.91
19	HSBC Bank Brasil	Brazil	10,408	Hong Kong Shangai Bank (UK)	99.00

Table 3.3. Top-25 banks' main shareholders in Latin American countries, 2004 (continued)

Position	Bank	Host country	Assets (billion dollars)	Shareholders	Participation (%)
20	Banco de Crédito e Inversiones	Chile	9,624	Empreas Juan Yarur S.A.C.	53.50
21	Citibank	Brazil	9,600	Citibank (USA)	n.a.
22	Nossa Caixa	Brazil	8,865	Brazilian local government	n.a.
23	Scotiabank Inverlat	Mexico	7,895	ScotiaBank (Canada)	91.00
24	Banco de la Provincia de Buenos Aires	Argentina	7,652	Argentinean local government	n.a.
25	Galacia y Buenos Aires	Argentina	7,229	Private local capital	n.a.

Source: Authors' elaboration from banks' websites and from the reviews *America Economia* and *Latintrade* websites.

The foreign presence in the principal Latin American economies exhibits different characteristics. In Mexico, for instance, its expansion began with the purchase of small banks. It was only in the late 1990s that the large domestic banks were acquired. Market expansion continued in the following years and, in addition, four of the five largest banks were acquired by foreign firms: BBVA–Bancomer (Spain), Banamex–Citibank (United States), Santander–Serfín (Spain), and HSBC (United Kingdom) (see Table 3.3).

In 2004, amongst the largest Latin American banks by assets, the fourth, sixth, and twelfth were also the three largest foreign banks in Mexico: BBVA acquired a majority share participation in Bancomer, although shortly after it acquired the remaining shares and secured full control of the latter bank. In addition, BBVA extended its acquisition spree with the Hipotecaria Nacional (mortgage state agency), which was the largest privatization in this market. BBVA also participated in the Latin American market in the United States, when it acquired some US banks in 2001. For instance, Banacci–Banamex was bought by Citigroup in 2001; Bital was acquired by HSBC and one share package was bought by Santander Central Hispano (Spain), which sold to

Bank of America 24 per cent of Serfín, which was acquired some months before (Economic Commission for Latin America and the Caribbean, 2005). Mexico is the country with the most concentrated foreign bank participation and, perhaps not incidentally, also the country in which bank credit contraction has been the largest.

In Brazil, the picture is certainly very different. The largest banks continue to be owned by public or private domestic capital, and the government has adopted policies to protect and support its domestic banking system: Bradesco, Itaú, and Unibanco are controlled by private domestic shareholders. In 2004, they were the second, fifth, and seventh largest banks in Latin America by assets. The state banks Banco do Brasil and Caixa Económica General are the first and the third in this ranking (see Table 3.2). During 2001 and 2002, Bradesco, Itaú, and Unibanco made equity buybacks, and Bradesco even participated in several privatizations and acquired, in 2003, the Brazilian branch of BBVA. Itaú and Unibanco bought banks and other financial firms, too. In general, the private domestic banks have been strengthened, including banks like Banco Safra and Votorantim. The foreign banks' market position reached 21.4 per cent of the total banking assets in December 2004. In this country, despite its relative stability after the most recent financial crises, interest rates and interest rate spreads gave rise to important returns to the banking system. As a result, the banking system in Brazil remains very much controlled by domestic interests.

In Argentina, by contrast, foreign bank participation grew rapidly in the 1990s, reaching more than 60 per cent of the market. Yet, the financial bankruptcy and instability in the years after the several banking crises led to an exodus of foreign banks. State banks have since then played an important role in the structural stabilization of the national banking system, such as Banco Nación, Galicia Bank, and Buenos Aires Bank.

Generally speaking, the important presence of foreign banks in LAc contributed to neither a deepening of the local financial markets nor an increased saving and investment financing, at least until the first half of the 2000s. Even so, the yield reached by these banks and other financial firms has been exceptionally high during these years, especially in Brazil, Chile, and Mexico.

Allegedly, the financial reforms of the 1990s should have diminished financial costs, granted much more confidence to depositors, and increased saving. These reforms were also presented as a means to achieve development and as a way out of poverty (World Bank, 2000). Nevertheless, the efforts for Latin American financial reforms, proposed as an economic stabilizer by the IMF, could neither prevent nor control the banking crises, but promoted a change in financial firms' ownership, including deposit banks, which can entail a systemic risk.

The IMF has faced criticism in recent years, because it pushed countries into a process of growing liberalization and financial opening that has led them down a path of financial and economic instability, banking crises, stagnation or slow economic growth, and growing denationalization of the whole economy. Until now, foreign bank subsidiaries in Argentina and Mexico, at least, have showed that they do not have a strategy of expanding and deepening national markets. On the contrary, these subsidiaries are merely taking advantage of a position that guarantees them capital expansion and better returns, especially in bonds and equity markets.

INSTABILITY AND FINANCIAL CONSTRAINTS

The progress made by the structural reforms in LAc has not yet led to a better economic performance, as free capital movements and exchange rate flexibility have not allowed consolidating a stable flow of financing in domestic markets and in local currencies, all of which remain reduced and expensive. At the same time, capital inflows and outflows have led to new periods of negative transfers, owing to the substantial increase of debt interests and FDI return payments (see Table 3.4).

Table 3.4. Latin America as a capital exporter (in billion dollars)

Year	Net capital inflows	Debt interest and FDI returns net outflows	Net capital transfers
1980	30.9	18.9	12.0
1990	16.1	34.2	−18.1
1995	61.1	40.8	20.2
2000	53.6	53.6	0.0
2001	51.8	54.7	−2.9
2002	10.3	51.2	−41.0
2003	21.4	55.8	−34.4
2004	−12.5	65.3	−77.8

Source: Economic Commission for Latin America and the Caribbean (2005), *Balance preliminar de las economías de América Latina y del Caribe*, Santiago de Chile: Economic Commission for Latin America and the Caribbean, Table A-13.

The financial reforms in Latin America, which occurred after the successive banking crises and the penetration of financial global corporations in most Latin American economies, from around 2002 were focused on the following elements:

1. Enlarging the investor base mainly through participation of mutual funds and hedge funds, as well as deepening the privatization of the pension system.
2. Advancing in the privatization process, including state banks (currently 20 per cent of the Latin American market).
3. Developing local institutional investors such as pension funds, insurance companies, and mutual funds.
4. Enlarging local securities markets through more local bonds and equity issues and derivative instruments. Developing domestic capital markets, including markets for interest rate and exchange rate hedging instruments.
5. Improving the legal and regulatory framework, while emphasizing creditors' legal protection.
6. Improving the credibility and uniformity of accounting standards, adopting international accounting standards, and implementing modern market infrastructures, such as clearing and settlement platforms.
7. Improving the valuation of assets, and regulations that support credit quality.
8. More competitive labour costs in order to avoid cyclical booms and busts in FDI.
9. Extending the maturity of external debt and avoiding a bunching of maturities, establishing benchmark external bond issues; improving secondary market liquidity and facilitating the pricing of external corporate debt issues; enlarging local debt markets.
10. Incorporating collective action clauses in international sovereign bonds issued under New York law, which implies that the voting threshold for an amendment of payment terms is set at 75 per cent of outstanding principal for the Italian, Korean, Mexican, and South African issues, and at 85 per cent for those of Belize and Brazil. The voting threshold for acceleration is set at 25 per cent and for deceleration at 50–66.3 per cent, to avoid debt market restructuration as Argentina did recently.
11. Improving market infrastructure, transparency, and corporate governance.
12. Making hidden debts (implicit debts and pension system debts) explicit. These explicit debts have to be financed voluntarily by capital markets.

13. Accumulating foreign exchange reserves with flexible exchange rate regimes, avoiding overvaluation, and minimizing the use of the dollar.
14. Encouraging firms to use formal financial system to pay for wages and salaries through banks.

With these reforms taking hold throughout Latin America, global financial corporations, institutional investors, investment banks, dealers, and brokers are expanding their operations, not only in the local markets but also in Chicago, New York, and other markets as well, taking multiple financial positions. Thus, an important part of the local assets revenues are taking the form of financial yields via an increase in all kinds of securities and financial assets (private and public bonds, equities, American Depositary Receipts (ADRs), Global Depositary Receipts (GDRs), other representative equity securities, and other financial instruments) (Correa, 1992).

Private and public debt issued in foreign currencies and even in local currencies are freely acquired by foreign investors, so that liquidation, principal, and generated returns involve foreign currency use. Thus, the difference between domestic and external debts is erased, even though the developing economies' capacity to generate foreign currency surpluses until now has been very limited. Hence the cyclical generation of current account deficits (including FDI returns and debt interests), which has been explained by the chronic insufficiency of savings and elicits a dependency on capital inflows in order to have the foreign currencies needed for debt service.

The largest Latin American corporations have developed schemes of financing through bond issues mainly in the North American market and in dollars. On the other hand, the greater presence of transnational corporations and global financial conglomerate subsidiaries has allowed for a change in the geographic location of financial operations (in legal and fiscal terms).

The results of these reforms are the consolidation of global financial conglomerates in domestic markets, the increasing pressure on LAc to hold net resources transfer positions (FDI returns and debt interests), which in the situations of developing Latin American economies harms domestic saving and investment capacities, especially in local currencies, and creates a trend of economic stagnation.

Therefore, new episodes of financial fragility are unavoidable, even with the considerable expansion of large foreign financial firms. Governments have less opportunities to stop the deepest consequences of these 'external shocks' when deposit banks are mainly foreign banks' subsidiaries. On the other hand, it has not been proven so far that these subsidiaries bring with them large volumes of financial resources at more competitive costs to Latin

America, and neither that the depositors see their savings grow with attractive interest rates.

CONCLUSION

The Latin American financial system has changed during the last 30 years. Since the 1980s, those financial reforms that were inspired by the Washington Consensus have had a tremendous impact and have significantly changed markets, institutions, and monetary as well as fiscal policies. With these changes, it has not been possible for many businesses and households in developing countries to count on the commercial banks for the financing of investment and productive capacity.

Moreover, these financial reforms have been further deepened following the successive banking and foreign debt crises. In particular with the second wave of banking crises in Latin America in the 1990s, important bank bankruptcies occurred, which led to different types of government support with high fiscal costs. This was also the period during which foreign control of the Latin American financial system grew. In the last half of the 1990s, foreign banks drastically increased their presence in Latin America, which coincided with FDI inflows bent on acquiring domestic companies in many economic sectors, especially telecommunications, electricity, oil, and gas.

Yet, despite the increased FDI and foreign banks in Latin America, there has not been a proportional increase in local financing and investment. Quite to the contrary, a financial structure has appeared that systematically leads to issues of debt instruments in foreign markets, whereas the local markets are dominated by government bond issues. Foreign banks become important government bond holders, since these bonds offer high interest rates.

Latin American economies must record a good economic performance in order to attract and maintain capital inflows, and at the same time create the conditions to repay these debts. The main point is that this performance creates a financial structure intrinsically fragile, in which new episodes of financial crises can appear. Therefore, the consolidation of global financial conglomerates as strong shareholders in the domestic financial markets of LAc increases the pressures on these countries in order to be net capital exporters (FDI returns and debt interests). This net capital export position for LAc limits their accumulation capacities and creates economic stagnation trends with dynamic economic growth concentrated in the exports and foreign investment sectors. The new financial structure that is emerging in LAc shows that the main problem of the financing process is not the shortage of savings as argued by the IMF and WB, but rather the constant and growing reduction of these savings owing to the unfair monetary, commercial, and financial international relations as Furtado and Prebish pointed out years ago.

ACKNOWLEDGEMENTS

The authors are grateful to Wesley Marshall and Fernanda Vidal for translating this chapter into English. The usual disclaimers apply.

REFERENCES

Armendáriz, P. and M. Mijangos (1995), 'Retos de la liberalización en el Tratado de Libre Comercio: el caso de los servicios bancarios', in A. Girón, E. Ortiz and E. Correa (eds), *Integración financiera y TLC: retos y perspectivas*, Mexico: Siglo XXI Editores, 258–301.

Banco Nacional de Desenvolvimento Economico e Social (1997), *Brazilian Privatization Program, Report of Activities 1997*, Rio de Janeiro: Banco Nacional de Desenvolvimento Economico e Social.

Banco Nacional de Desenvolvimento Economico e Social (1998), *Privatizações no Brasil 1991–1998*, Rio de Janeiro: Banco Nacional de Desenvolvimento Economico e Social.

Correa, E. (1992), *Los mercados financieros y la crisis en América Latina*, Mexico: IIEc–UNAM.

Correa, E. (1998), *Crisis y desregulación financiera*, Mexico: Siglo XXI Editores.

Correa, E. (2003), 'Los sistemas financieros en América Latina: algunas transformaciones', available at http://www.redcelsofurtado.edu.

Economic Commission for Latin America and the Caribbean (2003), 'La inversión extranjera en América Latina y el Caribe', available at http://www.eclac.org.

Economic Commission for Latin America and the Caribbean (2005), 'Preliminary overview of the economies of the Latin America and Caribbean', available at http://www.eclac.org.

Girón, A. (1995), *Fin de siglo y deuda externa: historia sin fin*, Mexico: Cambio XXI and IIEc–UNAM.

Gnos, C. and L.-P. Rochon (2004–05), 'The Washington Consensus and multinational banking in Latin America', *Journal of Post Keynesian Economics*, **27** (2), 315–31.

International Monetary Fund (2004a), 'Rules-based fiscal policy in emerging markets', available at http://www.imf.org/external/np/tr/2004/tr041006.htm.

International Monetary Fund (2004b), *El FMI en foco*, no. 33, available at http://www.imf.org/imfsurvey.

Kuczynski, P.P. and J. Williamson (2003), *After the Washington Consensus: Restarting Growth and Reform in Latin America*, Washington, DC: Institute for International Economics.

Mathieson, D. and J. Roldós (2001), 'The role of foreign banks in emerging markets', paper presented at the joint International Monetary Fund, World Bank, and Brookings Institution Conference, available at http://www.brooking.org.

Vidal, G. (2001), *Privatizaciones, fusiones y adquisiciones: las grandes empresas en América Latina*, Barcelona: Anthropos Editorial.

Vidal, G. (2002), 'Bancos, fortunas y poder: una lectura de la economía en el México del 2000', in E. Correa and A. Girón (eds), *Crisis y futuro de la banca en México*, Mexico: Miguel Ángel Porrúa Editor, 11–45.

Vilariño, A. (2001), 'La presencia de los bancos españoles en la economía mexicana', *Información Comercial Española*, Madrid, Ministerio de Economía, no. 795, 101–12.

World Bank (2000), *Global Development Finance Report*, Washington, DC: World Bank, available at http://www.wb.org.

4. East Asian Monetary and Financial Cooperation: The Long Road Ahead

Kok-Fay Chin

INTRODUCTION

The Asian financial crisis rekindled the interest in monetary and financial cooperation in East Asia.[1] Failure of international organizations, particularly the International Monetary Fund (IMF), to foresee the crisis and effectively deal with it led to renewed calls for some kinds of regional cooperation in the monetary and financial spheres. One might refer to financial cooperation as policy measures that facilitate cross-border financial flows by removing frictions and obstacles (Rajan, 2005). It can range from the creation of a regional bond fund to more intensive cooperation, involving agreement of a regional financial standards and prudential measures, cross-trading of financial instruments in various national markets, and facilitating intra-regional payments and settlements. Monetary cooperation, on the other hand, can range from steps to enhance regional financial surveillance and policy dialogue or swap arrangements to more intensive forms of monetary regionalism such as exchange rate coordination (including regional basket pegs or a regionally-harmonized exchange rate band) to full monetary integration incorporating a single currency and a common monetary policy (Eichengreen as cited in Rajan, 2005).

Among the main areas of monetary and financial cooperation that have been proposed or taken place, one should include the aborted Asian Monetary Fund (AMF), a series of bilateral swap and repurchase agreements under the Chiang Mai Initiative (CMI), the Asian bond market and Asian Bond Fund (ABF), as well as regional and multilateral surveillance. Each of these different forms of cooperation carries its own calculus of potential costs and benefits. It is important to recognize, in practical terms, that how monetary and financial cooperation will take place ultimately also depends on the prevailing regional and global political-economy factors, which impinge on the degree of cooperation.

This chapter begins with a discussion of the rationale for monetary and financial cooperation in the region, before examining the perceived costs and benefits of each regional initiative. We will then review its development since the Asian financial crisis. Owing to the political as well as economic divergences in East Asia, the following section attempts to identify the emerging issues and potential problems that influence regional monetary and financial cooperation, which seemingly revolves around the question of the economic gains, but its motivations and outcomes can be mainly driven by political concerns. The last section concludes this chapter with observation of recent positive signs of growing cooperation in the region.

RATIONALE FOR REGIONAL MONETARY AND FINANCIAL COOPERATION

It is not difficult to see why monetary and financial cooperation has been increasingly favoured by East Asian governments and scholars since the 1997 Asian financial crisis. Sussangkarn (2002) focuses on four reasons for monetary and financial cooperation among the East Asian economies:

- to prevent the recurrence of a crisis;
- to better manage a crisis should it occur;
- to have greater leverage in shaping the financial environment affecting the region;
- to facilitate economic integration of the region.

However, the rationale for such cooperation is not just economic but also institutional and political (Henning, 2002).

The crisis undoubtedly provided the strongest driving force for regional cooperation in money and finance. East Asian regionalism prior to the crisis had largely been limited to trade. The need for enhanced protection against financial crises is all the more justified as the existing regional institutional economic arrangements failed to provide regional public good of financial stability. Both ASEAN and APEC failed to address the major regional concern for financial volatility; they provided neither liquidity nor sound advice to their members (see Dieter and Higgot, 2003).

To the extent that the Asian financial crisis was due to illiquidity, some form of international liquidity enhancement measures in crisis conditions could minimize losses due to the crisis. As noted by Henning (2002, p. 8), '[t]o the extent that financial crises are driven by collapsing confidence, which played a larger role in some countries than others during the 1997–98 period, speed of disbursement is especially important'. As contagion often tends to have a regional as opposed to a global dimension, it provides a rationale for exploring regional solutions or approaches to tackling short-term liquidity difficulties (Rajan, 2003, p. 55). It strongly reinforces the common interest in crisis prevention and financial stabilization among the countries in the region.

As a defence against currency crises, East Asian economies have been bolstering their foreign reserves following their sharp decline in 1997. The abundant reserves have grown rapidly in 2003–4, as East Asian central banks intervened in markets to curb their currencies from rising too high against the falling US dollar, with an eye on protecting their exports. East Asian central banks control today more than two-thirds of global foreign exchange reserves, or more than 2.5 trillion US dollars (*International Herald Tribune*, 4 May 2005). Most of the reserves are held in US dollar-denominated assets. Nevertheless, reserve hoarding may not be an effective safeguard against external shocks and liquidity crises for two important reasons (Rajan, 2003, p. 56).

1. It carries high fiscal costs as the country effectively swaps high yielding domestic assets for lower yielding foreign assets.
2. Since foreign reserve holdings are an important determinant of creditworthiness, depleting them as a way of cushioning the effects of capital outflows on the exchange rate may worsen the situation by inducing further capital outflows.

Arguably, the mountain of reserves in East Asia would have been sufficient to deal with the liquidity crisis, if there had been a framework for cooperation to effectively pool together the total reserves in the region. Therefore, there is a rationale for countries in the region to look beyond domestic reserve management, to safeguard themselves from the vagaries of international capital markets.

It is also argued that the post-crisis financial cooperation initiatives are partly a reaction to the disappointment that 'most of the key measures that countries under the IMF program have had to follow to deal with the crisis were designed by individuals and institutions from outside the region, with little input from within the region and may not fully reflect the best interests of the affected countries' (Sussangkarn, 2002, p. 1). Weaknesses of the IMF

– notably its relatively slow decision making due to the diversity of its membership and its rigid programmes that are often not adapted to the local circumstances but reflect the interests of the United States – remain the major concern.

Regional monetary and financial cooperation is necessary, owing to the uncertainty about the future development of the international financial architecture, and the ability of the region's countries to access the resources of multilateral institutions. Regional facilities can supplement the resources of the IMF and other multilateral institutions. Regional financial cooperation can augment regional surveillance, supplementing the existing framework of the IMF. Interaction and exchange of views through regional arrangements serves as peer review exercise for regional economies to continuously review polices in order to strengthen resilience to adverse external shocks. This will contribute to better understanding, coordination, and technical standards all round (Grenville, 2000). The region as a whole stands to gain from its more superior and up-to-date information of what is happening in the region than multilateral institutions.

According to Japan's former Vice-Finance Minister, Dr Eisuke Sakakibara at the First East Asia Congress in Kuala Lumpur (*The Star*, 5 August 2003), East Asia needs to revive the idea of an Asian Monetary Fund – which was first mooted in late 1997 – to provide the region with financial stability and increased clout in a global arena dominated by the United States and Europe. Asia still lags behind Europe, where monetary and financial cooperation successfully led to the creation of a single currency and a common central bank. While the United States will promote the cause of those areas of principal interest to it (especially Latin America), and Europe will protect the interests of its Eastern European neighbours (including Russia) at the multilateral level, particularly at the IMF, the interests of Asian countries are left without a champion in the multilateral forum. It is obvious that the undersized quota of East Asian countries in the IMF does not properly reflect the current realities and their relative strengths in the world economy. Thus, East Asia needs a strong regional cooperation and representation as a way of refining, concentrating, and amplifying its voice so that 'the distilled wisdom of this interaction is heard more effectively in the multilateral forum' (Grenville, 2000, p. 1). Such cooperation not only would complement the development of East Asian regional cooperation in trade and direct investment, but also boost East Asian influence in multilateral organizations.

There is also a political rationale for monetary and financial cooperation. As Henning (2002, p. 9) puts it:

Although the Cold War is over in Europe, many political conflicts in Asia remain unresolved. Regional cooperation can nonetheless limit the damage to economic relations when political conflict breaks out. By raising the economic cost of political disputes, moreover, such cooperation provides additional incentives for peaceful resolution of conflicts. Regional cooperation would create a context in which the emergence of China could be managed, in particular.

OPTIONS FOR COPING WITH THE VOLATILITY OF CAPITAL FLOWS

Recent literature has clearly shown that one main attribute that accounts for the rising frequency of financial crisis concerns destabilizing capital flows, especially portfolio investment and other short-term capital flows. Hence, the relevant question asks what are the options to deal with financial globalization with its huge, volatile capital flows? Kohsaka (2005, pp. 304–7) discusses three policy options, namely, exchange rate arrangements, the strengthening of prudential regulation, and capital controls on volatile capital flows. He emphasizes, however, that a unique, all-weather solution does not exist.

There is no unique solution for an optimal exchange rate regime, as the choice would depend on the functions and governance of a country's foreign exchange markets and domestic markets. This is especially true for developing countries at different stages of development and with different economic environments. Kohsaka (2005, p. 304) argues that '[i]t is therefore impossible to recommend one unique optimal exchange rate regime applicable to developing economies in general. Even an optimal exchange rate regime for one country might become sub-optimal as the country's environment changes'.

On prudential regulation, Kohsaka (2005, p. 305) recognizes the importance of strengthening market discipline, supervision and regulation of public authorities, and internal governance of private financial institutions in order to avoid moral hazard. Each country should favour a system of closer prudential regulation intended to contain capital inflows and deter speculative surges. Nevertheless, not much improvement can be expected in developing countries in the short run, as these elements depend on the stage of development of markets and institutions across countries.

Capital controls, especially on destabilizing short-term capital, can be regarded as second best precautionary measures against international capital market failures, especially owing to information problems and their resulting external diseconomies (Kohsaka, 2005, p. 306; Arestis et al., Chapter 8 this volume). For Arestis et al. (Chapter 8 this volume) capital controls paradoxically have a role to play in the process of capital account liberalization. Since only the countries with sound institutions would benefit from capital account liberalization, capital controls must be maintained whilst the process of institutional reforms last. In the absence of sound institutions, capital controls can curb the adverse economic consequences arising from unfettered capital account liberalization, although they cannot avoid financial crises generated by domestic circumstances.

In addition, this chapter emphasises that these measures need to be accompanied by greater cooperation among monetary authorities in the region. First, capital controls would face serious political impediments from the most powerful actors in the international economy – from international financial institutions such as the World Bank and the IMF, to the governments of the wealthy nations of the world, particularly the United States, to the largest financial and non-financial corporations. As noted by Griffith-Jones (2003, p. 446), '[i]ndustry country governments seem to be the key stakeholder group, though banks and market actors are also influential. This pattern persists because the reforms of primary interest to developing countries would require industrial countries to provide resources or take other policy action.'

Secondly, while the developing countries have been urged by increasing calls, especially from the United States and the IMF, for reforms along with the neoliberal line, the progress of reform of the global financial architecture that includes the prevention, management, and resolution of financial crises in a timely and effective manner has been painfully slow. Thus, there should be more acceptance of regional cooperative arrangements as alternatives. Moreover, as pointed out by Jomo (2005, Internet site):

> Instead of trying to assert greater national control, with limited efficacy likely, cooperation among governments in a region is more likely to be effective than going it alone in the face of the larger magnitude and velocity of capital flows. The existence of such regional arrangements also offers an intermediate alternative between national and global levels of action and intervention, and reduces the likely monopolistic powers of global authorities. To be successful and effective, such regional arrangements must be flexible, but credible, and capable of effective counter-cyclical initiatives for crisis prevention as well as management.

Of course, this is not an easy, though not impossible, task, as we show in the following section.

THE JOURNEY SO FAR

The rationale above inspired several East Asian countries to take more serious initiatives to guard themselves against future crises, and to attain financial stability in the region. At the IMF annual meeting in Hong Kong in September 1997, Japan proposed to establish an Asian Monetary Fund, that is, a 100 billion US dollar fund aimed at providing trade finance and balance of payments support in order to assist the crisis economies in the region. While the proposal was supported by most of the ASEAN countries, Japan's pursuit of an AMF independent of the United States' influence drew strong objection from both the United States and the IMF. Their opposition was based on the premise that an AMF will lead to the moral hazard problem and duplicate the IMF functions. Failure to invite the regional key powerhouses, particularly China, for discussion before the AMF proposal also caused some countries to be suspicious of Japan in dominating the AMF in a similar manner as the United States dominates the IMF. Eventually, the Japanese proposal was aborted, although it brings more benefits than costs to the regional economies (see Table 4.1).

The United States effectively blocked the Japanese initiative in setting up an AMF, but did not contribute many resources to managing the regional crisis. Clearly, the United States wanted to dictate how Asian economies should be run without paying for its hegemony (Tadokoro, 2003). With the inclusion of the United States as a member, the Manila Framework Group (MFG), which was created in November 1997 in place of the AMF, was supposed to discuss monetary and financial cooperation, but it did not even have staff or financial resources. Thus, it turned out to be nothing more than a meeting group.

The latter half of 1998 saw a sudden change in the global economic environment. What was perceived earlier as a regional crisis now appeared to spread beyond East Asia, as financial turmoil spread even further to Russia and Brazil in August 1998, and the near bankruptcy of Long Term Capital Management (LTCM) – a hedge fund based in New York – surfaced in September.

After the LTCM crisis, the high-ranking officials in the United States and Japan agreed that the world economy was heading towards a 'serious crisis', and began working on counter-measures to combat it.

Table 4.1. Major areas of Asian monetary and financial cooperation

Area	Benefit(s)	Cost(s)	Progress	Chief impediment(s)
AMF	As a regional lender of last resort when it was first mooted, it provides a crisis-stricken country with rapid liquidity. It develops its own form of regional surveillance and policy dialogue according to the regional realities. A regional fund gives more appropriate advice due to more superior and up-to-date information. It is delinked from IMF conditionality.	It may lead to moral hazard. It is feared that Japan will dominate the AMF in the same way as the United States dominates the IMF.	The AMF proposal was aborted.	Strong objection from the United States and the IMF.
A network of BSAs under the CMI	It acts as a 'firewall' against future financial crises by providing countries facing the possibility of a temporary liquidity shortage with additional short-term hard currencies. It is likely to be a more effective strategy than reserve hoarding, which carries high fiscal costs, and less problematic than obtaining contingent credit lines from foreign banks and private financial institutions unilaterally.	It may lead to moral hazard on the part of potential borrowers (government and central banks), delaying the necessary adjustment in the region and hence worsening the severity of crises when they strike.	The current arrangements are insufficient in size to be effective in crisis periods. It is tightly tied to IMF conditionality. There has been little progress towards multilateralization of arrangements.	Difficulty moving beyond surveillance concerns owing to the lack of ASEAN+3's credible mechanism for surveillance of member countries.

70

Common currency arrangement (the yen bloc proposal)	It reduces currency volatility, contributing to regional financial stability. It reduces transaction costs of trade within the region. Less room for beggar-thy-neighbour devaluation.	Participating countries would have to give up independent monetary policy.	No initiative except a commitment to study the issues under the 'Kobe Research Project', proposed by Japan and endorsed in the third Asia–Europe Finance Ministers' meeting.	Difficult to find an optimal currency arrangement owing to substantial diversities within the region. Great resistance owing to loss of sovereignty over monetary policy.
Asian bond market	It recycles part of the region's surplus savings to finance development within the regional economies. It enables Asian central banks to diversify their investments beyond the more traditional reserve assets to enhance their returns. It is aimed at promoting bond markets in the region by investing in a basket of US dollar denominated bonds issued by Asian sovereign and quasi-sovereign issuers in EMEAP economies (except Japan, Australia, and New Zealand).	Public sector involvement in establishing and investing in local bond funds such as ABF2 may create moral hazard problems as it may serve as a mechanism for financing fiscal deficits of member countries and bailing out individual issuers.	Growth of local currency bond markets in East Asia in recent years has been skewed toward the government sector, largely driven by the need in many East Asian countries to finance post-crisis banking sector recapitalization programmes and provide fiscal stimulus to support economic recovery.	Corporate bond market development lags behind that of government bond markets in terms of size and liquidity owing to: • Narrow issuer and investor base • Underdeveloped hedging products and derivatives markets • Uneven disclosure standards and weak framework for creditor rights • Relatively poor transaction and general data reporting

Sources: Fabella (2002), Henning (2002), Rajan (2003), Amyx (2004), and Asian Development Bank (2005).

When the global financial disorder threatened the United States' stock market boom and economic stability, it appeared that the US policy rapidly shifted away from stringently imposing structural reform through IMF conditionality on crisis-stricken countries, in line with the Washington consensus, to giving priority to stabilization by opening public credit lines.

It is in this new context that the idea of establishing a framework that did not rely on involvement of the United States resurfaced in a variety of forms thereafter. A new Japanese proposal, the New Miyazawa Initiative (NMI), which was presented during the annual meeting of the IMF and World Bank in October 1998, did not meet the similar fate like the AMF proposed a year earlier. As noted by Tadokoro (2003, p. 232):

> The United States, in sharp contrast to its attitude towards the AMF, warmly welcomed the new Japanese proposal. The American endorsement of the Japanese proposal seemed to be a quid pro quo for Japanese support for a new short-term facility established within the IMF to bail out Latin American countries. With a financial crisis looming large in Latin America, the US Congress also finally agreed on the appropriation of $18 billion for an IMF capital increase.

The NMI was basically a package of bilateral assistance totalling 30 billion dollars from Japan, mainly in the form of loans and credit guarantees to help revive the countries hit by the crisis. It complemented the IMF assistance in countries having IMF programmes in place, whereas in countries where IMF programmes were not in place, it substituted for IMF aid rather than supplementing it. In 1999, the NMI was expanded beyond loans and credit guarantees, to include the establishment of backup facilities, in the form of currency swap agreements, with the central banks of South Korea and Malaysia (Amyx, 2002).

The NMI was seen as an initial step towards the revival of the notion of an AMF (Amyx, 2002). While welcoming a greater leadership role for Japan, the ten ASEAN countries at the same time hoped that Japan would consult more actively with regional leaders, to ensure that the region's concerns are reflected in the process. An informal regional grouping known as ASEAN+3[2] was formed when Japan, China, and South Korea were invited to their summit meeting in 1997 in Kuala Lumpur. Starting from 1999, this emerging regional grouping has gathered its momentum when it expanded the level of cooperation between its member countries to include an annual Finance Ministers meeting held in parallel with the annual Asian Development Bank (ADB) meeting of the board of governors (Amyx, 2002).

The following ASEAN+3 Finance Ministers meeting in Chiang Mai in May 2000 came up with a framework to increase the availability of liquidity through swap lines as defense against future currency crises. This framework, known as the Chiang Mai Initiative (CMI), involves:

1. The expansion of an existing ASEAN Swap Agreement (ASA) among the prior member countries of ASEAN to all its ten member countries, and enlargement of the funds in this network to one billion dollars.
2. The setting-up of a network of bilateral currency swap agreements (BSAs) that included Japan, China, and South Korea.

As a result, the CMI in principle provides for 33 BSAs to be negotiated: 30 agreements between each of the three North-East Asian countries and each of the ten ASEAN member countries, plus three agreements among the three North-East Asian countries themselves. As Table 4.2 shows, only 16 BSAs have been signed or are currently being negotiated among ASEAN+3 nations since 2001, collectively amounting to 36.5 billion dollars.[3] This framework provides short-term financial assistance in the form of swaps[4] to member countries facing short-term liquidity problems. Supplementing rather than replacing the existing international financial arrangements, countries that draw more than 10 per cent under their swap arrangements must have an IMF-supported programme in place.

As an effective regional surveillance mechanism is important to the working of the CMI arrangement, the ASEAN+3 finance forum adopted new mechanisms in order to enhance the surveillance processes under the CMI arrangement. These included deepening and broadening the exchange of economic reviews and policy dialogues among the ASEAN+3 countries, and strengthening regional capital-flow monitoring through data exchange and assessments of developments among members, and the training of personnel needed for these exercises.

Nevertheless, three dimensions of the CMI make it fall short of being a functional equivalent to the aborted AMF (Amyx, 2004). First, the amounts involved under the CMI remain small and insufficient for stopping speculative attacks. Secondly, the release of 90 per cent of the funds in the BSAs is subject to recipient countries already having an IMF programme in place. Thirdly, the arrangements remain bilateral rather than being multilateral.

Table 4.2. BSAs under the Chiang Mai Initiative

	Malaysia	Indonesia	Philippines	Singapore	Thailand	China	Korea
China	• 9 Oct. 2002[1] (US$1.5 billion)	• 30 Dec. 2003[1] (US$1 billion)	• 29 Aug. 2003[1] (US$1 billion)		• 6 Dec. 2001[1] (US$2 billion)		
Korea	• 26 July 2002[2] (US$1 billion)	• 24 Dec. 2003[2] (US$1 billion)	• 9 Aug. 2002[2] (US$1 billion)		• 11 June 2002[2] (US$1 billion)	o 24 June 2002[2] (US$2 billion)	
Japan	• 5 Oct. 2001[1] (US$1 billion) *Renewed on 5 Oct. 2004*	• 17 Feb. 2003[1] (US$3 billion)	• 27 Aug. 2001[1] (US$3 billion) *Renewed on 27 Aug. 2004*	• 10 Nov. 2003[1] (US$1 billion)	• 30 July 2001[1] (US$3 billion) *Under negotiation for renewal*	o 28 May 2002[2] (US$3 billion)	o 4 July 2001[1] (US$2 billion)

Notes: Dates indicate when the agreements have been signed (maximum drawing amount for each agreement is in parentheses).
[1] A one-way swap arrangement where the requesting country under the agreement can request the swap-providing country to enter into a swap transaction.
[2] A two-way swap arrangement where either party could request the other party to enter into a swap transaction under the agreement.
• Agreements signed between the Plus Three countries (People's Republic of China, Japan, and Korea) and ASEAN countries.
o Agreements signed among the Plus Three countries.

Source: Bank Negara Malaysia (2005, p. 231).

Regional financial cooperation went a step further when the proposal for the formation of an Asian bond market garnered strong support from leaders and central bankers in the region. In June 2003, the Executives' Meeting of East Asia–Pacific central banks (EMEAP), comprising 11 central banks and monetary authorities in the East Asia and Pacific region,[5] jointly launched the one billion dollar Asian Bond Fund to invest in US dollar sovereign and quasi-sovereign bonds issued in EMEAP countries (except Australia, New Zealand, and Japan). While the ABF addresses the demand side challenges, the Asian Bond Market Initiative (ABMI), which was later in the same year launched by the ASEAN+3, addresses the supply side issues by providing the necessary infrastructure for a well-functioning regional bond market. Six working groups have been set up, each addressing a key area for local currency bond market development (Asian Development Bank, 2004).[6] A focal group has also been established to coordinate and monitor the work of the six working groups. Following the successful launch of the first ABF, the EMEAP launched the second ABF (ABF2), amounting to two billion dollars, to invest in the local currency bond markets in the region (Asian Development Bank, 2005). Half of this amount was allocated to the Pan-Asia Bond Index Fund (PAIF)[7] and the balance for the Fund of Bond Funds (FoBF),[8] distributed to eight single-market domestic currency funds.

Although the idea was not new, previous efforts to develop an Asian bond market as an avenue for channelling Asian capital toward regional financing did not succeed (see Amyx, 2004). The idea is justified, since international financial intermediation has been taking place outside the region, particularly in the United States. Capital-exporting Asian countries like Japan, Taiwan, Singapore, and the Arab nations have been using bond markets in the United States and Europe to lend out their funds, while Asian countries requiring capital have to raise their funds from Western financial markets. The proposed Asian bond market is aimed to lessen the need for Asian countries to depend on Western financial markets to recycle their funds, hence contributing to economic growth in the region. A regional bond market also reduces reliance of Asian countries on the banking sector. It also addresses the currency mismatch problem that contributed to the regional crisis.

One aspect of surveillance that deserves priority, but has yet to show much progress, concerns the need of an effective dialogue among the participating countries about their expectations of as well as perspectives on exchange rate policy. Such a regional dialogue is essential to avoid potential currency conflicts that may arise owing to the different exchange rate regimes in the region. The recent conflict occurred after the 2001–02 depreciation of the yen against the dollar, which was favoured by Japan facing a sharp recession during the period. Most governments in the region allowed their currencies to depreciate, partly matching the depreciation of the Japanese currency (see Henning, 2002, p. 89). By contrast, China strongly protests against further depreciation of the yen, which, according to the Governor of the People's Bank of China (China's central bank), could create 'a domino effect of depreciations in Asia' (*Dow Jones International News* cited in Henning, 2002, p. 27).

Obviously, the region needs not only a more effective regional cooperation on exchange rate policy but also more concerted efforts toward a common currency arrangement that can benefit the region. In 2001–02, officials in Japan's Ministry of Finance (MoF) increasingly sought to use the cooperative framework within the ASEAN+3 as a stepping stone for introducing a common currency in the region (Amyx, 2004, p. 9). A common regional currency can contribute to the regional public good of financial stability (see Table 4.1). But it turned out to be problematic when the MoF saw it as a way to stimulate Japanese financial markets by pursuing a yen-centred regional exchange rate regime, eliciting deep suspicion of Japan's motives within the region. Owing to the widely diverse stages of economic development and structure of trade in the region, there clearly was no currency arrangement optimal to all players in the region. Thus, the idea was viewed as 'one that focused on regional integration through the prism of Japan's national interests rather than through the prism of greater regional collective interests' (Amyx, 2004, p. 9). Consequently, few regional players were keen to commit significant resources in this effort, other than engaging in study groups under the 'Kobe Research Project', proposed by Japan in 2001.

LONG ROAD AHEAD

Since the outbreak of the Asian financial crisis, enhanced sentiment in favour of cooperation within the region continues to flourish, with increasing efforts to strengthen monetary and financial cooperation in the region under various regional fora, of which the most significant include the ASEAN+3 and the EMEAP. What determines the direction of the journey so far? Put differently, what explains the variation in outcomes across the various regional monetary and financial cooperation initiatives pursued so far? Cost–benefit analysis of each regional initiative cannot account for the different progress made. There is no simple answer to this question. Yet understanding of this will help us to see what determines the journey ahead.

As the previous section has shown, one problematic obstacle in regional monetary and financial cooperation stems from the external impediment of hegemonic forces as in the case of the aborted AMF proposal. In contrast, the regional cooperation that has been materialized remained in two main areas, which did not incur opposition from key players outside the region: the establishment of mechanisms for short-term liquidity support in time of crisis, and the regional bond market development. The establishment of a fully-fledged regional bond market has progressed relatively fast, not only because it can be pursued without sacrifice of national sovereignty, but also as it elicited support from 'actors outside the region who are eager to benefit from its expected by-products, including financial liberalization and reform in ASEAN+3 economies' (Amyx, 2004, p. 3). In addition, it is unlikely to affect the United States in the near or medium term, so long as the dollar remains an important anchor currency for most Asian governments to maintain their currency pegs.

In the case of the absence of external impediment, the biggest problem emerged when the cooperation framework – such as the establishment of a common currency arrangement in the region – impinged on sovereignty of the participating countries. Owing to the heavy reliance on exports by the regional economies, exchange rate policy remains one of the most sensitive issues surrounding monetary and financial cooperation in the region. The journey to a common currency arrangement is, therefore, expected to be complicated, if not impossible. Even if the region advances to form a regional monetary system, there is no room for a yen-centred regional currency area. China and other key players in East Asia are not likely to agree with an effectively hegemonic role for the Japanese currency. In addition, Japanese monetary policy lacks the transparency and cohesion needed to achieve the status of a widely accepted reserve currency (Wang, cited in Dieter and Higgot, 2003, p. 440).

The road to enhanced regional cooperation in East Asia is not likely to be smooth. After all, it has taken Europe almost 50 years of slow progress to reach the integration levels it has today. A regional monetary arrangement for East Asia does not seem to be possible along the path that led to the European single currency: political as well as economic divergences – more intensive than within the European Union – point to the need to search for alternative strategies for East Asian monetary integration. The current global political-economy context shaping the East Asian regionalization is different from the framework under which European integration took place. As noted by Diehl (2005, p. 4), '[t]he global system is no longer defined by the bipolarity of the superpower rivalry, but rather by the unipolarity of the US dominance with perhaps some form of multipolarity on the horizon. More importantly, globalization has unleashed divergent forces on regional integration efforts'.

An important lesson to be drawn from the process of monetary cooperation in Europe is that:

> there is nothing better than an operational framework to promote and focus monetary cooperation. Such a framework could be a swap arrangement requiring accounting and settlement services, or it could be an ABF or some form of exchange rate mechanism. What matters is that any such arrangement makes it necessary to meet, to exchange views and to take decisions in common. This in turn builds knowledge and mutual trust, which provide the basis for getting through difficult moments in more ambitious cooperative undertakings (Baer, 2004, Internet site).

As the European experience shows, strong political will is surely a *sine qua non* condition for the move towards monetary union. It is important to try to get as much input into policy discussions as possible, so that the region's concerns are reflected in the process.

Despite some impediments, the journey so far has provided a foundation for more productive regional dialogue on further enhancement of financial and monetary cooperation in the future. This chapter ends with observation of recent positive signs that the CMI will progress leading to growing regionalism.

- Even though almost eight years have passed since the financial crisis hit the region, the East Asian countries have not forgotten the traumatic and costly experience, and hence tend to be more tolerant to set aside their differences in order to enhance regional cooperation so as to improve the region's resilience to future financial crises. The approaching East Asian Summit – the first milestone en route to the creation of the East Asian Community – to be held in Malaysia at the end of 2005 bears testimony to the growing consciousness of East Asian as a region.
- Although its performance in fulfilling its mandate for regional cooperation in the past was rather modest, the Asian Development Bank's (ADB) role in regional development as well as cooperation has been expanded. As an institutional arrangement to coordinate the activities of the CMI and other financial cooperation in the region, the ADB set up the Office of Regional Economic Integration in April 2005 (*ADB News Release*, 1 April 2005). This new institution will act as ADB's new focal point for regional bodies, fora, and initiatives related to regional cooperation and integration, including the ASEAN+3 Finance Ministers Process, the ASEAN

Surveillance Process, the APEC Finance Ministers Process, and the Asia–Europe Finance Ministers Process.

- One oft-cited impediment of regional monetary and financial cooperation concerns political conflicts and potential security disputes in the region, particularly the war legacy of Japanese occupation before as well as during World War II, and territorial disputes in the South China Sea.[9] Nevertheless, the recent souring Sino–Japanese and South Korean–Japanese relations, which hit a new low following Japan's approval of a revised controversial history textbook in April 2005, does not seem to affect the ASEAN+3 process.[10] In May 2005, finance ministers from ASEAN+3 agreed to expand their system of BSAs under the CMI to a more multilateral system, so that the relevant BSAs would be activated collectively and promptly in case of an emergency. If this materializes, coupled with the support of an effective surveillance system, the CMI constitutes a *de facto* regional monetary fund, which could further promote a higher level of cooperation, coordination, and integration. With their pledge to boost by up to 100 per cent the size of currency swaps, crisis-hit member countries would also be able to draw down as much as 20 per cent of the funds under the BSAs without having to go through the IMF.[11]

APPENDIX: EAST ASIAN POST-CRISIS MONETARY AND FINANCIAL COOPERATION TIMELINE

September 1997	Japanese proposal to establish a 100 billion dollar Asian Monetary Fund opposed by the United States and the International Monetary Fund.
November 1997	ASEAN leaders invite China, Japan, and South Korea to their summit meeting in Kuala Lumpur.
	Manila Framework Group (AMG) created for regional cooperation to enhance the prospects for financial stability.
October 1998	ASEAN finance ministers' meeting officially establishes the ASEAN Surveillance Process (ASP) based on the principles of peer review for all member countries, complementing the global surveillance undertaken by the IMF.
	Japan implements the New Miyazawa Initiative (NMI) as a bilateral support mechanism to assist Asian countries hit by the financial crisis.
November 1999	The ASEAN+3 summit declares a 'Joint Statement on East Asian Cooperation' that covers a wide range of possible areas for regional cooperation.
May 2000	Finance ministers of ASEAN+3 at their meeting in Chiang Mai agree to strengthen the existing cooperative frameworks in the

	region through the Chiang Mai Initiative (CMI), involving an expanded ASEAN Swap Arrangement (ASA) that includes all ASEAN members and a network of bilateral swap and repurchase agreement facilities among ASEAN countries, China, Japan, and South Korea.
January 2001	The third Asia–Europe Finance Ministers' meeting endorses the Kobe Research Project proposed by Japan, which is designed to facilitate interregional cooperative research and study activities on topics of mutual interest, such as regional monetary cooperation, exchange rate regimes, and public debt management under Asia–Europe cooperation.
January 2002	The Japanese Prime Minister, Junichiro Koizumi, conceptualizes an East Asian Community to create a community of 15 countries including Australia and New Zealand in addition to the ASEAN+3 countries.
June 2003	EMEAP launches the one billion dollar Asian Bond Fund.
August 2003	ASEAN+3 finance ministers endorse the ABMI.
May 2004	The Asian Bonds Online website is launched.
December 2004	EMEAP launches the Asian Bond Fund 2.
April 2005	The President of the Asian Development Bank announces the establishment of the Office of Regional Economic Integration.
May 2005	ASEAN+3 finance ministers agree to expand their system of BSAs under the CMI to a more multilateral system.

NOTES

1. East Asia includes North-East as well as South-East Asian countries.
2. ASEAN+3 is composed of the Association of South-East Asian Nations (ASEAN) plus the People's Republic of China (henceforth China), Japan, and South Korea.
3. This amount is based on the overall availability under the BSAs, where the maximum drawing amount under two-way swap arrangements is counted twice to reflect the swap amount available to both parties under the agreement.
4. A currency swap is an agreement to exchange one currency for another and to reverse the transaction in the future (see Henning, 2002, p. 16, box 3.1).
5. The countries involved are Indonesia, Malaysia, Thailand, the Philippines, Singapore, China, Hong Kong, Japan, South Korea, Australia, and New Zealand.
6. The six key areas include new securitized debt instruments, credit guarantee and investment mechanisms, foreign exchange transactions and settlement issues, issuance of bonds denominated in local currencies by multilateral development banks, foreign government agencies, as well as Asian multinational corporations, rating systems and dissemination of information on Asian bond markets, and technical assistance coordination.
7. PAIF is a single bond fund index investing in sovereign and quasi-sovereign local currency-denominated bonds issued in eight EMEAP countries.
8. FoBF is a two-tiered structure with a parent fund investing in eight sub-funds, each of which will invest in local currency sovereign and quasi-sovereign bonds issued in their respective markets.
9. The latest territorial dispute emerged in February 2005 after the Malaysian government awarded a contract to energy giant Shell to develop a deep water oil block in the disputed

oil-rich maritime area off East Kalimantan in the Sulawesi Sea. The Indonesian government has insisted the Ambalat oil block is outside Malaysian territory.

10. According to its critics, this controversial textbook whitewashed Japan's military past and wartime atrocities in the first half of the twentieth century, including forcing tens of thousands of women into sex slavery. Demonstrations against Japan, which subsequently erupted and spread in China, also included calls for a boycott of Japanese products. Meanwhile, Japan's relations with Korea have also deteriorated as a civics textbook approved by the Japanese government reiterated its claim to a chain of uninhabited rock islands held by Korea in the Sea of Japan.

11. See the Joint Ministerial Statement of the Eight ASEAN+3 Finance Ministers' Meeting, 4 May 2005, Istanbul, Turkey, available at http://www.aseansec.org/afp/113.htm.

REFERENCES

Amyx, J.A. (2002), 'Moving beyond bilateralism? Japan and the Asian Monetary Fund', *Pacific Economic Papers*, no. 331.

Amyx, J.A. (2004), 'A regional bond market for East Asia? The evolving political dynamics of regional financial cooperation', *Pacific Economic Papers*, no. 342.

Asian Development Bank (2004), *Asian Bond Monitor 2004*, November, available at http://asianbondsonline.adb.org.

Asian Development Bank (2005), *Asian Bond Monitor 2005*, April, available at http://asianbondsonline.adb.org.

Baer, G. (2004), 'Asian financial cooperation as seen from Europe', speech given at the Korea University and Bank for International Settlements international conference on 'Asian Bond Markets: Issues and Prospects', Seoul, 21–23 March, available at http://www.bis.org/speeches/sp040323.htm.

Bank Negara Malaysia (2005), *Annual Report 2004*, Kuala Lumpur: Bank Negara Malaysia.

Diehl, P.F. (2005), 'Can East Asia be like Europe? Exploring selected conditions for regional integration', paper presented to the international conference on 'The Emerging East Asian Community: Economic and Security Issues', organized by the Institute of Malaysian and International Studies (University Kebangsaan Malaysia) and the Center for East Asian and Pacific Studies (University of Illinois), Urbana-Champaign, 19–20 May.

Dieter, H. and R. Higgot (2003), 'Exploring alternative theories of economic regionalism: from trade to finance in Asian co-operation?', *Review of International Political Economy*, **10** (3), 430–54.

Fabella, R. (2002), 'Monetary cooperation in East Asia: a survey', *ERD Working Paper*, no. 13.

Grenville, S.A. (2000), 'Notes on East Asian financial cooperation', paper presented at the ANU international conference on 'Financial Markets and Policies in East Asia', Camberra, 4 September.

Griffith-Jones, S. (2003), 'International financial stability and market efficiency as a global public good', in I. Kaul (ed.), *Providing Global Public Good: Managing Globalization*, Oxford: Oxford University Press, 435–54.

Henning, C.R. (2002), *East Asian Financial Cooperation*, Washington, DC: Institute for International Economics.

Jomo, K.S. (2005), 'Sovereign debt for sustainable development', *News Analysis*, International Development Economics Association, 9 March, available at http://www.networkideas.org.

Kohsaka, A. (2005), 'A quest for a new international financial architecture: an Asia–Pacific perspective', in L.K. Tae (ed.), *Globalizaiton and the Asia Pacific Economy*, London and New York: Routledge, 300–317.

Rajan, R.S. (2003), 'Liquidity enhancing measures and monetary cooperation in East Asia: rationale and progress', in *Economic Globalization and Asia: Essays on Finance, Trade and Taxation*, Singapore: World Scientific, 27–82.

Rajan, R.S. (2005), 'Sequence of financial, trade, and monetary regionalism', in Asian Development Bank (ed.), *Asian Economic Cooperation and Integration: Progress, Prospects, and Challenges*, Manila: Asian Development Bank, 77–92.

Sussangkarn, C. (2002), 'East Asian financial cooperation: an assessment of the rationales', paper presented at the conference on 'East Asian Cooperation' organized by the Institute of Asia Pacific Studies and the Center for APEC and East Asian Cooperation, Chinese Academy of Social Sciences, Beijing, 22–23 August.

Tadokoro, M. (2003), 'The Asian financial crisis and Japanese policy reactions', in R. Geoffrey, D. Underhill and Z. Xiaoke (eds), *International Financial Governance under Stress: Global Structures versus National Imperatives*, Cambridge: Cambridge University Press, 223–40.

5. Does Financial Liberalization Affect the Distribution of Income between Wages and Profits?

Domenica Tropeano

INTRODUCTION

This chapter reviews different approaches of the transmission channel from financial liberalization to the distribution of income. The second section considers the empirical evidence on the effects of financial liberalization. As we will see, the findings of the empirical literature contradict most propositions of the neoclassical theory about the effects of financial liberalization. The increase in investment and saving, and in output growth, resulting from improved efficiency does not often materialize. Although there is a broad consensus on the mostly disappointing results of the implementation of financial liberalization policies, no agreement exists so far on the possible explanations for these failures. This chapter focuses on the worsening in income distribution that, according to many studies (Behrman et al., 2000; Cornia and Kiiski, 2001; Morley, 2001; Cornia, 2004a, 2004b), occurs after liberalization processes, in particular financial liberalization. Although another important channel of worsening income distribution is the rise in financial rents (see Yeldan, 2004), this aspect will not be addressed in this chapter, which rather deals with the worsening in the functional distribution of income between wages and profits.

In the third section, we discuss why, from a post-Keynesian perspective, financial liberalization worsens the distribution of income. The conclusion here is that the increase in saving, as a result of financial liberalization, creates a lack of effective demand, excess capacity, and falling profits, consistent with the paradox of thrift established in post-Keynesian models. In the fourth section, we investigate another possible link between financial liberalization and income distribution, starting from the stylized fact that real interest rates have risen everywhere after financial liberalization. We will explain the link between higher real interest rates and lower wages using the monetary theory of distribution. We will also discuss the limitations of this theory in an environment with growing international competition. The last section concludes.

STYLIZED FACTS AND EMPIRICAL EVIDENCE

According to neoclassical theory (see McKinnon, 1973), financial liberalization fosters the mobilization of savings and investment. The rise in the interest rate on deposits would increase savings deposited at banks, and hence the supply of credit to finance investment. Another, more recent strand of literature, which follows the same approach, argues that financial liberalization fosters investment and growth, not only through the increase in the supply of credit, but also through the gains in efficiency for the whole economic system that would stem from a more efficient financial system. A financial system with lower costs and a better managerial organization, both due to the increase in competition, would imply lower costs of the services it provides and thus higher investment (see King and Levine, 1993; Demirguc-Kunt et al., 1998; Levine, 2001).

In this section, we compare the predictions of this theory with the facts. In light of the results of the empirical literature, we consider the extent of financial deepening and the cost of capital after financial reforms. Then we discuss whether saving and investment have increased. In the last subsection we focus on the issue, rather unsettled up to now, of whether – and indeed how – financial reforms affect income distribution and inequality.

Financial Deepening

A number of empirical studies have established that the increase in money and credit supply favours growth (King and Levine, 1993; Levine, 1997; Levine and Zervos, 1998; Beck et al., 2000). These studies are cross-country analyses that use data from many different countries and over considerable periods of time. Given that industrial development goes hand in hand with financial capital development, these findings indeed are not surprising. While the old literature on the subject (see McKinnon, 1973) stresses the financial deepening effect, the new literature (see Levine, 2001; Demirguc-Kunt et al., 1998) argues that financial liberalization fosters growth not only because it increases the supply of credit but also because it improves the efficiency of the financial system. A more efficient financial system would in turn contribute through various channels to the overall efficiency of the economic system. In particular, if growth is related more to productivity increase than to capital accumulation, then the beneficial effects of the improved productivity of banks will spill over the whole economy. It is then assumed that the rise in productivity will foster growth. Both Demirguc-Kunt et al. (1998) and Levine (2001) refer to the case of South Korea.

It is not clear how the link between a decline in banks' profits, which would result from increased competition, and efficiency should be interpreted. If efficiency is just the efficiency of the whole banking sector, then its weight over the whole financial system is so low that it seems unlikely that it could boost growth. In fact, in that country, after financial liberalization, the share of both assets and liabilities of banks versus non-bank financial institutions declined dramatically (see Tropeano, 2001). Generally speaking, it cannot be claimed that liberalization increases the efficiency and the size of the financial system in all countries. Although financial deepening has occurred in developing countries, which have liberalized in the 1990s, in some countries, in particular in Asia, this has increased the efficiency of a small part of the financial system only. Certainly, there has been an expansion of the supply of credit, but the quality and the conditions of this credit were very poor, for the weight of traditional bank credit has decreased in the total credit supply. Most of the new credit was provided by non-bank financial institutions and consisted in underwriting commercial papers issued by firms. This credit was therefore legally granted as underwriting of short-term securities. The institutions that were active in this market for commercial papers were not efficient at all. On the other hand, the banks, with so many competitors, suffered losses in profits and, to recover, have entered new and risky areas of business. In fact, financial systems have not become more efficient, and their imbalances have often led to painful financial crises. For instance, the banking systems of East-Asian countries, which had successfully supported industrial development for decades, were terribly shaken and eventually broke down (see Tropeano, 2001).

The stylized facts are an expansion in the supply of credit that follows the first steps of liberalization, then a financial crisis, and a costly restructuring of the financial system with the closures of many financial institutions and the merger of the few healthy banks left with foreign banks. After the crisis, banks usually show both a more prudent attitude towards lending and improved accounts, while the supply of credit is falling (for Latin America, see Moguillansky et al., 2004). For example, in Mexico, after various financial crises, the ratio of money supply to output is today one of the lowest in the world (see Bonturi, 2002). Honohan (2001) also finds that in a sample of developing countries, for the period 1980–98, inflation, financial deepening (measured as the ratio of M2 to GDP), and output growth did not change significantly with respect to the previous period.

If we consider the medium-term effects of financial liberalization in developing countries, it cannot be asserted that financial deepening occurs as a consequence of liberalization. The argument that the increased efficiency of the financial system will spill over to the whole economic system as reduced costs for credit, thus enhancing overall productivity, does not seem convincing: the reason is that the increased efficiency of a part of the financial system gets along with reduced lending to the domestic economy and higher interest rates (Table 5.1).

Table 5.1. Real rates of growth of credit and real rates of interest in Latin America, 1997–2001

Country	Real rate of growth of credit		Real rate of interest on loans		
	1997–2000	2000–2001	1997–2000	2000	2001
Argentina	1.4	–17.6	11.0	12.7	27.0
Brazil	11.4	14.4	66.6	48.1	46.4
Chile	6.8	9.1	11.0	9.7	9.5
Colombia	–1.5	12.9	16.1	9.5	12.4
Mexico	–4.5	–7.5	9.6	9.4	8.6
Peru	4.2	–2.6	23.8	23.2	21.4
Venezuela	0.2	26.4	6.1	11.2	9.0

Source: Moguillansky et al. (2004, p. 28).

According to the various versions of the neoclassical theory, the positive effects of financial liberalization on investment and growth would be due to the increase in both the supply of credit and in the efficiency of the financial system, which in turn implies lower costs for borrowers. In fact, efficiency may increase, but at the same time the supply of credit contracts and the costs for borrowers rise. An alternative explanation for these findings is that the fall in credit has led to a fall in bank deposits rather than the other way round.

The Evolution of Real Interest Rates after Financial Liberalization

Interest rates on loans tend to increase almost everywhere after financial liberalization has occurred.[1] Among the factors behind this fact are the increased mark-ups and the rise in money market interest rates (see Honohan, 2001). Honohan (2001) found that, between 1980 and 1998, wholesale interest rates, such as interbank rates and treasury bill rates, have gone up after financial liberalization in a sample of developing countries, and their volatility has increased as well. This results in the widening of the spread between lending and deposit rates, which responds to an increase in money market rates, and converges slowly to an equilibrium relationship. The equilibrium spread is in turn positively related to the general level of interest rates (both wholesale rates and deposit rates matter). Thus the increase in both deposit and lending rates has the same cause in the long run: an increase in wholesale rates. It must be added that the increase in the volatility of wholesale rates is not limited to the period following financial liberalization but lasts forever. Official interest rates, at which the central bank lends to commercial banks, increase too after financial liberalization and, in contrast to the past, are higher than treasury bill rates.[2] Even in high inflation countries, where real interest rates were zero or negative, real interest rates have risen, after liberalization, to very high levels. Double-digit real rates of interest have become the rule rather than the exception (see Honohan, 2001). The influence of foreign interest rates, by contrast, is not so strong. In the Appendix provided by Honohan (2001), it is not clear which retail interest rates are used in the analysis; the only information available is that they are not averages but quoted rates for large transactions. The maturity of these loans and deposits, to which the interest rates refer, is not given either. But, on the basis of this information, one can guess that average interest rates on loans might be higher rather than lower after financial liberalization.

The reason why real interest rates have risen has not been explained in a consistent way until now. Honohan (2001) hints at varying conditions within the time period to which his estimates refer. He also considers increased loan risk. In Caprio et al. (2001) there are some attempts at solving this problem, which, however, refer only to particular cases. In Mexico, for example, the way banks were privatized matters. They were bought with money borrowed by the same banks, and the new owners had to raise interest rates in order to repay their own loans (see Montes-Negret and Landa, 2001). There may be a more general reason for the rise in average lending interest rates. This could be linked to the increase in interbank loans, which causes an increase in the layering of the financial system. An increase in the ratio of interbank loans to total loans could be a suitable explanation. Most loans, before reaching the final borrower, pass through the balance sheets of many financial institutions. The higher the number of passages, the higher the final cost of loans. The reason is that many new financial institutions are neither allowed to take deposits nor, in some cases, to obtain refinancing from the central bank. They depend therefore on commercial banks and foreign banks for the supply of funds. These institutions are risky, and can therefore collect funds only at high interest rates and with short maturity (see Tropeano, 2001, for the case of financial liberalization in Asia). In these circumstances it is not strange at all that interbank interest rates have increased. The transactions in the interbank market were not considered as safe and risk-free as Honohan (2001) assumes.[3] In some countries, some non-bank financial institutions were not eligible at all for central bank refinancing at any rate.[4]

In most middle-income countries where financial liberalization was put into practice, the supply of credit went mainly to non-traded goods sectors; credit to consumers is sometimes considered as credit to non-traded goods sectors (see Tornell and Westermann, 2003) (Table 5.2).

Table 5.2. Bank lending by sectors (%)

Country	Loans to non-tradable goods sectors	Loans to tradable goods sectors
Argentina (1995)	67.1	32.9
Chile (1985)	60.1	39.9
Korea (1997)	74.8	25.2
Mexico (1995)	66.1	33.9
Peru (1996)	59.2	40.8
Thailand (1997)	65.5	34.5
Turkey (1993)	34.0	66.0

Source: Tornell and Westermann (2003, p. 13).

According to Grubel (1995), the high rates of interest resulting from liberalization would worsen the composition of borrowers by pricing out the projects with a profile of low expected return and low risk, and letting only the more risky projects to be financed. This in turn would favour only speculative investment and lead to a pattern of speculative growth.

Saving and Investment

The notion that financial liberalization gives rise to more investment has not been proven so far by empirical studies. First, there are important doubts that the cost of capital has fallen after financial liberalization, and, even in that case, that investment has increased. The only fact that emerges from almost all studies is that saving tends to decrease after financial reforms (see for instance Bayoumi, 1993; Jappelli and Pagano, 1994; Bandiera et al., 2000). In most countries the main effect of the fall in the propensity to save has been linked to the relaxation of liquidity constraints for households. It would not be linked to the interest rates behaviour. For many developing countries, Bandiera et al. (2000) find that there is no significant effect of the rise in interest rates on saving. Yet another study concludes that:

> With greater certainty, financial liberalization appears to deliver: higher real interest rates (possibly reflecting the allocation of capital toward more productive, higher return projects); lower investment, but not lower growth (again, possibly owing to a shift to more productive uses of financial resources); a higher level of foreign direct investment; and high gross capital flows – the catch is that occurs only in the higher income countries. Liberalization appears to deliver financial deepening, as measured by the credit and monetary aggregates – but, again, low income countries do not appear to show clear signs of such a benefit. As regards saving, anything goes. In some regions saving increased following financial sector reforms; but in the majority of cases saving declined following the reforms (Reinhart and Tokatlidis, 2002, p. 21).

Two questions are crucial in this respect. First, do high real interest rates reflect the allocation of capital towards higher return projects? Secondly, can the co-existence of lower investment and higher growth be due to a shift to more productive uses of financial resources? Taylor (2001) provides valuable answers to these questions. It appears that the most common sources of income growth in countries that have liberalized are consumption and government expenditures. Moreover, in most countries the productive structure has shifted towards the production of non-traded goods, which usually does not show a return higher than that of other sectors.

Summing up, the main results of the empirical literature on financial liberalization are: a fall in the propensity to save; an increase in short-term debt, often in foreign currency and via securitization; an increase in interest rates, both money market and retail rates. It remains to assess whether and how the financial reform has affected income distribution and inequality, an issue to which we now turn.

Income Distribution and Inequality

The evidence on income distribution and inequality is scant and contradictory. For instance, Clarke et al. (2003) show that there is a negative correlation between (some index of) inequality and (some measures of) financial development. The time span and the country coverage of this study are, however, very wide. As a result, no inference can be made for those developing countries that have liberalized in the last 20 years. To the extent that financial liberalization increases financial deepening, that result might apply to this case, too. Cornia and Kiiski (2001) calculate that inequality has increased in many countries in the last 20 years, while reforms were being introduced. The data set they use is different from that used by Clarke et al. (2003), which is the Deininger and Squire data set. Cornia and Kiiski (2001) measure the relationship between an index of all reforms and an index of inequality, so that no conclusion on the relation between financial reform, as such, and inequality can be drawn.

In another study, Behrman et al. (2000) show that both financial and capital account reforms increase the wage gap of workers with different education levels. The difference in the hourly real wages of workers with different levels of education is chosen as a measure of wage inequality. This study refers in particular to the wage gap between workers with primary and higher education levels. Surprisingly, the index of trade reform does not explain the wage gap at all, while the indexes of capital account, financial, and tax reforms do so. The index of financial reform includes the interest rates and the ratio of reserves to deposits. The index of capital account reform reflects the decline in restrictions. The index of tax reform measures the decline in marginal income tax rates and the rise in indirect taxes, while the index of trade reform is related to the decrease in tariffs for imported goods. Finally, the index of privatization measures the extent to which previously state-owned firms were being privatized. The latter is the only index that tends to reduce rather than increase the wage differential. Before interpreting these results, it is better to look at the rough data. The privatization index has no time trend, for its graph is almost a straight line, while the others are rising and, in the time span 1989–95, their rise is steeper.

Although the reforms appear to increase the wage gap and thus inequality, they were badly needed – so conclude Behrman et al. (2000). These authors argue that it would be false to claim that all reforms are bad for equality, since privatization increases it. Yet, the privatization index does not show a rising trend with respect to equality. It is therefore difficult to agree with this conclusion. Another reason why reform policies should increase social welfare, according to the authors, is that they may decrease monopolistic rents and thus profits. This positive effect, however, cannot be ascertained in their study, which deals only with wages. This in turn would require an increase in the share of wages and a decrease in the share of profits in national income. The authors, however, find that the same indexes, capital and financial account, cause a decline in the wage share and an increase in the profit share.[5]

According to the same authors, another reason why these results should not worry is that they last only for five years after the reforms have been accomplished. This, however, is not obvious at all, because once wage inequality has increased, it remains at a higher level than before, even if it stops increasing further. In this case we mean by inequality the standard deviation of wages.[6] The Gini index of general income distribution might behave differently if the different sources of income had an opposite trend.

Whether and how financial liberalization changes the distribution of income between quintile shares is at the heart of Das and Mohapatra (2003). For a number of developing countries, these authors show that after stock market liberalization the income of the highest quintile increases, and correspondingly decreases the income of the middle quintiles (that is, the second, third, and fourth). The lowest quintile's share of income, however, remains constant. This effect, it must be stated, only lasts for the two years following liberalization. According to the authors, this is because the ownership of shares is concentrated in the first quintile. Yet, their data set is mixed, because it contains observations both from the Deininger and Squire data set and the WIID data set.

Das and Mohapatra (2003) also calculated Gini coefficients of income inequality in the years after stock market liberalization. They found that they generally have increased, although not in all countries – and to varying extents. In their study, they considered Brazil, India, Malaysia, Mexico, Nigeria, Pakistan, Philippines, South Korea, Sri Lanka, Thailand, and Turkey.

Generally speaking, studies on developing countries that have liberalized show a tendency for the wage share to fall with respect to the profit share. In these contributions, however, the focus is on the effects of trade liberalization on the labour market (see Taylor, 2001).

In a sample of both developed and developing countries, Diwan (2000) shows that the wage share has declined between 1980 and 1995. The author uses data on the 'compensation of employees' by the United Nations, which are calculated before taxes. He finds that capital controls have a strong positive impact on the wage share in the North, while they have a small negative impact in the South. Using an index of capital account restrictions calculated by the International Monetary Fund, the author finds a positive trend in the South but a negative trend in the North. This means that capital account restrictions were increasing in the South while decreasing in the North. In the whole sample, the effect of relaxing capital controls on the wage share is negative. Trade openness has a small positive impact, less than one percentage point, on the wage share. What affects the wage share more in developing countries are financial crises, which decrease it in a persistent way. The reintroduction of capital controls during financial crises mitigates the fall in the wage share.

To summarize, the effect detected by Behrman et al. (2000) should lead to an increase in inequality as measured by either the variance of wages or a Gini index of labour income. The effect of stock market liberalization instead should lead to an increase in the share of profit and interest in national income, while the effect on the Gini index of total incomes is uncertain. If both effects would work, we should find both an increase in the variance of wages and a decrease in the share of wages in national income.

If we neglect for a while the peculiarities of each work, it is not clear at all within which theory the results obtained could be made meaningful. Clarke et al. (2003) clearly draw on the financial deepening argument; while the other contributions, although interesting, are not so easy to understand from the perspective of the theory. Behrman et al. (2000) open an unexplored field of research, for they show that financial factors have affected the labour market much more than real factors have done. While the link between trade liberalization and wages has been extensively studied, not so much ink has been spilled on financial liberalization and wages. The same authors are also not clear on bridging the gap between theory and reality. Some of their conclusions, if carefully discussed, are in contrast with what they have found out in their empirical work.

LESSONS DRAWN FROM THE EMPIRICAL LITERATURE

Perhaps the most important fact emphasized in the empirical literature is the rise in real interest rates. What then is the link between interest rate increases and income distribution? A direct link concerns the increase in the share of output that does not arise from labour. Another link suggests that higher interest rates lead to higher prices. Higher interest rates could be passed on to consumers by mark-up increases. Thus, while the rise in the share of interest income and the fall in the propensity to save (see above) may cause an increase in demand and imports, the rise in real interest rates and the worsening in the maturity of credit cut the incomes of the middle classes and of self-employed workers, who cannot pass these costs on to others. Since these agents account for a high and rising share of labour in most countries, this effect is assumed to be large. This is the reason why financial liberalization may increase the wage differential.

The result that financial reform increases the wage differentials has been obtained in a study (see Behrman et al., 2000) using data from households surveys, where informal sector wages and self-employed people's income were reported, too. Firms in the formal sector are not as affected by the interest rate increase, either because they have high profit margins and do not need to borrow to finance their activity, or because they can pass this increase to workers through lower wages.

As a result, inequality increases for two reasons: the accumulation of financial assets favours the richest households, and, within the labour share, those with lower remunerations. These two sources of inequality show a different trend during the passage from boom to crisis, and from that to post-crisis. While the rate at which rich people accumulate financial assets may slow down after a crisis, the monetary squeeze that usually follows it lets the incomes of informal and self-employed workers fall down further.

Although a great deal of evidence on the effects of financial liberalization draws on wage differentials, a rather smaller part of it deals with the distribution of income between wages and profits. In what follows, we will explain why financial liberalization may change the ratio of wages to profits. The share of interest is of course an important distributive variable, too, but the inclusion of it in this reasoning would presume an explanation of why financial liberalization may increase public and private debt, which goes beyond the scope of this chapter.

THE CONTRIBUTION OF POST-KEYNESIAN ANALYSIS ON FINANCIAL LIBERALIZATION, GROWTH, AND DISTRIBUTION

In the earlier literature on the effect of financial liberalization on income distribution it is claimed that financial liberalization may worsen distribution through its positive effect on aggregate saving and its negative effect on aggregate demand in a context of less than full capacity utilization.

Dutt (1990) puts forward a model in which the supply of savings depends on the saving propensity of capitalists, on the profit share – which is inversely related to the real wage – and on capacity utilization. In the short run the real wage is considered as fixed. The demand for investment depends negatively on the interest rate, positively on the profit rate in real terms and on capacity utilization (Figure 5.1).

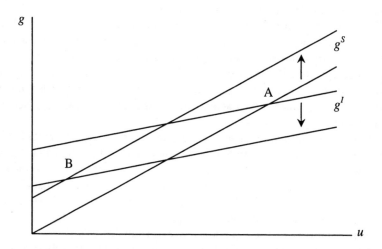

g^s = rate of growth of savings; g^I = rate of growth of capital; u = capacity utilization

Figure 5.1. The effect of a higher rate of interest on capital accumulation and capacity utilization

A higher real wage elicits a downward shift of the curve representing the supply of savings, because it implies a redistribution of income from capitalists to workers, who do not save. At the same time the curve representing the demand for investment moves up, because the inflation rate rises and the real interest rate falls. The result is a new equilibrium with a higher utilization of capacity and a higher growth of the capital stock. The opposite occurs if the real wage falls. In the short run a rise in the nominal interest rate, if it is supposed to imply a change in the same direction in the real interest rate, will cause a new equilibrium with a lower rate of capacity utilization and a lower rate of capital accumulation (see Figure 5.1, point B).

The curve representing the rate of growth of savings goes up because of the positive effect of the interest rate on the savings of capitalists, while the curve representing the rate of growth of capital shifts down because of the negative effect of the interest rate on investment (see Dutt, 1990, p. 221).

In the long run the real wage is no longer fixed but depends on the firms' desired wage rate, which in turn depends positively on the interest rate. In the long run the impact on capacity utilization is higher than in the short run, because of the change in the real wage desired by firms and imposed to workers. This means that the long-run effect on the rate of capital accumulation is greater than the short-run effect.

The conclusions that Dutt (1990) draws with respect to the effects of financial liberalization in developing countries are that an increase in the rate of interest does not imply a higher rate of growth in the economy. On the contrary, under conditions of less than full employment, this increase is likely to reduce the rate of growth, to worsen the distribution of income, and to increase the inflation rate. All this would happen even if the real interest rate increases, the saving rate rises, and efficiency increases.

In contrast to previous models, Dutt (1990) assumes that after financial liberalization both the deposit and lending rates of interest increase. There is a single rate of interest in his model. In the short run, since the real wage is fixed, the negative effects on growth come out of the fall in aggregate demand caused by the increase in capitalists' savings and by a negative effect on investment caused by the higher real interest rate. In the long run, by contrast, the main effect comes from the fall in the real wage desired by firms, which depends on the interest rate increase, which in turn causes a fall in aggregate demand and in capacity utilization. The same results do not hold, however, under the condition of full capacity utilization where financial liberalization, through the rise in the interest rate, succeeds in improving income distribution in the long run. This occurs because in conditions of full capacity utilization a fall in demand lowers inflation and thus the real wage in the long run (output gap equation). The result of the model therefore is strongly linked to the assumption of less than fully-utilized capacity.

If we compare the assumptions of the models with the stylized facts summarized in the previous section, we notice that the main assumption that the savings of capitalists increase is not supported. The assumption that both deposit and lending rates increase appears realistic. Thus, if saving does not increase, the main contracting force in the short run is the effect of the rise in real interest rate on the demand for investment, which may not be so big. In any case, a fall in investment demand with an unchanged supply of saving would induce a downward adjustment in output and prices. The effect on the rate of capital accumulation would be negative. In the long run, however, the negative effect of a fall in real wage on capacity utilization would persist.

In conclusion, since the two transmission channels from financial liberalization to output growth and income distribution would pass through the negative effect of the rise in interest rates on aggregate demand – both because saving increases and because real wages fall – the only effect left if we look at the data would be the falling real wages. In turn, this effect would depend on the parameter linking the desired real wage rate by firms to the interest rate. If this parameter is not so high, the effect may not be so strong.

Burkett and Dutt (1991) offer a slightly different model. In their model the aim of the authors is again to show that, even if financial liberalization succeeds in raising saving, it depresses aggregate demand and thus the level of equilibrium output. The modelling of the financial sector is different from Dutt (1990), because Burkett and Dutt (1991) assume a loanable funds demand and supply of savings, where the interest rate is seen as the variable that clears the market. A rise in the interest rate will increase the supply of savings, and therefore the excess demand for savings (owing to financial repression) disappears. The deposit rate of interest increases while the lending rate does not, since banks now have more funds to lend, and thus the unit cost of loans will fall. In this model all savings increase, not only those of capitalists.

This description of the market for loans can be criticized with respect to both theory and the stylized facts noted above. While the rate of interest on deposits has increased, banks have passed on this increase to their customers, and often even the spread between loan and deposit rates has increased. Both the money supply and the lending rates have increased, although the increase in the money supply is not linked to the increase in deposits but rather to the increase in loans, which create in turn more deposits (as in the theory of endogenous money). The increase in money supply does not depend on domestic savings, owing to liberalization of the capital account and the increase in the number of financial institutions. These institutions borrow from each other and thereby expand the credit supply. Another factor causing a higher lending rate has been the increase in risk both in the corporate sector and in the financial sector linked to the liberalization process.

In the remainder of their paper, Burkett and Dutt (1991) assume that, increases in savings and loans notwithstanding, equilibrium output falls. Their main point is that the reduction in effective demand caused by a higher rate of interest on deposits, and thus on the rate of profit, may reduce investment, output, and savings enough to more than offset the positive effects of the reduced loans rate. Of course, the negative effect on demand will be higher if it is assumed that the lending rate rises, too.

Now, once the fundamental assumption that savings decrease as a result of financial liberalization is dropped, the depressionary effects of that decrease disappear as well. If one drops the assumption that the interest rate on loans does not rise, one can take into account some contraction of investment, although the elasticity of investment to the interest rate may not be so high.

THE MONETARY THEORY OF DISTRIBUTION APPROACH

Another possible approach to investigate the effects of financial liberalization is to start from the fact that the real interest rate has risen almost everywhere as a consequence of financial liberalization. The rise in the real interest rate could bring about a rise in the profit rate and a fall in the real wage rate.

In this case, if goods are produced by means of other goods, an increase in the profit of the intermediate goods sector means an increase in the prices of those goods that are produced by using them. This amounts to closing the mathematical system that determines relative prices by fixing the profit rate outside the system, as Sraffa (1960) suggested by linking it to monetary factors or conventions. In practice, however, this means an increase in the mark-up, and in a small open economy this increase may not be allowed by international competition unless firms manage to lower nominal wages. This is particularly relevant for the economic environment in which developing countries liberalized their economies in the period between the end of the 1980s and the beginning of the 1990s. Since financial liberalization was often preceded by trade liberalization, the abolition of tariffs on home-produced industrial goods would mean increased competition from foreign goods. Given this and the likely fall in domestic aggregate demand owing to lower wages, the increase in the mark-up is not a solution for firms operating in the tradable goods sectors. This may favour, however, the expansion of firms operating in the non-tradable goods sectors.

A more general statement is that a higher rate of interest will increase profits with unchanged techniques of production and nominal wage rates. The dynamic process that is implicit in this idea, however, can be compatible with very different changes in the industrial structure.

For instance, a persistent change in the rate of interest would cause a change in the same direction of the price level in relation to nominal wages, thus changing in the same direction, too, the rate of profit and in the opposite direction the real wage (see Pivetti, 2004). A reappraisal of this thesis has been proposed by Nardozzi (2002), who argues that the high real rates of interest have caused a rise in the profit rates, and, given the constancy of the capital–output ratio, even in the profit share. The author shows, using some econometric testing, that a positive relationship exists between the rate of return on capital and long-term real interest rates; a negative relationship would by contrast link the rate of return on capital and the real wage per worker. His sample consists of developed countries, including the United States and European countries. Yet, the process through which these relations are generated in this particular episode is not clear. Ciocca (2002) refers to the work of Sraffa (1960), in which the equalization of profit rates, as well as that between the profit rate and the money rate of interest, result from competition among production sectors. Nardozzi (2002), however, does not work out in detail the circumstances favouring this process in developed countries. In developing countries, by contrast, this link may be easier to understand. The higher rate of interest, if agents believe it will last in the future, will tend to increase the rate of profit. Since tradable goods sectors, or more precisely sectors that produce importable goods, are more subject to foreign competition, they will move to the (now more profitable) non-tradable goods sectors.[7] The equality between the interest rate and the profit rate will require a reshuffling of the production structure.

In the tradable goods sectors, competition from foreign producers being higher than in the non-tradable goods sectors, prices cannot be increased. In the non-tradable goods sectors, by contrast, this can be – and is – often done. Another solution would be a change in regulation that allows the lowering of the nominal wage rate.[8] Yet, lowering nominal wages, even if possible, would not bé so easy for entrepreneurs in the tradable goods sectors. In fact, if capital and skilled labour were complementary, the option of hiring low skilled and low paid workers would not work.

Post-Keynesian economists (see Rowthorn, 1982; Dutt, 1984; Taylor, 1985) argue that a redistribution of income in favour of wages may result in a higher capacity utilization and in higher profits. The classical assumption of an inverse relationship between wages and profits is revised.[9] The simple use of price theory by Sraffa (1960) does not make clear, however, how this inverse relation is justified in reality. If there is excess capacity, then a fall in demand caused by lower nominal – as well as real – wages should in any case affect profits negatively, if we assume an investment function depending on profitability.

Blecker (1996) gives some hints at how this process occurred in recent times in developing countries that have liberalized their financial system and their capital account. Even in countries with excess capacity in the modern sector, a profit-led growth may set in, if some conditions are satisfied. There must be an investment demand that is very sensitive to the profit rate, and a possibility of expanding exports driven by the increase in competitiveness owing to falling labour costs.

Even in this case, a redistribution of income from wages to profits would have a big underconsumption effect, and would thus require a big increase in investment demand and in net exports to give rise to an expansionary effect on output (see Blecker, 1996, p. 28).

In many countries that have liberalized, the first stage after liberalization has been characterized by a fall in investment in the manufacturing sector, which usually rises again only after an inflow of foreign direct investment. Because of the competition between different locations, these inflows are accompanied by lower nominal wages.

Another problem arises, however, because if the increase in profit were passed on to prices, as the Sraffa (1960) model assumes, competitiveness would be lower, and the above-depicted strategy could not be set in motion. A way out of this impasse would be to increase only the prices of the goods that workers consume, keeping the price of exports low. To show how this works in the real world, let us consider the case of Mexico.

Wages and Profits

According to the monetary theory of distribution, as noted above, a rise in the interest rate should raise the rate of profit as well as prices, thus lowering real wages. But what are real wages? How can we define them in this context? As we will see, this is not an easy question to answer. To wit, the real wage for each branch may be calculated by dividing the nominal wage by the price of the branch product or by dividing it by a cost-of-living index.

If the ratio of tradable to non-tradable goods prices decreases, because the denominator grows faster than the numerator, then the real wage of the workers in the non-tradable goods sectors, calculated in terms of their own product, falls. The real wage, calculated as the nominal wage divided by the consumer price index, might well increase, or remain unchanged, reflecting opposite tendencies in the prices in the index. If, following some technical innovation, prices in the tradable goods sectors fall, then the real wage rate of the workers in these sectors would rise, if divided by the sectoral price index. Of course, the same would not occur if the real wage were calculated as the nominal wage divided by the cost-of-living index, since prices of non-tradable goods do not fall with respect to the tradable goods but instead tend to rise.[10]

This, however, does not take into account the productive linkages among different production sectors. A reason for this is that these linkages tend to be weakened by trade liberalization, because most intermediate goods are imported rather than bought from other domestic producers.

If workers with lower wages tend to consume more non-tradable goods, mainly food and housing, then their real wage in terms of the consumption basket they demand falls. Likewise, if those workers with higher wages tend to consume more tradable and imported goods, then their real wage may rise, since their own products have fallen in price and the price of imports may have fallen, too, owing to trade liberalization. In this reasoning we leave aside exchange rate considerations. As a matter of fact, in many countries the exchange rate has been pegged to a foreign currency, at a level that is usually quite high. As a result, the price of imported goods in domestic currency falls and thus also the purchasing power of those who consume them. If high wage earners and capitalists were those who consume more tradable and imported goods, then they would be favoured, because the ratio of tradable to non-tradable goods prices usually falls. Economists often neglect the way liberalization through relative price changes affects factor shares, concentrating instead on real wage inequalities. In the latter case, nominal wages are made real by dividing for the same consumer price index (for a criticism of this approach see Williamson, 2002).

Table 5.3. The distribution of income in Mexico, 1982–96

Year	Profit and interest*	Tradable goods sectors	Non-tradable goods sectors
1982–87	53.4	33.8	19.6
1988	56.5	25.1	31.4
1989	56.0	21.3	34.7
1990	54.5	19.1	35.4
1991	52.9	17.5	35.4
1992	51.8	16.0	35.8
1993	50.4	14.2	36.2
1994	49.8	13.8	36.0
1995	54.6	17.0	37.6
1996	55.9	19.2	36.7

* Operating surplus (excluding oil, agriculture, commerce and other services) less property income abroad plus interest on public debt.

Source: Ros and Lustig (2001, p. 222).

If the flow of resources through sectors is very rapid, then the whole economy will experience a fall in the wage share and a rise in the profit share. If different sectors with different pricing and wage policies survive, the ratio of the wage share to the profit share for the whole economy may be constant, rise, or fall according to what happens to the wage/profit share ratio in each sector. A case in point is Mexico. In this country the aggregate wage share was constant, owing to the combination of a falling wage share in the non-tradable goods sectors and a rising wage share in the tradable goods sectors (see Table 5.3).

If capitalists in the tradable goods sectors were to adopt a strategy of competing with low wages rather than improving technology, the wage share would decrease in all sectors and then in the aggregate, too. Low wage earners in the tradable goods sectors would not enjoy the benefits of unchanged prices of their own products if, as we assumed, they consume mainly non-tradable goods.

CONCLUDING REMARKS

This chapter has reviewed some stylized facts of financial liberalization, the policies of which have been implemented in recent times, and put forward a theory that may explain them.

The undisputable facts on financial liberalization in developing countries are the increase in interest rates and credit supply, the worsening in income distribution with a fall in the wage share, and an increase in inequality, as measured by the Gini indexes of labour income.

Post-Keynesian models put forward by Dutt (1990), and Burkett and Dutt (1991) explain this pattern of distribution by arguing that financial liberalization tends to cause a fall in aggregate demand; such policies are stagnationist. In some cases, since prices may increase because of the higher interest rates, the overall result would be stagflation, with falling rates of growth of output and increasing inflation. This type of explanation fails to capture some of the most important evidence on recent financial liberalization. In fact, the most important reason why aggregate demand falls according to these authors is that saving increases after financial liberalization. The evidence available on saving, however, does not support this assumption. Hence, if stagnation is the result of increased saving, liberalization cannot be blamed. Moreover, with the financial liberalization of the 1990s, inflation rates have been reduced by using a strategy based on a high exchange rate as a nominal anchor. Restrictive monetary and fiscal policies have also helped to reach this objective. This type of explanation needs to be updated, to take into account the characteristics of these recent episodes of financial liberalization.

An alternative explanation, which could be borrowed from the monetary theory of distribution, is that the increase in interest rate translates itself into a higher profit rate, and implies a falling real wage. The application of this theory, however, requires some caution, owing to the type of competition prevailing in international goods markets. A rise in the mark-up, if it increases the prices of the products, may worsen the competitiveness of the sectors producing exportable goods, and may favour the expansion of those sectors not subject to international competition. A possibility of getting out of this problem would be that workers consume only non-tradable goods, so that their real wage falls while the price of the tradable goods they produce is not increased. Another possibility is that nominal wages grow at falling rates (see Tropeano, 2005). All this would cause at the aggregate level a fall in the wage share and an increase in the profit share. This explanation, although it needs some further elaboration, might account for some stylized facts of recent financial liberalization processes. In particular, with respect to the alternative explanation mentioned above, it has the advantage of not requiring an increase in saving to justify the fall in aggregate demand.

Another possible explanation is that, through liberalization, developing countries are pursuing a growth strategy based on exports. The rise in the rate of profit in a context of excess capacity is made possible through the expansion in exports. This expansion, however, requires a continuous fall in domestic demand, and thus in both nominal and real wages.

NOTES

1. According to Arestis et al. (2003), the relation between the number of financial institutions, on the one hand, and the deposit and lending rates spread, on the other, is positive in some episodes of financial liberalization.
2. Official interest rates, however, are not included in the set of the independent variables in the equations, in which the spread between lending and deposit rates is the dependent variable.
3. 'Assuming that quoted inter-bank money market rates relate to lending that is highly liquid and virtually free of credit risk, Treasury bill rates at the same maturity should be very close to money market rates' (Honohan, 2001, p. 69).
4. This is the case of merchant banks in South Korea.
5. Behrman et al. (2000, p. 26, fn. 31) state in a footnote that '[t]o address the question of whether reforms have affected the share of wages as compared to profits, we used IMF data on the wage share reported in the National Accounts, by country and year, to estimate the effect of the reform indexes on the wage share (the ratio of wages to GDP) under a country fixed effects specification. Because we are not confident in the quality and comparability of the wage share data and we are not able to control for time-varying country characteristics, we do not wish to overstate the importance of these results, and so discuss them only in this footnote. The estimates suggest that the average reform index is associated with a reduction

in the wage share with the index lagged for one through five years; after five years the negative effect is no longer statistically significant. Among the separate indexes it appears to be capital and financial sector reforms that are reducing the wage share'.
6. The Gini index of wages income should rise proportionally to the standard variation in the case of a log-normal distribution (see Bourguignon, 2003, p. 8).
7. This process may not be instantaneous; the adjustment may take a shorter or longer time.
8. The classical theory of distribution considers the wage rate fixed by real factors and thus cannot envisage such a solution. In reality minimum wages have been lowered by a considerable amount in many developing countries.
9. See on this Blecker (1989, p. 395).
10. Such a mechanism seems at work in Italy if one considers the wages in the manufacturing sector. These wages lose value since the ratio of the price of value added to the cost of living falls (see Levrero and Stirati, 2004).

REFERENCES

Arestis, P., M. Nissanke and H. Stein (2003), 'Finance and development: institutional and policy alternatives to financial liberalization theory', *Jerome Levy Economics Institute Working Paper*, no. 377.
Bandiera, O., G. Caprio, P. Honohan and F. Schiantarelli (2000), 'Does financial reform increase or reduce savings?', *Review of Economics and Statistics*, **82** (2), 239–63.
Bayoumi, T. (1993), 'Financial deregulation and households savings', *American Economic Review*, **103** (421), 1432–43.
Beck, T., R. Levine and N. Loyaza (2000), 'Finance and the sources of growth', *Journal of Financial Economics*, **58** (1–2), 261–300.
Behrman, J., N. Birdsall and M. Szekely (2000), 'Economic reform and wage differentials in Latin America', *Inter-American Development Bank Working Paper*, no. 435.
Blecker, R. (1989), 'International competition, income distribution and economic growth', *Cambridge Journal of Economics*, **13** (3), 395–412.
Blecker, R. (1996), 'NAFTA, the peso crisis and the contradictions of the Mexican growth strategy', *Center for Economic Policy Analysis Working Paper*, no. 3.
Bonturi, M. (2002), 'Challenges in the Mexican financial system', *OECD Economic Department Working Paper*, no. 339.
Bourguignon, F. (2003), 'Growth, inequality and poverty: basic facts and mechanisms', paper presented at the workshop on 'Inequality and Economic Integration', Siena, 30 June–6 July.
Burkett, P. and A. Dutt (1991), 'Interest rate policy, effective demand, and growth in LDCs', *International Review of Applied Economics*, **5** (2), 127–53.
Caprio, G., P. Honohan and J.S. Stiglitz (eds) (2001), *Financial Liberalization: How Far, How Fast?*, Cambridge: Cambridge University Press.
Ciocca, P. (2002), 'Comment', in G. Nardozzi (ed.), *I rapporti tra finanza e distribuzione del reddito: un'interpretazione dell'economia di fine secolo*, Roma: Luiss Edizioni, 155–61.
Clarke, G., L.C. Xu and H.F. Zou (2003), 'Finance and income inequality: test of alternative theories', *World Bank Research Paper*, no. 2984.
Cornia, G.A. (2004a), 'Changes in the distribution of income over the last two

decades: extent, sources and possible causes', *Rivista Italiana degli Economisti*, **9** (3), 349–87.

Cornia, G.A. (ed.) (2004b), *Inequality, Growth and Poverty in an Era of Liberalisation and Globalisation*, Oxford: Oxford University Press.

Cornia, G.A. and S. Kiiski (2001), 'Trends in income distribution in the post WWII period: evidence and interpretation', paper presented at the UNU–WIDER conference on 'Growth and Poverty', Helsinki, 24–25 May.

Das, M. and S. Mohapatra (2003), 'Income inequality: the aftermath of stock market liberalization in emerging markets', *Journal of Empirical Finance*, **10** (1–2), 217–48.

Demirguc-Kunt, A., R. Levine and H.G. Min (1998), 'Opening to foreign banks: issues of stability efficiency and growth', in S. Lee (ed.), *The Implications of Globalization of World Financial Markets*, Seoul: Bank of Korea, 83–115.

Diwan, I. (2000), 'Labour shares and globalization', paper presented at the OECD conference on 'Poverty and Income Inequality in Developing Countries', Paris, 30 November–1 December.

Dutt, A. (1984), 'Stagnation, income distribution and monopoly power', *Cambridge Journal of Economics*, **8** (1), 25–40.

Dutt, A. (1990), 'Interest rate policy in LDCs: a post Keynesian view', *Journal of Post Keynesian Economics*, **13** (2), 210–32.

Grubel, I. (1995), 'Speculation-led economic development: a post-Keynesian interpretation of financial liberalization programmes in the Third World', *International Review of Applied Economics*, **9** (2), 127–49.

Honohan, P. (2001), 'How interest rates changed under liberalizations: a statistical review', in G. Caprio, P. Honohan and J.S. Stiglitz (eds), *Financial Liberalization: How Far, How Fast?*, Cambridge: Cambridge University Press, 63–95.

Jappelli, T. and M. Pagano (1994), 'Saving, growth and liquidity constraints', *Quarterly Journal of Economics*, **109** (1), 83–109.

King, R.G. and R. Levine (1993), 'Finance and growth: Schumpeter may be right', *Quarterly Journal of Economics*, **108** (3), 717–38.

Levine, R. (1997), 'Financial development and economic growth: views and agenda', *Journal of Economic Literature*, **35** (2), 688–726.

Levine, R. (2001), 'International financial liberalization and economic growth', *Review of International Economics*, **9** (4), 688–702.

Levine, R. and S. Zervos (1998), 'Stock markets, banks and economic growth', *American Economic Review*, **88** (3), 537–58.

Levrero, S. and A. Stirati (2004), 'Quote distributive, profittabilità e prezzi relativi', paper presented at the workshop on 'La distribuzione del reddito in Italia', Bologna, 4 June.

McKinnon, R. (1973), *Money and Capital in Economic Development*, Washington, DC: Brookings Institution.

Moguillansky, G., R. Studart and S. Vergara (2004), 'Foreign banks in Latin America: a paradoxical result', *CEPAL Review*, no. 82, April, 21–37.

Montes-Negret, F. and L. Landa (2001), 'Interest rate spreads in Mexico during liberalization', in G. Caprio, P. Honohan and J.S. Stiglitz (eds), *Financial Liberalization: How Far, How Fast?*, Cambridge: Cambridge University Press, 188–207.

Morley, S. (2001), *The Income Distribution Problem in Latin America and the*

Caribbean, Santiago de Chile: Economic Commission for Latin America and the Caribbean.

Nardozzi, G. (2002), 'Interesse, profitto e borsa negli anni Ottanta e Novanta', in G. Nardozzi (ed.), *I rapporti tra finanza e distribuzione del reddito: un'interpretazione dell'economia di fine secolo*, Roma: Luiss Edizioni, 11–69.

Pivetti, M. (2004), 'La teoria monetaria della distribuzione e il caso americano', *Rivista italiana degli economisti*, no. 2, August, 225–44.

Reinhart, C.M. and I. Tokatlidis (2002), 'Before and after financial liberalization', paper presented at the World Bank conference on 'Financial Globalization', May.

Ros, J. and N. Lustig (2001), 'Mexico: trade and financial liberalization with volatile capital inflows: macroeconomic consequences and social impact during the 1990s', in L. Taylor (ed.), *External Liberalization, Economic Performance, and Social Policy*, Oxford: Oxford University Press, 217–50.

Rowthorn, R (1982), 'Demand, real wages and economic growth', *Studi Economici*, **37** (18), 3–53.

Sraffa, P. (1960), *Production of Commodities by Means of Commodities: Prelude to a Critique of Economic Theory*, Cambridge: Cambridge University Press.

Taylor, L. (1985), 'A stagnationist model of economic growth', *Cambridge Journal of Economics*, **9** (4), 383–403.

Taylor, L. (ed.) (2001), *External Liberalization, Economic Performance, and Social Policy*, Oxford: Oxford University Press.

Tornell, A. and F. Westermann (2003), 'Credit market imperfections in middle income countries', *CESIFO Working Paper*, no. 960.

Tropeano, D. (2001), *Liberalizzazioni e crisi finanziarie*, Roma: Carocci.

Tropeano, D. (2005), 'Financial liberalization, growth and distribution in developing countries: some notes on a different approach', *Economia Politica*, **22** (3), 439–56.

Williamson, J.G. (2002), 'Winners and losers over two centuries of globalization', *National Bureau of Economic Research Working Paper*, no. 9161.

Yeldan, E. (2004), 'The impact of financial liberalization and the rise of financial rents on income inequality: the case of Turkey', in G.A. Cornia (ed.), *Inequality, Growth and Poverty in an Era of Liberalisation and Globalisation*, Oxford: Oxford University Press, 355–75.

6. Crisis Avoidance: The Post-Washington Consensus Agenda

Louis-Philippe Rochon

INTRODUCTION

The collapse of the Bretton Woods system changed dramatically the way in which foreign exchange markets operate. While it marked the end of almost three decades of global stability and growth during which currency crises were few and far between, it also paved the way for the dramatic rise of the US dollar as international reserve currency. In this sense, the collapse of the Bretton Woods system led to the development of the current international financial structure centred on the hegemonic role of the US dollar. Around the globe, countries compete for US imports as a way of accumulating US-dollar reserves, and export-led policies are now favoured above all others as a way to foster growth.

Yet, the road after the end of the Bretton Woods system was not all paved with gold. The last 30 years have witnessed some remarkable contradictions, and in particular the last 15 years. While the United States and many other advanced economies saw some impressive growth with strong employment, low inflation, and high productivity gains, emerging and developing economies were hit by a string of financial crises (for instance, the Mexican crisis in 1994, followed by Brazil in 1999, and Argentina in 2001), which led some countries to experiment with alternative exchange rate systems, such as dollarization and currency boards. Perhaps now more than ever, we are witness to a growing economic schism between advanced and developing countries. And while it remains still an important obstacle, there appears to be no quick solution to narrowing the income gap between countries. Given the last few years, it is certainly difficult to remain optimistic about the economic prospect of emerging market economies in the near future.

One of the more remarkable policy developments in the post-Bretton

Woods era was the so-called Washington Consensus. Proposed by John Williamson in 1989, but published in 1990, it was meant as a general blueprint for economic growth in Latin American and other developing economies, and was proposed as a consensus among economists and policy makers at the International Monetary Fund, the World Bank, and the US Treasury (to name only the most well-known institutions). Yet, consensus relative to its success is certainly far from reached. Once heralded as the beginning of a new era, the Washington Consensus has failed to deliver on its most basic promises of growth. Indeed, while many economists were hopeful as to the anticipated growth prospects in Latin America, the news is disappointing at best. The last 15 years have not been kind to Latin America. Some would dare say that these years were a scourge for this part of the world, contributing largely to a second 'lost decade' in it.

In honour of the fifteenth anniversary of the Washington Consensus, I was fortunate enough to edit (with Claude Gnos; see Gnos and Rochon, 2004– 05a) a special symposium for the *Journal of Post Keynesian Economics*, which included articles by Williamson himself, but also by Philip Arestis, Ha-Joon Chang and Ilene Grabel, Paul Davidson, Jose Antonio Ocampo, Luiz Bresser-Pereira, Claude Gnos and myself, among others. The emerging consensus, at least from the heterodox contributions to that symposium, points to a rather disappointing conclusion: the Washington Consensus experience of developing countries has not been a success. In fact, it has been an utter failure.

The structure of this chapter is quite simple. The next section criticizes the existing Washington Consensus. The third section exposes the 'Augmented Consensus' (see for instance Naim, 2000, 2002), as simply 'more of the same'. The fourth section proposes some policy prescriptions from a post-Keynesian perspective. While there still needs to be considerable debate around the precise nature of what would constitute an alternative to the Washington Consensus, this section is meant to be a starting point for future dialogue among post-Keynesians. The last section concludes.

THE WASHINGTON CONSENSUS AND EMERGING ECONOMIES

In his original paper, Williamson (1990) proposed ten policy prescriptions that were met with alarming enthusiasm from economists and policy makers. Meant as a blueprint for growth in emerging economies, his prescriptions were intended 'to refer to the lowest common denominator of policy advice being addressed by the Washington-based institutions to Latin American countries as of 1989' (Williamson, 2000, p. 251). It was, as Williamson (2000, p. 251) saw it, 'an intellectual convergence' of ideas on development economics, and represented, as Williamson (2002) would explain later, 'motherhood and apple pie'.

The ten policy prescriptions are as follows (Williamson, 2004–05, p. 196):

1. Budget deficits . . . should be small enough to be financed without recourse to the inflation tax.
2. Public expenditure should be redirected from politically sensitive areas that receive more resources than their economic return can justify . . . toward neglected fields with high economic returns and the potential to improve income distribution, such as primary education and health, and infrastructure.
3. Tax reform . . . to broaden the tax base and cut marginal tax rates.
4. Financial liberalization, involving an ultimate objective of market-determined interest rates.
5. A unified exchange rate at a level sufficiently competitive to induce a rapid growth in non-traditional exports.
6. Quantitative trade restrictions to be rapidly replaced by tariffs, which would be progressively reduced until a uniform low rate in the range of 10 to 20 percent was achieved.
7. Abolition of barriers impeding the entry of FDI.
8. Privatization of state enterprises.
9. Abolition of regulations that impede the entry of new firms or restrict competition.
10. The provision of secure property rights, especially to the informal sector.

Overall, the chief concern of these ten proposals was with fiscal prudence, liberalizing financial flows, deregulation, and privatization. In other words, the core of the Washington Consensus was about market-friendly reforms. In fact, in his contribution to the *Journal of Post Keynesian Economics* symposium I edited, Williamson (2004–05, p. 197) describes what he calls the 'strange history' of the Consensus. In that paper, Williamson explains how he wanted to contrast the Western orthodoxy of 'macroeconomic discipline, outward orientation, and the market economy' with the Latin American orthodoxy of 'inflation tolerance, import substituting industrialization, and a leading role for the state' (p. 197). The Williamson paper was clearly meant to contrast two very opposite views of economics. At the core of his paper is a rejection of macroeconomic policies that were practised in Latin American in the previous decades.

The underlying argument is that, in the age of globalization, the only possible or logical solution to avoiding a financial crisis is to open goods and financial markets, including the national banking system and other financial institutions, to market-friendly policies. Trade and exports would inevitably lead to higher growth. Other policies, such as any policy proposed by post-Keynesians for instance, can perhaps bring some stability in the short run, but can only result in a disastrous economic situation in the long run. These are old, tired refrains not unknown to post-Keynesians.

At the core of the Washington-Consensus approach is the notion that all markets, at all times, must be treated the same way. It is in this sense that this approach adopts a 'one-size-fits-all' development strategy, or what I called elsewhere 'ready-to-wear' policies. It is a belief that all markets at all times behave the same way, and that therefore no special consideration is needed when it comes to emerging markets. In a sense, it is placing blind faith on market forces. It is in this way that the Washington Consensus has been termed 'ideological', or as Stiglitz (2002) claimed, was steeped in neo-liberal ideology, an epithet Williamson (2002, 2004–05) rejected and, in fact, could never understand.

In the years following the Williamson (1990) paper, these policy prescriptions became enshrined into IMF philosophy. In fact, IMF loans and financial assistance to emerging economies were tied to strict adherence to the principles of the Consensus. While they were meant as a recipe for growth in emerging economies in Latin America, time has not been kind. It is generally agreed today that the Washington Consensus as originally designed by Williamson has not delivered the strong growth that it once promised. In fact, if consensus there is, it is perhaps over the conclusion that the Washington Consensus has been a failure. According to Williamson (2004–5, p. 202) himself, '[t]he economic performance of most Latin American countries (Chile aside) in the decade and a half since I first enunciated what became known as the Washington Consensus has been pretty disappointing'.

Indeed, the string of financial crises in recent years has cast doubt on the benefits of unrestricted capital flows and on the merits of the Washington Consensus. Since the opening of emerging market economies and liberalized capital markets, the volume and pace of international capital mobility has been nothing short of astonishing. Yet, it is clear that globalization has not had its desired effects and, some would argue, has actually worsened an already fragile system.

A good number of economists today, including many with the mainstream pedigree, readily acknowledge the failure of the Washington Consensus approach. Indeed, the economic performance of developing economies over the last 15 years has been at best disappointing, and alarming at worst. In fact, the poor performance of many emerging economies – along with the string of financial crises in the later part of the 1990s – has led Stiglitz (2002) to argue in no uncertain terms that the current system is broke and that changes are urgently needed. According to Stiglitz (2002, p. 20), 'the net effect of the policies set by the Washington Consensus has all too often been to benefit the few at the expense of the many, the well-off at the expense of the poor'. Among post-Keynesians, Davidson (2003a, p. 3) also argued that the 'evidence of the last 10–20 years, however, has demonstrated that attempting to implement the ten reforms of the Washington Consensus has ultimately proven to be a disaster for developing nations'.

Globalization is quickly redefining the international currency stage. From one crisis to another, countries have adopted various solutions to deal with the ravages left behind by foreign exchange instability, from monetary union to currency board and dollarization. From one crisis to another, however, the debate remains strikingly the same: economists have not left the confines of debating the virtues and merits of fixed versus flexible exchange rates; and competing schools of thought propose solutions that always consider one form or another of these two only possible choices. If anything, recent turmoil has only solidified economists' respective views about exchange rate arrangements. Even as Argentina's experimentation with a currency board proved to be disastrous, the debate never moved beyond the narrow framework of exchange rate regimes. For instance, Hausmann (2001), while acknowledging inherent problems in the international financial system for developing countries unable to borrow in their own currencies, nonetheless suggests that the solution is the pesofication of Argentina's economy and debt in order to eliminate the currency mismatch, such that both its assets and liabilities are in the same currency. As for the case of dollarization in Ecuador and El Salvador (in 2000 and 2001 respectively), it is still too early to tell whether that experiment will follow the path of Argentina.

As the subsequent international flows of capital to emerging economies reversed, national economies were left holding the bag and forced to adopt policies that have ranged from eliminating budget deficits and adopting highly restrictive fiscal stances to severely cutting current account deficits by forcing recessions and currency depreciations to cut back on imports. With the International Monetary Fund imposing such policies in return for financial aid, the complete collapse of aggregate demand ensued. The collapse of the Argentinean currency board was inevitable.

AN AUGMENTED CONSENSUS

As stated in the previous section, the underlying theme of the Washington Consensus is that only orthodox policies – what Williamson refers to as Western orthodoxy – can lead to economic growth and avoid financial and economic crises. Yet, the aftermath of the Washington Consensus has not been an encouraging situation. Indeed, the economic performance of emerging economies has been dismal, leading some to refer to the 1990s as a 'lost decade' in Latin America. How can we therefore reconcile the weak performance of many Latin American economies in recent years and the adoption of the Washington Consensus?

Generally, among policy advocates of the Consensus, three arguments are put forward. Many have argued that the Washington Consensus was simply not sufficient, and that its policy recommendations needed to be broadened or 'augmented'. Secondly, many have claimed that the policies of the Washington Consensus were never really followed in the first place. In other words, the poor performance in Latin America in the 'lost decade' of the 1990s cannot be blamed on the Washington Consensus, because very few countries really followed the policies advocated by this Consensus. Finally, some have argued that the Washington Consensus is not really to blame, although the pace at which the policies are implemented is crucial to the success of this Consensus.

Let us consider these three arguments in turn.

Williamson certainly accepts at least two versions that explain the failure of the Washington Consensus, although he never acknowledged that this Consensus led to the failure of Latin American economies to grow. First, he acknowledges some shortcomings with the original Consensus, but refuses to admit complete defeat. Indeed, according to him, the original reforms were not wrong as much as they were 'incomplete'. As he claims (Williamson, 2004–05, p. 199), 'the proposition that there is a need to supplement what I laid out as the Washington Consensus seems to me unobjectionable, indeed compelling'. This echoes the same statement the author made earlier: 'the way forward is to complete, correct, and complement the reforms of a decade ago, not to reverse them' (Kuczynski and Williamson, 2003, p. 18). It is an attempt to place a 'human face' on the policies of the Washington Consensus.

For instance, Rodrik (2002, 2005), who coined the expression 'Augmented Washington Consensus', argues that there now exists an 'augmented' Washington Consensus, which, in addition to the items listed above, would contain the additional ten policy proposals covering the following areas:

1. Corporate governance
2. Anti-corruption
3. Flexible labour markets
4. World Trade Organization agreements
5. Financial codes and standards
6. 'Prudent' capital-account opening
7. Non-intermediate exchange rate regimes
8. Independent central banks and inflation targeting
9. Social safety nets
10. Targeted poverty reduction

The second argument, namely, that the policies advocated by the Washington Consensus were never followed, is one that is shared by many economists. For instance, the issue comes down to the interpretation of these policies. Indeed, what exactly the Washington Consensus represented, or meant, is not clear. Naim (2000), in fact, wondered whether it is more reasonable to be talking about some sort of Washington Confusion? The meaning of the reforms became entangled in a spirited debate over the intent of the reforms, but also the intellectual bias they portrayed. Williamson (2004–05, p, 199) echoed this sentiment:

> One problem is that many people do not mean what I meant when they refer to the Washington Consensus. . . . The Washington Consensus has been denounced as a policy agenda that has brought misery and ruin in its wake, for example by causing the collapse in Argentina. This I find quite extraordinary because the Argentinean crisis was quite clearly a consequence of hanging on to an unrealistic exchange rate (what Argentineans referred to as 'convertibility') combined with a reluctance to implement the extremely deflationary fiscal policy that would have been needed to stick with a fixed, overvalued exchange rate. Look at items 1 and 5 on the list above, and you will see why I resent people trying to blame the Washington Consensus for the Argentinean collapse.

Williamson (2004–05) offers two different interpretations of the Washington Consensus, which may have contributed to the confusion. The first, which may be labelled the 'Bretton Woods institutions' approach, refers to the policies advocated by the Bretton Woods institutions, and the US Treasury, toward their country clients. This approach, however, is not the same as the Washington Consensus, since it emphasized corner – or bipolar – exchange rate solutions. According to Williamson (2004–05, p. 200) '[t]his is directly counter to my version of the Washington Consensus, which called for a competitive exchange rate, which necessarily implies an intermediate regime since either fixed or floating rates can easily become overvalued'.

The second approach, which we may call the 'market fundamentalist' approach, is, in the words of Williamson (2004–05, p. 201), a 'thoroughly objectionable perversion of the original meaning' of the Washington Consensus. For him, market fundamentalism is defined as supply-side economics, monetarism, or minimal government. Yet, the author of the Consensus sees no connection between his proposals and what he considers as neo-liberal policies.

Finally, regarding the pace of implementation of the reforms, the camps are divided among those advocating a 'shock therapy' (or big bang) approach, and those preferring 'more therapy and less shock', that is, a more gradual implementation of the reforms. Despite this, there is today a clear recognition that a 'human face' should complement the original Washington Consensus, involving, for instance, policies designed to better distribute income among as well as between countries.

THE POST-KEYNESIAN SOLUTION: TIME FOR REFORM

Irrespective of whether the original Washington Consensus has been misunderstood or should be augmented, from a post-Keynesian perspective it changes very little. Indeed, adding a 'human face' changes very little to the original intent of this Consensus. In spite of Williamson's rejection of the 'market fundamentalist' approach, the policy reforms are certainly rooted in market-friendly, neoclassical economics. It is difficult to comprehend how the Washington Consensus can be interpreted in any way but ideological. From a post-Keynesian perspective, faith in market forces, balanced budgets, privatization, elimination of trade barriers, and other tenets of neoclassical theory are ideological in nature, as many post-Keynesian economists have argued relentlessly for many years.

From a post-Keynesian stance, adding a 'kindler, gentler' face on what is fundamentally a neoclassical, supply-side set of economic policies would not change the fate of emerging market economies. In fact, macroeconomic discipline, a market economy, and openness to the world may be accepted by a large number of economists, but these policies are at the root of the economic crises striking emerging market economies. Consider the fact that the average annual growth rate in Latin American has fallen from 3 per cent during the activist years (1960–80) to only 1.5 per cent per year since the 1980s (Chang and Grabel, 2004–05).

Hence, a new consensus is really needed, one that takes into consideration the special characteristics of Latin America, and its openness. In fact, there is a credible alternative, and this alternative can be found in the writings of post-Keynesians. Such an alternative aims at promoting stability, economic growth, and minimizing the possibility of financial crises.

Not only have post-Keynesians criticized the pace of economic reforms, they have also criticized the reforms themselves. They notably criticize the Washington Consensus as being a blueprint that ignores the specific historical and institutional conditions prevailing in developing countries and, more importantly, completely abandons the Keynesian notion of aggregate demand and income distribution set within a non-ergodic world. In particular, they argue that a policy blueprint cannot be applicable to all circumstances in all times. No policy prescription can be 'prêt-à-porter', but rather must be tailor-made to take into account the specific problems inherent to emerging and/or developing countries.

The concerns of this 'Main Street alternative' (see Palley, 1998) cannot be taken lightly. Indeed, alternative voices have not been a component of the economic dialogue, yet many of their concerns and arguments have proven to be warranted, at least in part. In this sense, are the risks of ignoring their concerns and questions too great a price to pay? Is there room for dialogue?

The Post-Keynesian 'Main Street' Consensus

The 'Main Street' consensus is part of a growing post-Keynesian literature that seeks to 'reclaim development', to use Chang and Grabel's (2004–05) more than apt expression.

The main concerns of a number of post-Keynesians can be reduced to two mutually reinforcing arguments. First, several post-Keynesians believe that there is a need to regulate the international movement of capital. In this sense, they are strong advocates of a new international financial architecture (see Davidson, 2003b). The precise make-up of this new institutional setting, however, remains to be clarified. Secondly, they argue that there is an overemphasis on inflation targeting and that little attention has been paid to output and employment stabilization. Stiglitz (1998, pp. 13–15, emphasis in original) has already outlined the disadvantages of fighting inflation when inflation rates are lower than 40 per cent. 'Below that level, however, *there is little evidence that inflation is costly.* . . . Minimizing or avoiding major economic contractions should be one of the most important goals of policy'. Post-Keynesians would therefore argue that it is not sufficient to soften the strict reliance on market forces by developing a social agenda including poverty and income inequality reductions. What is needed is a thorough debate on the fundamental causes of the current economic performance of developing countries.

What is becoming increasingly clear is the need for a new consensus that emphasizes Keynesian aggregate demand policies, exchange rate stability, income distribution, employment growth, and crisis avoidance. This is not the same as an 'Augmented Washington Consensus', but rather a new 'Main Street Consensus' that requires more than 'plumbing' (Davidson, 2003b). After all, the real world is fundamentally Keynesian, and as such only Keynesian economic policies can succeed in creating and promoting a stable international environment. Only when domestic full-employment policies are adopted will the world have a more stable international environment. This is one of Keynes's most fundamental open economy policies. 'It is the simultaneously pursuit of these policies by all countries together which is capable of restoring health and strength internationally, whether we measure it by the level of domestic employment or by the volume of international trade' (Keynes, 1936, p. 349).

For starters, it is important to recognize that emphasis should be placed foremost on reforming the domestic economy, rather than relying on the development of export industries. Indeed, the limits of export-led growth strategies are well known to post-Keynesians, and thus policies encouraging domestic enterprises that meet the needs of local residents are the primary focus of 'reclaiming development'. Emphasis should be placed therefore on effective demand, both in the short and long run. This implies emphasizing fiscal policy, domestic investment, and consumption, through a much-needed redistribution of income in favour of workers.

Alone, these effective demand policies might not be sufficient to prevent financial crises. After all, strong economic growth may not be sufficient to prevent the ravages of destabilizing financial flows. Therefore, there needs to be another set of policies that deal with financial flows. Let us consider these policies in turn.

While there might be much to say about fiscal policy, land reform, wages, and income distribution, let us only discuss here two particular issues: first, the need to guarantee long-term financing of domestic investment; secondly, the role of foreign direct investment and capital controls.

The Need to Finance Long-Term Investment

In discussing the need to finance long-term investment, let us place the discussion in its proper context. Indeed, within a post-Keynesian framework of endogenous money, it is not savings that finance investment, as in neoclassical growth models, but rather bank credit. Banks finance the needs for both the payment of wages and investment by firms. Firms usually arrange for lines of credit to pay for wages (short-term credit) and borrow longer for capital purchases. Hence, the solution for encouraging domestic investment from local residents is not to find ways of increasing savings, as in the original and augmented versions of the Washington Consensus (we are all familiar with the paradox of thrift), but rather to encourage banks to finance investment.

In many developing economies, however, there is an important obstacle: the domestic banking system is within the hands of foreign interests. Indeed, the dramatic increase in multinational banks in the late 1990s is a direct result of Washington Consensus-type policies that emphasize the removal of barriers to the free flow of financial capital. Currently, in Latin America, foreign banks control almost half of the total banking activity.

Indeed, from 1990 to 2002 the increased presence of foreign banks in Latin America, or indeed in all emerging economies, has been nothing but remarkable. In particular, in the second half of the 1990s, there has been a dramatic increase of involvement of foreign banks, either by a measure of their participation in domestic banking or more directly by their ownership and control of the domestic banking industry. In 2001, for example, foreign banks accounted for 47 per cent of total loans and 43 per cent of total deposits, up from 38 per cent and 36 per cent respectively in 2000. As empirical evidence shows, there is however a marked difference across countries in the degree of foreign ownership of the domestic banking sector. Nonetheless, the available data show that for some countries multinational banking can reach nearly 75 per cent of total banking activity. On average, it is close to 50 per cent (see Gnos and Rochon, 2004–05b).

The conclusion is undeniable: 'For many emerging markets, one of the most striking structural changes in their financial systems during the 1990s has been the growing presence of foreign-owned financial institutions, especially in the banking system. ... In some Latin American countries, almost one-half of total bank assets are controlled by foreign institutions' (International Monetary Fund, 2000, p. 152).

Two questions are of particular interest at this juncture.

1. Does this presence of foreign banks change the structure of bank lending? In other words, does an increased presence of foreign banks lead to a crowding-out of local or smaller borrowers?
2. Does an increased presence of foreign banks tend to stabilize or destabilize the banking system? Is there more systemic risk as a result?

Since the adoption of the Washington Consensus – which corresponded to the rise of globalization – financial deregulation and economic liberalization policies have taken centre stage. As a result, many barriers to the free flow of capital have been eliminated. With the rise of these policies, financial institutions found profitable the possibility of expanding to other countries. This intense competitive pressure led to the increased multinationalization of the financial industry seeking potential new borrowers.

Many countries, in the past, have had regulatory policies and substantial barriers to entry, which prevented foreign ownership of the domestic banking sector especially in emerging markets. Examples of such barriers include number of branches, controls over permissible activities, and strict limits to the percentage of foreign ownerships of domestic banks. But, as Eichengreen and Mussa (1998) argue, many emerging economies have eliminated a number of such barriers especially since the early/mid 1990s, specifically to attract foreign banks in the belief that such policies would stabilize the domestic banking sector (foreign banks are seen as 'better' banks).

As Weller (1998, p. 1) points out, however, 'the spread of global banking has contributed to the financial instability of many nations and led to the disruption of domestic credit markets'. This is because foreign multinational banks tend to follow their multinational clients (Cull et al., 1999; Clarke et al., 2000). After all, as Clarke et al. (2001, p. 11) argue, 'multinational enterprises are expected to be customers of larger banks'. This is not surprising, and it is not surprising either that the trend in multinational banking followed greater economic integration. As multinational corporations are increasingly opening factories in emerging market economies, banks will follow their clients to finance their operations.

Moreover, as foreign banks set up shops in emerging markets, they begin to attract the local larger firms. Because of their better reputation, large blue-chip corporations prefer banking with blue-chip (reputable) banks. This implies that foreign banks will be able to capture the 'best' part of the market or the more creditworthy borrowers, both foreign and domestic. This is evidenced by Belaisch et al. (2001), who have argued that since foreign banks rely on the assessment and quantification of risk, smaller local (non-oligopolistic) banks are disadvantaged, because their lending operations depend more on developing long-term relationships with the clients. In this sense, the increase in multinational banking leads to an oligopolization of credit supply.

To the extent that they lend to small borrowers, large banks are likely to employ standardized methods for assessing creditworthiness based on readily available information. For smaller banks, it may pay to grant loan officers greater latitude to use idiosyncratic borrower information, most of which is not easily quantified or transferable, in assessing creditworthiness. This flexibility makes it easier to create and maintain a relationship between small banks and small borrowers (Clarke et al., 2001, p. 21; see also Focarelli and Pozzolo, 2000).

This practice, known as 'cherry picking', suggests therefore that foreign banks will lend only to the more profitable industries and borrowers – both domestic and foreign – thereby leaving the more risky borrowers to local banks. In this sense, foreign banks are able to pick and choose their borrowers, and do not contribute to the improvement of local banks' balance sheets, but often will lead to their worsening. 'Foreign banks are viewed as focusing their lending on wealthy individuals and the most creditworthy corporates. . . . Experience in the early stages of financial liberalizations . . . in many countries suggests that this is not an unwarranted concern' (International Monetary Fund, 2000, pp. 163–4; see also Demirgüç-Kunt and Detragiache, 1998). Clarke et al. (2001, p. 20) found evidence to this effect. Clarke et al. (2000) conclude that foreign banks devote almost twice as much of their loan portfolio to manufacturing firms.

Hence, if the demand from creditworthy borrowers does not change, a shift from local to foreign banks by the larger firms will lead to a crowding-out effect, and local banks lose an important source of lending. This in turn can lead to two possible outcomes, each contributing to the instability of the local banking system.

On the one hand, local banks will face a decline in their credit supply. As their more creditworthy customers move to multinational banks, local banks will be crowded out of the loan market, which will translate not only in a decline of their loans, but also of their profits. Indeed, in an extensive study using bank-level data from 80 countries for the period between 1988 and 1995, Claessens et al. (2001) have shown that multinational banking has led to a general decrease in the profits of local banks. Weller (2001, p. 11) precisely points to this scenario in South Korea, Hungary, and Poland (see also Euh and Baker, 1990; Anderson and Kegels, 1998; and Weller, 2000). With depressed profits and capital structures, local banks are thus less likely to raise the necessary capital, thereby paving the way for increased foreign banks entry in the future.

On the other hand, or, in fact, perhaps as an eventual result of the first scenario, local banks may indeed react by increasing their supply of credit. This is perhaps the more problematic of the two scenarios. As their balance sheets deteriorate, local banks may be forced to react to increased competition by lending to riskier borrowers, or by financing riskier projects, thereby increasing the overall risk of the lending pool (Darity and Horn,

1998). This is especially true if existing local banks already have weak or deteriorating capital positions. Riskier projects or riskier borrowers are seen as the only possible way of rebuilding the local banks' capital position.

In an alternative scenario, local banks may lend not only to riskier projects, but also to projects that are in fact more short-term and speculative in nature, which could then translate into financial and speculative bubbles.

From this analysis we can draw two conclusions. First, small, local borrowers will not be able to have access to bank credit. Secondly, the domestic financial system will be more unstable. This is certainly disquieting. Large borrowers tend to operate in the export industries. Hence favouring the financing of large businesses goes hand in hand with a more export-oriented growth strategy.

While the above analysis is rarely considered by post-Keynesian authors, it is nonetheless consistent with Chang and Grabel (2004–05), who, in fact, emphasize the need to finance long-term projects as well. They also emphasize that an industrial strategy is required too, where selected industries are singled out. We absolutely agree with this assertion. Yet, the authors also suggest the creation of development banks. According to them (Chang and Grabel, 2004–05, p. 280):

> Another means of ensuring the provision of stable, long-term finance to particular sectors/firms is through the creation of development banks that specialize in long-term financing. Development banks can be publicly financed and managed as in Brazil and Korea, or can be privately financed as in the case of German industrial banks. It is also conceivable that these banks could be organized as a public–private hybrid, and could raise capital on international markets and even from private sources. Development banks are the institutional counterpart of the industrial policies and public investment programs that are critical to late development, as the experiences of several countries suggest.

By encouraging the development of a strong local banking sector, this may contribute to two important aspects. First, it may channel much needed credit to small, local borrowers and thus encourage the development of local firms. Secondly, it may also reduce the dependence on either foreign borrowing or borrowing in foreign currencies.

Foreign Direct Investment and Capital Controls

The second issue that needs to be emphasized is the role of foreign direct investment and, in particular, the role of capital controls. In this context, the divisions between exchange rate regimes are of secondary importance. What is of particular interest is the specific objective of economic policy.

Preferences over a specific exchange rate arrangement are linked to specific macroeconomic policies, in particular to whether economists prefer full employment policies to policies guaranteeing price stability. In this sense, the old dichotomy between Keynesian (full employment) economists and neoclassical/monetarist economists (focusing on price stability) is still fully appropriate (see Rochon and Vernengo, 2000).

The absence of capital controls imposes important deflationary pressures on economic systems. Steady outflows of capital, which can be caused by a number of variables such as uncertainty and speculative forms of behaviour, tend to devalue the national currency. Moreover, if one of the objectives of the monetary authority is to prevent the value of the local currency from depreciating, it will more than likely intervene and raise the interest rate. In turn, high or rising rates of interest will affect negatively effective demand, and depress the economy.

Post-Keynesians argue that deregulation and liberalization of capital markets will tend to create a tendency towards higher rates of interest, because once capital flows can move freely from one country to another in search of higher returns, central banks that are not willing to allow their currency to depreciate – that is, which do not want capital flight – will have to increase the attractiveness of their currency by bidding up interest rates. The increase in the rate of interest, in turn, not only depresses the economy but also increases the burden of government debt by increasing the financial component of the fiscal deficit.

In order to be able to control interest rates for domestic purposes, restrictions on the free mobility of capital are an essential component of macroeconomic policy. Otherwise, the negative effects that these movements of financial capital will have on interest rates, and hence on the economy, can be devastating.

Keynes (1980, p. 276) advocated these restrictions. In fact, he argued that 'we cannot hope to control rates of interest at home if movements of capital moneys out of the country are unrestricted'. He saw capital controls as an essential policy instrument in developing aggregate demand, full employment policies. Once these controls are adopted, countries can expect to maintain control over their interest rate policy. If full employment is a desirable goal, then a policy of low real rates of interest ought to be put into practice. In the *General Theory*, Keynes favoured such a policy, since it would lead to what he called the 'euthanasia of the rentier' (1936, p. 376). Keeping interest rates low would also allow for the 'socialization of investment' as well as full employment.

CONCLUSION

The purpose of this chapter was to offer a criticism of the Washington Consensus that is distinct from mainstream criticism. The economic performance of Latin American economies in the last two decades is nothing short of disastrous. The string of financial crises that have occurred in recent years provides evidence of the failure of the Washington Consensus.

Financial crises are grounded on poor economic performance. The strategy of this chapter was to offer an alternative 'Main Street' consensus that would help in the stabilization of Latin American economies and, hopefully, prevent future financial crises. It rests primarily on the need to stabilize the economic performance of emerging and developing countries, based on policies of aggregate demand. In this sense, we discussed two important aspects worth considering: banking sector reforms and the need for capital controls.

While there are a great many other arguments that need to be thoroughly discussed, we think that the greatest impact can be achieved if the elements pointed out in this chapter are taken into account, with future reforms needed as the economies stabilize.

REFERENCES

Anderson, R.W. and C. Kegels (1998), *Transition Banking: Financial Development of Central and Eastern Europe*, Oxford: Oxford University Press.

Belaisch, A., L. Kodres, J. Levy and A. Ubide (2001), 'Euro-area banking at the crossroads', *International Monetary Fund Working Paper*, no. 01/28.

Chang, H.J. and I. Grabel (2004–05), 'Reclaiming development from the Washington Consensus', *Journal of Post Keynesian Economics*, **27** (2), 273–91.

Clarke, G., R. Cull, L. D'Amato and A. Molinari (2000), 'On the kindness of strangers? The impact of foreign entry on domestic banks in Argentina', in S. Claessens and M. Jansen (eds), *The Internationalisation of Financial Services: Issues and Lessons for Developing Countries*, Boston: Kluwer Academic Press, 351–64.

Clarke, G., R. Cull, M.S.M. Peria and S.M. Sánchez (2001), 'Foreign bank entry: experience, implications for developing countries, and agenda for further research', *World Bank Policy Research Working Paper*, no. 2698.

Claessens, S., A. Demirgüç-Kunt and H. Huizinga (2001), 'How does foreign entry affect domestic banking markets?', *Journal of Banking and Finance*, **25** (5), 891–911.

Cull, R., L. D'Amato, A. Molinari and G. Clarke (1999), 'The effect of foreign entry on Argentina's domestic banking sector', *World Bank Policy Research Working Paper*, no. 2158.

Darity, W.A. and B.L. Horn (1998), *The Loan Pushers: The Role of Commercial*

Banks in the International Debt Crisis, Cambridge: Ballinger Publications.

Davidson, P. (2003a), 'What is wrong with the Washington Consensus and what should we do about it?', paper presented at the international conference on 'Reforming the Reforms: What's Next for Latin America?', Rio de Janeiro, 25 July.

Davidson, P. (2003b), 'The future of the international financial system', paper presented at the international conference on 'The Future of Economics', University of Cambridge, 18 September.

Demirgüç-Kunt, A. and E. Detragiache (1998), 'Financial liberalization and financial fragility', *World Bank Policy Research Working Paper*, no. 1917.

Eichengreen, B. and M. Mussa (1998), 'Capital account liberalization: theoretical and practical aspects', *International Monetary Fund Occasional Paper*, no. 172.

Euh, Y.-D. and J.C. Baker (1990), *The Korean Banking System and Foreign Influence*, London and New York: Routledge.

Focarelli, D. and A.F. Pozzolo (2000), 'The determinants of cross-border bank shareholdings: an analysis with bank-level data from OECD countries', *Federal Reserve Bank of Chicago Proceedings*, May, 199–232.

Gnos, C. and L.-P. Rochon (2004–05a), 'What is next for the Washington Consensus? The fifteenth anniversary, 1989–2004', *Journal of Post Keynesian Economics*, **27** (2), 187–93.

Gnos, C. and L.-P. Rochon (2004–05b), 'The Washington Consensus and multinational banking in Latin America', *Journal of Post Keynesian Economics*, **27** (2), 315–31.

Hausmann, R. (2001), 'Plan B: a way out for Argentina', 28 October, available at www.nber.org/~confer/2002/argentina02/hausmann.pdf.

International Monetary Fund (2000), 'International capital markets developments, prospects, and key policy issues', *World Economic and Financial Surveys*, September.

Keynes, J.M. (1936), *The General Theory of Employment, Interest, and Money*, London: Macmillan.

Keynes, J.M. (1980), *The Collected Writings of John Maynard Keynes* (vol. XXV *Activities 1940–1944. Shaping the Post-War World: The Clearing Union*), London and New York: Macmillan and Cambridge University Press.

Kuczynski, P.-P. and J. Williamson (eds) (2003), *After the Washington Consensus*, Washington, DC: Institute for International Economics.

Naim, M. (2000), 'Washington Consensus or Washington Confusion?', *Foreign Policy*, March, **118**, 86–103.

Naim, M. (2002), 'The Washington Consensus: a damaged brand', *Financial Times*, 28 October.

Palley, T.I. (1998), 'Goodbye Washington Consensus, hello Main Street alternative', available at http://www.fmcenter.org/site/pp.asp?c=8fLGJTOyHpE&b=264083.

Rochon, L.-P. and M. Vernengo (2000), 'Disentangling the confusion: exchange rate regimes, capital controls and the revenge of the rentiers', *Challenge*, November–December, 76–92.

Rodrik, D. (2002) 'After neo-liberalism, what?', *Taipei Times*, 5 October, available at http://www.taipeitimes.com/News/editorials/archives/2002/10/05/170814.

Rodrik, D. (2005), 'Growth strategies', in P. Aghion and S.N. Durlauf (eds), *Handbook of Economic Growth*, vol. 1A, Amsterdam: Elsevier B.V., forthcoming.

Stiglitz, J.E. (1998), 'More instruments and broader goals: moving toward the post-Washington Consensus', United Nations University, World Institute for Development Economics Research, Annual Lecture 2, January.

Stiglitz, J.E. (2002), *Globalization and its Discontents*, New York: W.W. Norton & Co.

Weller, C.E. (1998), 'Global banking', *Foreign Policy*, **3** (9), 1–3.

Weller, C.E. (2000), 'Financial liberalization, multinational banks and credit supply: the case of Poland', *International Review of Applied Economics*, **14** (2), 193–211.

Weller, C.E. (2001), 'The supply of credit by multinational banks in developing and transition economies: determinants and effects', *Department of Economic and Social Affairs Discussion Paper*, no. 16.

Williamson, J. (1990), 'What Washington means by policy reform', in J. Williamson (ed.), *Latin American Adjustment: How Much Has Happened?*, Washington, DC: Institute for International Economics, 5–20.

Williamson, J. (2000), 'What should the World Bank think about the Washington Consensus?', *World Bank Research Observer*, **15** (2), 251–64.

Williamson, J. (2002), 'Did the Washington Consensus fail?', speech given at the Center for Strategic and International Studies, Washington, DC, 6 November.

Williamson, J. (2004–05), 'The strange history of the Washington Consensus', *Journal of Post Keynesian Economics*, **27** (2), 195–206.

PART TWO

From Financial Instability to
Macroeconomic Performance

7. Reforming the International Payment System: An Assessment

Claude Gnos

INTRODUCTION

For several decades now, a small number of post-Keynesians (Davidson, 1991, 2002; D'Arista, 2004) and monetary circuit authors (Schmitt, 1973, 1975; Cencini, 1995; and recently Rossi, 2005, and Chapter 10 this volume) have been arguing for a structural reform of the international system of payments with reference to Keynes, who once advocated setting up an International Clearing Union complete with a currency of its own (Keynes, 1942/1980). Despite the obvious failings of the present system, though, today's proponents of change have so far been no more successful than their mentor was some 60 years ago at the Bretton Woods Conference. Their failure might be ascribed to (i) the scant influence post-Keynesians and monetary circuit authors wield in both academic and political circles, (ii) more general political and ideological factors, notably the hegemony of the United States, which is unlikely to be enthusiastic at the idea of the dollar losing its status as a key currency, and (iii) the belief, shared by a majority of authorities, that the unrestricted operation of markets, provided it is guaranteed, can provide solutions to any economic problem that might arise. However, we believe these reasons conceal another, more fundamental reason, which also explains the current deficit in support for post-Keynesians and monetary circuit authors.

In his Preface to the *General Theory*, Keynes (1936/1973, p. viii) advised readers that what he was proposing was a new way of thinking. He also warned them that escaping from habitual modes of thought and expression is a very difficult exercise.[1] This chapter argues that it is this sort of difficulty that still besets proposals for reform of the international payment system. Where money is concerned, especially, mindsets have remained highly conservative. Although money has been dematerialized and its linkage to any physical yardstick has been abandoned (even if the reference to gold in the international arena was not officially abandoned until 1976), most economists and the general public still think of it as a thing that is somehow comparable to real goods and assets. In this respect, several crucial issues, which we shall be examining, stand in the way of the proposed reform.

The next section concentrates on Keynes's struggle to renew the conceptual approach to money and the role of banks in the face of common conceptions. The third and fourth sections illustrate our argument by showing that these conceptions stood in the way of reforms both at the Bretton Woods Conference and after the collapse in the 1970s of the system that conference begat. The fifth section concludes.

KEYNES'S RENEWED APPROACH TO MONEY AND THE ROLE OF BANKS

It should be emphasized that money is usually, that is to say, in mainstream economics, conceived of as a good. This conception undoubtedly derives from the idea that present-day bank money is no more than a refinement of commodity money; it is also enshrined in a representation inherited from Smith (1776/1976) and extended by Walras (1926/1954), by which market transactions may ultimately be seen as exchanges of goods and productive services for one another. In this view, money is a medium of exchange, that is, a commodity subdividing trade into two sets of transactions, with goods (or services) being exchanged for money, and then money for goods. Even paper and bank monies are to be considered as goods (albeit immaterial ones), the quantity of which is exogenously determined. The quantity-theory-of-money equation eventually completes the model by determining the level of prices. In issuing greater or lesser amounts of money, it is argued, banks vary the level of demand in respect of a given quantity of available goods and so act on prices.

Back in 1925, when preparing his *Treatise on Money*, Keynes (1930/1971) challenged this view. He dismissed the quantity-theory-of-money equation, and conceived of deposits as resulting from bank loans, that is, from credit. He emphasized the role of the money of account in terms of which debts and contracts are currently expressed. Although he did not expand much on the nature of money in the *General Theory*, he went on elaborating on his innovative views in the latter book and in his subsequent writings, especially his 1937 articles (see Keynes, 1937a/1973, 1937b/1973).

Among Keynes's findings, we may first cite the equality of saving and investment:

> The prevalence of the idea that saving and investment, taken in their straightforward sense, can differ from one another, is to be explained, I think, by an optical illusion due to regarding an individual depositor's relation to his bank as being a one-sided transaction, instead of seeing it as the two-sided transaction which it actually is. It is supposed that a depositor and his bank can somehow contrive between them to perform an operation by which savings can disappear into the banking system so that they are lost to investment, or, contrariwise, that the banking system can make it possible for investment to occur, to which no saving corresponds (Keynes, 1936/1973, p. 81).

This means that, fundamentally, banks are financial intermediaries between borrowers and depositors. When granting credit to their customers, they do not create resources that they lend to customers and that these customers then exchange for goods. The resources that are actually lent come from deposits, that is, from depositors. For the post-Keynesians, Moore (1988) emphasized that this assertion is confirmed by double-entry bookkeeping in which the existence of bank money is enshrined: the double-entry principle does not allow banks to extend credit to borrowers without gaining an equivalent credit from depositors. On the side of monetary circuit authors, Schmitt (1984a) insisted that money creation has to be seen for what it really is: bookkeeping entries – debits and credits that banks record in their books in nominal units of account and that resolve into liabilities and assets denoting (indirect) financial relations between borrowers and depositors.

We may secondly cite the distinction between cash and saving Keynes made in his 1937 articles when defining what he termed the 'finance motive'. He drew the readers' attention to the fact that, when starting production, firms have to secure finance, which may be provided by banks (in the form of overdraft facilities) or by the market (Keynes, 1937a/1973, pp. 208–9). Such finance, he claimed, amounts to 'a provision of cash', and, in conformity with what we just pointed out, generates saving in the form of bank deposits when used in payments of the factors of production. In other words, deposits are a dual entity. As noted before, they are assets denoting indirect (that is, through the intermediation of banks) financial relationships between borrowers and depositors. They are also, in the first instance, claims on banks that entitle their holders to ask banks to make payments on their behalf. All in all, banks are both financial intermediaries and, so to speak, monetary intermediaries, in that they make payments in crediting and debiting accounts on their customers' behalf.

The two features of Keynes's analysis of money and the role of banks we have just cited were crucial foundations for his proposal for establishing an International Clearing Union. As Keynes (1943a, p. 210) argued, '[m]odern banking has developed . . . to a very fine degree of perfection within a given country. But we have, broadly speaking, continued with the uncivilised practices of the Middle Ages as between countries'. He then proposed to apply what he termed 'the essential principle of banking' in the international arena: 'The idea underlying such a Union is simple, namely, to generalise the essential principle of banking as it is exhibited within any closed system. This principle is the necessary equality of credits and debits' (Keynes, 1942/1980, p. 171).

In keeping with his analysis of money creation, Keynes insisted that the constitution of capital is not a prerequisite when establishing the Clearing Union (Keynes, 1943a/1980, p. 210). Namely, contrary to a belief that was still prevalent in his days, it is not bank deposits that create loans, but loans that create bank deposits. Keynes had to set out his views at a meeting of the European Allies:

> It is perplexing to some people at first that that should not be necessary. In the first days of banking great stress was laid on the possession of capital but we have learned as time goes on that that is of insignificant importance (Keynes, 1943a/1980, p. 210).

It is true, however, that bankers must, in practice, keep a watch on the quantity of deposits they currently receive from the general public. This is so, as Keynes (1930/1971, p. 21) explained in the *Treatise*, because, in domestic banking systems, a given bank may become indebted towards other banks when the general public comes to deposit with other banks the cash it obtained from this bank. But this constraint does not hold in the international arena, where the Union would be the sole bank (Keynes, 1941/1980, p. 44, and 1943a/1980, pp. 210–11).

The next two sections show that the persistency of the conventional view was the main impediment both to the adoption of Keynes's proposals at the Bretton Woods Conference and to the search for new ground rules after the collapse of the Bretton Woods system.

THE PERSISTENCY OF THE CONVENTIONAL VIEW AS THE MAIN IMPEDIMENT TO THE ADOPTION OF KEYNES'S SCHEME AT THE BRETTON WOODS CONFERENCE

The responsibility borne by the conventional view in the rejection of Keynes's scheme is very clear if we consider the main arguments that the US experts raised against it. First of all, being the main potential creditor of the system, the United States feared it might be unable to exercise control over the size of its financial commitments. Deficit countries would be granted credits labelled in bancor (that is, the international currency unit in Keynes's plan) by the Union, which the United States would then have to convert into US dollars on demand. Creditor countries would become the 'milch cow' of the system. This fear was all the more acute, because the creditor countries 'might find themselves with a minority of votes' (Horsefield, 1969, p. 30). Allied to this, as the British negotiator reported, US officials feared 'that the open-ended obligation to provide credit, involved in the Clearing Union, might have an inflationary effect in the United States, with adverse results on the dollar' (p. 49).

Keynes (1943b/1980, p. 276) replied to the US experts by claiming that:

[t]here is one important respect in which the British proposals seem to be gravely misunderstood in some quarters in the United States. There is no foundation whatever for the idea that the object of the proposals is to make the United States the milch cow of the world in general and of this country [the United Kingdom] in particular. In fact the best hope for the lasting success of the plan is the precise contrary. The plan does not require the United States, or any other country, to put up a single dollar which they themselves choose or prefer to employ in any other way whatever. The essence of it is that if a country has a balance in its favour which it does not choose to use in buying goods or services or making overseas investment, this balance shall remain available to the Union – not permanently, but only for just so long as the country owning it chooses to leave it unemployed. That is not a burden on the creditor country. It is an extra facility to it, for it allows it to carry on its trade with the rest of the world unimpeded, whenever a time lag between earning and spending happens to suit its own convenience.

Keynes's reply provides a good example in support of our general argument. If it were possible for banks, specifically for the Clearing Union Bank, to provide borrowers with financing of their own, then US fears as regards its potential financial commitments would have been legitimate. On the conventional view, the Clearing Union Bank would issue bancor to the benefit of deficit countries, which the latter countries would then convert at will into key currencies, that is, creditor countries' currencies. By Keynes's renewed approach to money and the role of banks, which is grounded not in fantasy but in actual double-entry bookkeeping, such a situation cannot arise. No country would be committed to supplying its own currency in exchange for deposits labelled in bancor, because money creation in no way forms bank deposits designed to be exchanged for goods or assets. What the Clearing Union Bank would be able to do is to provide cash to a country buying goods or assets from another country. So the relation of cause-and-effect is reversed compared to the direction it is assumed to take on the conventional view. Namely, the need and use of cash is subordinated to an economic – commercial or financial – transaction being made between both countries. Then, and only then, would the creditor country grant credit to its partner through the Clearing Union Bank. As a consequence, the creditor country would hold deposits with the Bank, which, as Keynes emphasized, far from being a burden would represent a facility: in this way countries operating a surplus can save their foreign earnings until such time as they decide to spend them. As he wryly put it, '[t]his is not a Red Cross philanthropic relief scheme, by which the rich countries come to the rescue of the poor' (p. 277). To achieve this outcome, however, one condition must be met: the spheres of circulation of national currencies and of the international currency should be kept strictly apart. Let us examine this latter point.

The core proposal of Keynes's scheme is to substitute a special-purpose currency for domestic currencies in the international arena. This does not mean that foreigners should be prohibited from holding deposits labelled in domestic currencies in the corresponding economies, and from changing currencies into one another (more on this below), but that they should have no means of depositing domestic currencies with foreign banks. In other words, no domestic currency should circulate between countries. Where this condition does not hold, any country (say, A) borrowing cash from the Clearing Union Bank may use it to obtain currencies from given countries (B) that will allow it to settle its debts vis-à-vis third countries (C). In this way, 'key' currency countries (B) become both creditors of the Clearing Union Bank and debtors of C countries, just because they are members of the Clearing Union and committed to providing their currencies on demand. Not so when domestic currencies are prevented from circulating between countries. This means that, when obtaining cash from the Clearing Union Bank, country A cannot avoid financing a bilateral transaction involving it and either country B or country C. Country A does not get country B's currency, which it would then be able to transfer to country C. So, if debtor countries tend to accumulate debts while creditor countries accumulate large bancor balances, as Keynes highlighted, this is a problem of maladjustments of balances of payments that each country should deal with on its own (p. 277). The International Clearing Union should be concerned with this problem only insofar as it may make use of its position to press its member countries to find means to reduce their balance-of-payments deficits or surpluses. This is a rule devised to ensure the smooth functioning of the international system, not a threat to any country's sovereignty. It should be clear, too, that arguing that the Clearing Union Bank would provide cash that countries would use in bilateral transactions is not contradictory to multilateral compensation between debts and assets labelled in bancor and held by any country.[2]

As regards inflation, the US experts' argument amounted to saying that their country would have to create US dollars as a counterpart to the bancor issued by the Clearing Union Bank, and would in this way increase the quantity of dollars in circulation and so possibly inflate prices both at home and abroad. Inflation would, in its turn, bring about a depreciation of the US dollar. Our analysis above clearly shows that this fear is unfounded. The Clearing Union Bank would not create resources of its own in addition to the resources supplied by its member countries.

THE PERSISTENCY OF THE CONVENTIONAL VIEW AS THE MAIN IMPEDIMENT TO THE SEARCH FOR NEW GROUND RULES AFTER THE COLLAPSE OF THE BRETTON WOODS SYSTEM

In the 1970s, when the Bretton Woods system was falling apart, the member countries of the International Monetary Fund (IMF) began thinking about reforming the international monetary system. One of the possibilities they examined, especially those countries of what was known as the Committee of Twenty (C-20) in 1973 and 1974, was to promote the Special Drawing Rights (SDR) to the rank of an international currency. This possibility was part of a scheme to ensure more symmetry and flexibility in the setting of exchange rates, and to allow IMF member countries greater macroeconomic autonomy.

Commenting on the ultimate failure of the negotiators to reform the international monetary system, McKinnon (1993, p. 25) notes that:

> the C-20 was renegotiating in the original spirit of the Bretton Woods articles. . . . Still under the sway of Keynes' views as of 1943–44, officials and academic economists in 1973–74 had not really changed their mindset for 30 years.

We cannot but agree with this statement: there is no doubt that the common view still prevailed, just as it did at the Bretton Woods Conference. Moreover, Keynes certainly bears some share of responsibility for this, despite his genuinely revolutionary message.

As McKinnon (1993) emphasizes, two main problems stood in the way of the expected reform. On the one hand, the existence of 'hot' money made long-term flexibility in exchange rates incompatible with their short-run stability, except if foreign exchange controls were introduced.

> As long as world financial markets remained (modestly) open, speculative hot money flows would tend to anticipate any discrete change in official par values. And, certainly by 1973–74, the negotiators did not want a return to the draconian exchange controls that Keynes had in mind in 1943 (McKinnon, 1993, p. 25).

It is true that Keynes recommended implementing strict capital movement controls, especially in the early versions of his scheme. In subsequent versions of it, however, he was more moderate: 'the universal establishment of a control of capital movements cannot be regarded as essential to the operation of the Clearing Union; and the method and degree of such control should therefore be left to the decision of each member state' (Keynes, 1942/1980, pp. 185–6).

Here we run into a difficulty with which post-Keynesian authors are quite familiar. Namely, while he developed quite innovative insights, Keynes did not always draw the full conclusions from his analysis. This is particularly so in the case of the endogeneity of money, which is acknowledged in the *Treatise*, but partly discarded in the *General Theory* (see Moore, 1988). And it is the case here, because we can show that capital movement controls would not have been required at all, if the bancor had been substituted for national currencies in international payments.

To make our point about the irrelevance of capital flow controls, suppose that a resident of country A, holding a deposit with a domestic bank, wants to convert it into a deposit with a bank in country B, for whatever reason. When there is no international money, this transaction amounts to supplying money A against money B in the foreign exchange market, and may cause money A to depreciate against money B. The establishment of an international money breaks this logic. From his viewpoint, the resident of country A still supplies money A and demands money B. But neither money A nor money B leaves its own country. The Clearing Union Bank is substituted for the foreign exchange market, and acts in such a way that the banking system of country A cannot but recycle the money supplied by its customer, in the domestic monetary and financial markets, while the supply of money by the banking system of country B is part of the money supply in the domestic monetary and financial markets. As Schmitt (1984b) puts it, national currencies are then the objects of 'absolute exchanges', as opposed to 'relative exchanges'. Despite individuals' experience, currencies are not actually exchanged for one another in the foreign exchange market. In changing its currency against bancor, each country considered as a whole simultaneously supplies and takes back its own currency. In this way, the conversion of one money into another may affect the quantities and prices prevailing in domestic markets, including monetary and financial markets, but not the par values of the currencies, that is, their value in terms of the bancor. The circulation of capital in the international arena could not affect par values, and so there would be no need to restrict it.

As reported by McKinnon (1993, p. 25), though:

> the negotiators refused to recognize the nature of Mundell's redundancy problem. In an N country world without any generally accepted purely international money such as gold, there can only be $N-1$ independent official targets for the exchange rate, balance of trade, balance of payments, and so on. Symmetry, in the sense of each of the N countries choosing its targets independently, is simply impossible.

This point is particularly interesting: McKinnon is claiming that the general goals of the negotiators – ensuring more symmetry and flexibility in the setting of exchange rates, and greater macroeconomic autonomy for member countries – could not be achieved unless an international money was established. This confirms that, far from being utopian, the establishment of an International Clearing Union endowed with a money of its own would best suit member countries' requirements.

To illustrate the argument, let us consider in more detail the setting of par values. As we have just seen, changing currencies into one another would not affect par values, if an international currency were to substitute for them in international payments. This does not mean, however, that par values should be kept permanently fixed. On the contrary, a legitimate goal, which was actually shared both by Keynes and the promoters of the IMF, was to ensure by means of changes in par values long-term equilibrium in countries' foreign payments. Keynes on his part emphasized that the state of the foreign trade of countries is linked to changes in their production costs. He made the ensuing link between par values and production costs a rule to ensure that countries could conduct their own social policies without jeopardizing the competitiveness of their industries. He made it clear, however, that competitive devaluation should be prevented by strictly defining the rules of play.

It is to be noted that Keynes's rule would still be relevant in today's world economy. Production costs, essentially wages, are notoriously higher in Western countries, particularly in Western Europe, than in Eastern Europe, South-East Asia, or China. These higher production costs prompt Western companies to relocate their plants at the expense of employment in their home countries. According to mainstream economists, the only way to restore full employment in Western countries is to cut wage costs. Unfortunately, this would only induce a vicious circle, with lower wages meaning lower demand for goods produced in Western countries (see Gnos, 2003, 2005). In these circumstances, the recourse to exchange-rate management is the only alternative. This is what the G-7 member countries recently (February 2004) realized when asking China for 'some appropriate changes' in its exchange rate policy. But, of course, this is a very superficial approach to the problem for which the only satisfactory solution is that advocated by Keynes and his followers.

CONCLUSION

It is well known that Keynes eventually watered down the innovative character of his scheme, especially in the face of US proposals. He went so far as to declare that the International Clearing Union he was advocating and the International Monetary Fund that actually came to be implemented under the guidance of US experts were 'two arrangements represent[ing] alternative technical set-ups, capable of performing precisely the same functions' (Keynes, 1944/1980, p. 437). He did so for diplomatic reasons, and this certainly did not help much in passing on his views to new generations of economists. However, this is not the crucial reason why his proposal for the creation of an international currency was, and still is, discarded. Fundamentally, we believe, as argued in this chapter, that the explanation for this situation lies in the thinking habits Keynes warned of in the Preface to his *General Theory*.

In particular, this chapter shows that the two main impediments to the creation of an international currency may be dispelled when we adhere to Keynes's renewed approach to money and banking. These impediments proved to be firmly tied in with the conventional view. For one thing, the claim that creditor countries would become the 'milch cow' of the system has proved to be inconsistent. On the contrary, just as Keynes argued, the sovereignty of member countries of the International Clearing Union would have been preserved and even strengthened, because the redundancy problem would have been solved. For another thing, although Keynes did not draw this conclusion, this chapter has shown that capital flow controls are irrelevant in the proposed international system. Therefore, to advocate Keynes's proposal is not to challenge globalization or to hanker for the past.

Is it a safe bet that Keynes's innovative views will triumph in the foreseeable future? In the face of the real challenges raised by globalization, especially that of unemployment, the very survival of Western economies may well hinge on the introduction of an international currency along the lines once defined by Keynes and currently developed by post-Keynesians and monetary circuit authors (see also Gnos and Rochon, 2004). However, it is not the case that necessity knows no law. Moreover, whilst this chapter has emphasized the dangers of habitual modes of thought with regard to money and banking, it should be mentioned that Keynes's proposals are also connected with more general issues concerning his method compared with the neoclassical approach (see notably his paper on 'Professor Tinbergen's method'; Keynes, 1939/1973). Given that neoclassical economics continues to hold sway in the world, we ought not to be over-optimistic.

NOTES

1. 'The difficulty lies, not in the new ideas, but in escaping from the old ones, which ramify, for those brought up as most of us have been, into every corner of our minds' (Keynes, 1936, p. viii).
2. 'It is a great advantage of the proposed Currency Union that it restores unfettered multilateral clearing between its members' (Keynes, 1941/1980, p. 51).

REFERENCES

Cencini, A. (1995), *Monetary Theory, National and International*, London and New York: Routledge.

D'Arista, J. (2004), 'Dollars, debt and dependence: the case for international monetary reform', *Journal of Post Keynesian Economics*, **26** (4), 557–72.

Davidson, P. (1991), 'What international payments scheme would Keynes have suggested for the twenty-first century?', in P. Davidson and J.A. Kregel (eds), *Economic Problems of the 1990s: Europe, the Developing Countries and the United States*, Aldershot, UK and Brookfield, USA: Edward Elgar, 85–104.

Davidson, P. (2002), *Financial Markets, Money and the Real World*, Cheltenham, UK and Northampton, MA, USA: Edward Elgar.

Gnos, C. (2003), 'The employment issue: Post Keynesian economics challenging New Keynesian economics', in E. Hein, A. Heise and A. Truger (eds), *Neu Keynesianismus: Der neue wirtschaftspolitische Mainstream?*, Marburg:

Metropolis, 117–33.

Gnos, C. (2005), 'Analysing and fighting recession with reference to Keynes', in L.R. Wray and M. Forstater (eds), *Contemporary Post Keynesian Analysis*, Cheltenham, UK and Northampton, MA, USA: Edward Elgar, 301–9.

Gnos, C. and L.-P. Rochon (2004), 'Reforming the international financial and monetary system: from Keynes to Davidson and Stiglitz', *Journal of Post Keynesian Economics*, **26** (4), 613–29.

Horsefield, J.K. (1969), *The International Monetary Fund, 1945–1965: Twenty Years of International Monetary Cooperation*, Washington, DC: International Monetary Fund, Vol. I.

Keynes, J.M. (1930/1971), *A Treatise on Money*, London: Macmillan. Reprinted in *The Collected Writings of John Maynard Keynes*, Vols V and VI, London and Basingstoke: Macmillan.

Keynes, J.M. (1936/1973), *The General Theory of Employment, Interest and Money*, London: Macmillan. Reprinted in *The Collected Writings of John Maynard Keynes*, Vol. VII, London and Basingstoke: Macmillan.

Keynes, J.M. (1937a/1973), 'Alternative theories of the rate of interest', *Economic Journal*, **47** (186), 241–52. Reprinted in *The Collected Writings of John Maynard Keynes*, Vol. XIV, London and Basingstoke: Macmillan, 201–15.

Keynes, J.M. (1937b/1973), 'The "ex ante" theory of the rate of interest', *Economic Journal*, **47** (188), 663–9. Reprinted in *The Collected Writings of John Maynard Keynes*, Vol. XIV, London and Basingstoke: Macmillan, 215–23.

Keynes, J.M. (1939/1973), 'Professor Tinbergen's method', *Economic Journal*, **49** (195), 558–68. Reprinted in *The Collected Writings of John Maynard Keynes*, Vol. XIV, London and Basingstoke: Macmillan, 306–18.

Keynes, J.M. (1941/1980), 'Proposals for an International Currency Union', in *The Collected Writings of John Maynard Keynes*, Vol. XXV, London and Basingstoke: Macmillan, 42–61.

Keynes, J.M. (1942/1980), 'Proposals for an International Clearing Union', in *The Collected Writings of John Maynard Keynes*, Vol. XXV, London and Basingstoke: Macmillan, 168–96.

Keynes, J.M. (1943a/1980), 'Speech to a meeting of the European Allies', in *The Collected Writings of John Maynard Keynes*, Vol. XXV, London and Basingstoke: Macmillan, 206–15.

Keynes, J.M. (1943b/1980), 'House of Lords debates', in *The Collected Writings of John Maynard Keynes*, Vol. XXV, London and Basingstoke: Macmillan, 269–80.

Keynes, J.M. (1944/1980), 'Explanatory notes by United Kingdom experts on the proposal for an International Monetary Fund', in *The Collected Writings of John Maynard Keynes*, Vol. XXV, London and Basingstoke: Macmillan, 437–42.

McKinnon, R.I. (1993), 'The rules of the game: international money in historical perspective', *Journal of Economic Literature*, **31** (1), 1–44.

Moore, B.J. (1988), *Horizontalists and Verticalists: The Macroeconomics of Credit Money*, Cambridge: Cambridge University Press.

Rossi, S. (2005), 'The Bretton Woods institutions sixty years later: a "glocal" reform proposal', in P. Arestis, J. Ferreiro and F. Serrano (eds), *Financial Developments in National and International Markets*, Basingstoke: Palgrave Macmillan, 56–76.

Schmitt, B. (1973), *New Proposals for World Monetary Reform*, Albeuve: Castella.

Schmitt, B. (1975), *Théorie unitaire de la monnaie, nationale et internationale*,

Albeuve: Castella.

Schmitt, B. (1984a), *Inflation, chômage et malformations du capital*, Paris and Albeuve: Economica and Castella.

Schmitt, B. (1984b), *La France souveraine de sa monnaie*, Paris and Albeuve: Economica and Castella.

Smith, A. (1776/1976), *An Inquiry into the Nature and Causes of the Wealth of Nations*, in *The Glasgow Edition of the Works and Correspondence of Adam Smith*, Vol. II, Oxford: Oxford University Press.

Walras, L. (1926/1954), *Elements of Pure Economics*, London: George Allen and Unwin (translation by W. Jaffé).

8. Is There a Role for Capital Controls?

Philip Arestis, Jesús Ferreiro and Carmen Gómez

INTRODUCTION

The decades of 1980s and 1990s witnessed a deep transformation in national and international capital markets. Most countries, both developed and developing, began a process of liberalizing their capital accounts hoping to achieve a sustained acceleration in economic growth, mainly in the case of developing economies. This was essentially based on the premise that capital controls was an inefficient way of conducting policy; removing such controls would boost capital inflows. The outcome of capital account liberalization, however, could not have been more disappointing. International capital markets have become highly volatile and unstable, characterized by speculative short-term capital flows. Systemic risks and contagion effects have turned out to be a sword of Damocles over most economies, especially over developing countries, which are precisely the economies that are more dependent on foreign capital for promoting growth and development.

In reality, the generalized process of capital account liberalization has not led to higher capital flows toward developing countries. On the contrary, the flows have been in the opposite direction: from developing to developed countries. Moreover, international capital markets and flows have not proved to be as efficient as initially believed. Most of the countries that liberalized their capital accounts, developing countries in particular, were subsequently shocked by a wave of currency and financial–banking crises (the 'twin crises'), over the last three decades or so. Therefore, financial liberalization seems to have been accompanied by an increased vulnerability of developing economies to financial and currency crises.

In this sense, the theoretical and empirical literature on the consequences of capital account liberalization is not merely controversial, but increasingly sceptical about the consequences of financial liberalization on growth. It is remarkable how former proponents of capital account liberalization have modified, and in some cases changed, their views on the matter. They now do not support this liberalization for its positive direct consequences on growth and efficiency (productivity-enhancing), but rather for other indirect consequences in terms, for instance, of lower corruption (DeLong, 2004), or indeed for purely ideological reasons.

Actually, the controversy and the lack of consensus appear to be widespread. Consider, for example, quotes from Mishkin (2001), who is able to pose two opposite conclusions about the role of capital controls! The first quote is pretty standard:

> Exchange controls are like throwing out the baby with the bath water. Capital controls have the undesirable feature that they may block funds from entering a country, which will be used for productive investment opportunities. Although these controls may limit the fuel supplied to lending booms through capital flows, over time they produce substantial distortions and misallocation of resources as households and businesses try to get around them. Indeed, there are serious doubts as to whether capital controls can be effective in today's environment in which trade is open and where there are many financial instruments that make it easier to get around these controls (Mishkin, 2001, p. 28).

However, the second quote is not as supportive:

> The above arguments suggest that the economy would be far less prone to financial crises and could recover far more easily if the issuance of foreign-denominated debt was discouraged. Because much foreign-denominated debt is intermediated through the banking system, regulations to both restrict bank lending and borrowing in foreign currencies could greatly enhance financial stability. Similarly, restrictions on corporate borrowing in foreign currency or tax policies to discourage foreign-currency borrowing could help make the economy better able to withstand currency depreciation without undergoing a financial crisis. Krueger (2000) has suggested that restrictions should be placed on financial institutions in industrialized countries to limit lending to emerging market countries using industrialized country currencies (p. 31).

As we point out below, a number of authors now defend the use of capital controls in some economies and under certain circumstances. In fact, they no longer support a generalized removal of capital controls under any circumstances, as they used to do. The basis of their argument is that capital controls could help these economies protect themselves from a variety of threats, such as financial and currency crises generated by unexpected, and sudden, capital stops and reversals, as well as the systemic risk and contagion effects that pervade the workings of international capital markets.

Eichengreen (2001) argues that, just as in the case of the generalized trend of intense capital account liberalization, which developed in the last three decades, the opposite can happen. Generalized capital account liberalization is explained by a set of reasons that give rise to a kind of contagion effect, thus making national decision makers respond in the same way to economic and political events (competition for foreign investments, deregulation of domestic financial institutions and markets, regional integration processes, greater exchange rate flexibility, democratization processes). The opposite kind of circumstances and events (disenchantment with financial liberalization, disaffection of flexible exchange rates, ineffective democratic governance, poor outcomes in terms of net capital inflows, poor outcomes in terms of economic activity growth, development of information and communication technologies, and so on) could easily reverse the trend toward capital account liberalization in the future.

We pursue these arguments in the remainder of this chapter. The next section sets out the arguments for capital account liberalization, while the arguments against capital account liberalization are discussed in the third section. The fourth section deals with the available empirical evidence. Finally, the fifth section summarizes and concludes.

ARGUMENTS FOR CAPITAL ACCOUNT LIBERALIZATION

Proponents of free international capital movements base their proposals on the positive economic consequences expected from financial liberalization. Capital account liberalization is claimed to increase long-term economic growth through various channels, discussed below.[1]

The first transmission channel of capital account liberalization is the impact on the size of capital flows. The basic argument is that financial liberalization would increase capital inflows, thus leading to higher investment, productivity, production, and economic growth (Forbes, 2004). First, financial liberalization would raise the supply of loanable funds in those economies with capital scarcity. Capital would flow from countries rich in capital resources (where the rate of interest is low) to countries poor in these resources (where rates of interest are high, or at least higher): capital inflows would add to domestic savings, hence increasing capital resources available for domestic borrowers. The higher volume of capital inflows would reduce domestic rates of interest (cost of borrowing) and increase the available amount of funds, thereby increasing aggregate demand in view of the stimulus to private investment.

The second argument with respect to the first channel is that capital inflows would enhance the competitive advantages of the host country, namely, knowledge and technology (Prasad et al., 2003). In this case, it is not portfolio inflows but foreign direct investment (FDI) that would be the vehicle that would enable these competitive advantages, transferring them from advanced and developed economies to emerging and developing economies. FDI flows would be stimulated not only through the liberalization process, but also because the capital account liberalization acts like a signalling of friendlier policies to be pursued for foreign investment in the future (Prasad et al., 2003), thereby reducing the inherent long-term risk of FDI operations. Multinational enterprises (MNEs) that possess more advanced knowledge and technology are expected to be more competitive than local firms. In the emerging and developing countries where MNEs operate, the foreign subsidiaries are more competitive than their domestic rivals, and, therefore, the host economy can take advantage of the presence of foreign subsidiaries and thus enhance competitiveness. Foreign subsidiaries have easy access to the advanced knowledge and technologies of their parent companies. Furthermore, these elements are spread to the host economy in view of the spillovers generated by the presence and operations of the MNEs in the host economy. On the one hand, domestic clients of and suppliers to these firms can benefit directly from the competitive advantage enjoyed by the foreign subsidiaries. Yet, on the other hand, via an imitation effect, domestic rival firms can be forced to adopt a similar competitive strategy to that of the MNEs, in order for them to survive in the new, more competitive, environment. Finally, the presence of MNEs has the potential to crowd-out the less competitive domestic firms, liberating productive resources that can be more efficiently used in other firms or activities.

In both cases, less developing countries (LDCs) suffer from the structural problems of capital scarcity and lack of knowledge and technology. These are the economies that would most benefit from capital account liberalization. By promoting private investment, capital inflows (both portfolio and FDI) would boost production and productivity, giving rise to higher rates of economic growth, thereby helping to reduce the gap between the LDCs and developed economies.

The second transmission channel is the improvement in the efficiency of domestic sectors. Capital account liberalization would lead to a more efficient resource allocation. This is especially true in the case of the financial and banking sectors. To the extent that capital account liberalization promotes financial development (Prasad et al., 2003), it could help to increase the size of both bank lending and capital (equities and bonds) markets. Domestic financial and banking firms would experience improved efficiency, and thus reduce the possibility of an endogenously-induced domestic banking crisis.

The third transmission channel operates through the increased efficiency of international capital markets. Efficient international capital markets do not only imply a higher volume of capital flows but also a more efficient international allocation of these resources. This can arise through mitigating the problems of asymmetric information and of instability of capital flows, now depending on long-term fundamentals. Perfect capital markets are able to distribute the amount of funds and their cost for each borrower, reduce the systemic risk of the international markets and the contagion effect (which is due to problems of asymmetric information and uncertainty), and limit the possibility of exogenous currency crises (explained by changes in foreign determinants of capital flows, that is, wild fluctuations in interest rates).

Both through the increased efficiency of domestic sectors and international capital markets, capital account liberalization facilitates the diversification of risks by increasing the opportunities of investment (Forbes, 2004). The lower induced volatility in the value of wealth and incomes reduces the volatility of consumption and finance, thus leading to a more stable level of economic activity. Consequently, countries that liberalize capital movements would benefit from risk sharing and consumption smoothing, and enjoy higher and more stable paths of growth.

The fourth transmission channel is the discipline mechanism that capital account liberalization produces for domestic macroeconomic policies (Prasad et al., 2003). Macroeconomic policy must generate an economic environment that helps create and maintain a stable supply of foreign funds. Inflation, high public sector deficits, and a high stock of public sector debt are believed to affect adversely the evolution of exchange rates. If exchange rates stability is a determinant of international capital flows, fiscal and monetary policies must avoid both inflation and public sector imbalances that could lead to potential currency crises.

The above channels operate directly in favour of financial liberalization. Many authors, however, defend capital account liberalization simply because of the 'high' costs of capital controls. Although these authors accept the doubts about the consequences of free capital mobility, they argue that the costs resulting from capital controls are higher than their benefits, that is, the costs elicited by capital account liberalization (Mishkin, 2001; Forbes, 2004). For proponents of free capital movements, capital controls are an ineffective and inefficient instrument, having the following undesirable consequences.

- They cannot avoid undesirable capital inflows or outflows (in terms of amount and/or kind of flows), since these controls can be by-passed easily.

- They contribute to a worsening of the corruption problem in the economies that implement them. The incentives and opportunities they offer to the agents that wish to avoid them produces a situation characterized by bribing the officials in charge of controlling capital flows. Furthermore, the administrative costs of managing capital controls increase over time as both agents and markets exploit the potential loopholes in the system (Ariyoshi et al., 2000; Cordella, 2003; Gallego and Hernandez, 2003). In this sense, the removal of capital controls would improve the quality of domestic institutions in general, and those of the government in particular. The overall result is the improvement in the efficiency of the private sector (DeLong, 2004).

- They discriminate between agents, affecting more those agents that do not have the capacity or ability to elude capital controls (poor people, and small and domestic-oriented firms) (Gallego and Hernandez, 2003).

- By restricting capital inflows, capital controls reduce the available capital resources and result in higher domestic interest rates than otherwise. They therefore reduce productive investment and the level of economic activity (Mishkin, 2001; Gallego and Hernandez, 2003).

- By restricting capital outflows, capital controls keep interest rates artificially low, thus promoting excessive borrowing. Also, capital controls that restrict capital outflows create a captive capital supply that can feed a loose fiscal policy leading to excessive levels of government deficit and debt.

- Although most capital controls restrain short-term capital inflows, they change the composition of capital flows in favour of long-term flows (De Gregorio et al., 2000; Reinhart and Smith, 2002; Cordella, 2003; Gallego and Hernandez, 2003; Forbes, 2004). However, long-term capital inflows, as in the case of FDI inflows, can also be negatively affected by capital controls (Asiedu and Lien, 2004).

- Even though there could be circumstances in which the implementation of capital controls could be justified, they are affected, nonetheless, by the possibility of government failure. The experience with capital controls shows that they generate costs that more than offset any possible benefits from their implementation (Mishkin, 2001).

ARGUMENTS AGAINST CAPITAL ACCOUNT LIBERALIZATION

The argument that capital account liberalization and, therefore, the removal of capital controls, may have a positive effect on economic growth is only valid when the assumption of perfectly competitive capital markets (domestic and international) is adopted. However, if we recognize that capital markets are characterized by monopolistic tendencies, ruled by asymmetric information and uncertainty, capital account liberalization can generate a misallocation of resources and a lower level of economic activity and growth than otherwise. In markets defined by the existence of distortions (protection for import-competing industries, downward rigid real wages, information asymmetries, and so on), capital controls can act as a second-best solution, avoiding not only undesirable (excessive) levels of capital inflows and/or outflows but also reducing the instability of capital flows. They generate disincentives to volatile capital flows, that is, short-term speculative flows associated with short-term expectations of profitability and to external shocks (Eichengreen and Leblang, 2003; Eichengreen and Voth, 2003; Klein, 2005; Arestis, 2006, and the references therein).

In this sense, the literature on the consequences of capital account liberalization is rather controversial. Neither theoretical nor empirical studies have been able to reach a clear-cut conclusion about the consequences of capital account liberalization and capital controls on a number of aspects: economic growth, size of capital flows, stability of capital flows, financial and banking development, and so on (Eichengreen, 2001; Chinn and Ito, 2002; Edison et al., 2002; Eichengreen and Voth, 2003; Forbes, 2004; Prasad et al., 2004). As Eichengreen and Leblang (2003, p. 205) state, 'theory yields no unambiguous prediction of whether opening the capital account is growth enhancing or growth inhibiting. And, despite the very considerable attention lavished on the subject, the evidence is generally inconclusive'.

A further problem with most studies concerned with the consequences of financial liberalization on growth is that they assume that there exists a strong relationship between growth and the total volume of capital flows. As Prasad et al. (2003) show, however, not all kinds of capital flows have the same consequence on growth: FDI flows would be the form of capital inflows with the strongest and more robust positive consequences for the host economies. However, not even in the case of FDI is there a consensus about the long-term consequences of FDI inflows on the economic growth in host countries. Macroeconometric studies, using cross-section, time series, or panel data, provide conflicting results not only about the existence of a significant link between FDI and growth, but also about the causal relationship between both variables (Carkovic and Levine, 2002; Economic Commission for Latin America and the Caribbean, 2004; Navaretti and Venables, 2004; Xiaoying and Xiaming, 2005).

The lack of consensus as described above also affects the direction of the impact of financial liberalization, namely, the type of economies that would benefit from financial liberalization. According to the general argument for capital account liberalization, all economies, both developed and developing, would benefit from the process (Edwards, 2004).[2] However, empirical evidence shows that the existence of different consequences depends on the level of development of the economies included in the sample analysed. Whilst for some authors developing countries would benefit more from the process of removing capital controls (Edison et al., 2002), other authors reach opposite conclusions: only developed countries benefit from financial liberalization, while developing countries would remain unaffected by capital account liberalization at best, or would be damaged at worst (Klein and Olivei, 2000; DeLong, 2004; Dell'Ariccia et al., 2005). In the case of developing economies, some studies pose the existence of differences among them depending on the relative degree of development: emerging countries would benefit from capital account liberalization and the less developing economies would be damaged (Edwards, 2001; Chinn and Ito, 2002). For other authors, the conclusion is even more mixed: only intermediate countries would benefit from capital account liberalization, and neither the less developing countries nor the most advanced economies would benefit from that process (Edison et al., 2002; Klein, 2005). Finally, other studies conclude that the consequences of financial liberalization in developing and emerging countries are contingent on the region where they are located. Basically, considering Africa, East Asia, Central and Eastern Europe, and Latin America, only East Asia countries would benefit from capital account liberalization.

The controversy between the theoretical models that conclude in favour of positive effects of capital account liberalization on growth, and the rather mixed results of the empirical studies is partly explained by the failure of some basic assumptions of the theoretical models. Basically, the neoclassical foundation of these models leads them to conclude that growth is enhanced by financial liberalization because the latter (i) leads to consumption smoothing, (ii) generates a higher equilibrium level of capital resources by the higher capital inflows, and because (iii) higher capital resources promote and finance more productive investment. These assumptions, however, are severely suspect.

As indicated above, international capital mobility, by enhancing the opportunities for international risk diversification, is assumed to reduce the volatility of prices, especially those of financial assets. As far as these variables are key determinants of private consumption decisions, more stable prices of financial assets would lead to a less volatile evolution of consumption and, consequently, economic growth. However, recent experience shows that financial markets are highly volatile, with high instability in the prices of financial assets, in interest rates and exchange rates. Furthermore, capital inflows are not counter-cyclical but pro-cyclical, exacerbating the fluctuations of private consumption related to the domestic business cycle. As a result, instability in the evolution of consumption and, therefore, lower economic growth ensues (Prasad et al., 2003, 2004).

On the other hand, it is also assumed that increased supply of capital resources leads to stable equilibrium outcomes. However, capital inflows can have an excessive size, thus leading to a substantial fall in interest rates, below the level corresponding to long-term equilibrium. These excessive capital inflows can have also a negative impact on the host economy in the form of overheating this economy (growing above the potential level), thus increasing inflationary pressures. Further implications include appreciation of the exchange rate leading to a deficit in the current account balance, and the costs of sterilization of the capital inflows that can lead to higher interest rates in order for the monetary authority to offset a rising money supply and inflation, thus affecting economic activity.

The excessive size of capital inflows is a distinct possibility if capital inflows are not only, or mainly, determined by domestic fundamentals, essentially by the domestic absorption capacity of a higher capital supply, but by foreign elements, for instance the case of a lower rate of interest abroad or expectations of depreciation of a foreign currency. In this sense, capital account liberalization can increase the external dependence of host economies. In as much as the size and direction of capital flows depend not only on domestic valuations but also mainly on the evolution of foreign determinants, capital account liberalization can increase the possibility of sudden stops and capital account reversals. Therefore, untrammelled capital mobility can increase the possibility of financial and/or currency crises, thereby depressing economic activity and growth (Eichengreen and Leblang, 2003; Prasad et al., 2003, 2004; DeLong, 2004; Forbes, 2004). In that case, capital controls can help to keep the degree of autonomy of domestic macroeconomic policy. This is of vital importance in periods when international capital markets are more unstable and volatile (Ariyoshi et al., 2000; Eichengreen and Leblang, 2003).

Finally, experience shows that sudden and big capital inflows do not lead to higher investment, and therefore to higher long-term growth, but to higher private and public consumption. Thus the consequences of international capital mobility on growth, which can come through the increase in private investment that is caused by lower interest rates and higher capital supply, are not established. This higher consumption can produce potential macro and microeconomic imbalances in the economy. These include higher inflation rates, higher public deficits and debts, higher foreign borrowing, higher current account deficits, excessive lending, increases in non-performing loans, and so on. All these factors enhance the probability of currency and banking crises.

EFFECTS OF CAPITAL ACCOUNT LIBERALIZATION AND CAPITAL CONTROLS: EMPIRICAL EVIDENCE

In the case of empirical studies, the conclusions about the consequences of capital account liberalization depend heavily on a number of different qualifications. These include the econometric method used, the period of time analysed, the size of the sample of countries, the level of development of the countries included in the sample, the legal and institutional framework, the level of financial development, the stability of the international capital markets, the microeconomic or macroeconomic perspective of the analyses of the costs and benefits, and so on (Chinn and Ito, 2002; Edison et al., 2002; Eichengreen and Leblang, 2003; Forbes, 2004; Klein, 2005).

Even if we accepted that capital account liberalization had a positive effect on growth, the actual size of that impact would be conditioned by the size of net inflows, an argument at the heart of the discussion over the empirics of capital account liberalization. Figure 8.1 shows the evolution of private capital flows since 1980 for a number of emerging market and developing countries (including the so-called 'selected advanced economies', namely, Hong Kong, Israel, Korea, Singapore, and Taiwan). Although there is a clear growth in the absolute size of these flows, only FDI flows have increased. On the contrary, portfolio flows are in 2005 at the same level as in 1981. In addition, the dynamics of the latter flows is quite volatile, with a dramatic fall since the late 1990s. We must also account for the fact that these figures include the so-called advanced economies, which can account for 21.7 per cent of total FDI inflows in developing economies in 1980–2003, a share that rises to 44.5 per cent if we include China.[3]

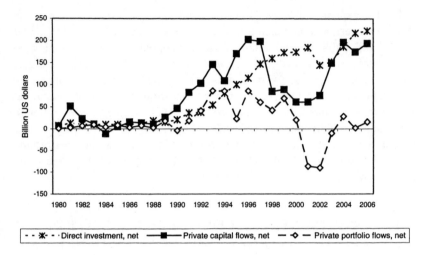

Source: International Monetary Fund, *World Economic Outlook* database (April 2005).

Figure 8.1. Net capital flows in emerging market and developing countries (billion US dollars)

This outcome worsens when we analyse the size of capital flows as a percentage of GDP (Figure 8.2). It is remarkable that private capital flows peaked in 1993 and 1996, and private portfolio flows peaked in 1993, at the early stages of the financial liberalization process. Since then, the relative weight of capital flows has diminished substantially.[4]

Another feature to be considered is the concentration of capital flows in a small number of countries (Table 8.1).

In 2004, Central and Eastern European countries and the developing Asian countries received 97 per cent of total private capital flows to emerging market and developing countries. In that same year, FDI was more evenly distributed in Latin America, although these flows were highly concentrated in Brazil and Mexico. In the case of private portfolio flows, however, only the Central and Eastern European countries and the developing Asian countries received inflows of capital.

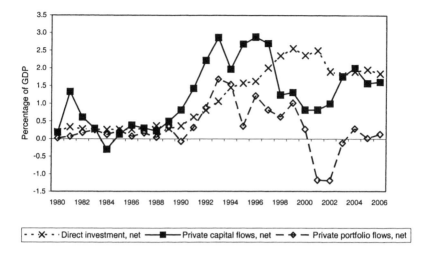

Source: International Monetary Fund, *World Economic Outlook* database (April 2005).

Figure 8.2. Net capital flows in emerging market and developing countries (as a percentage of GDP)

In terms of the share of capital flows in the GDP of the host regions (Table 8.2), it is clear that the only regions that have a good record are Central and Eastern Europe, and Asia (the latter owing to FDI flows).

With the exception of Asia, since the wave of currency and financial crises of the late 1980s, the weight of private capital flows has fallen dramatically and, as mentioned above, only the higher stability of FDI flows has avoided an even higher fall.[5]

In fact, one extended conclusion among different recent studies is that there is a threshold effect in the relationship between financial liberalization and growth. Only those economies that cross this threshold benefit from the capital account liberalization. For the countries below this threshold, financial liberalization has a nil effect at best, or even a negative impact on growth at worst (Prasad et al., 2003, 2004; Forbes, 2004).

Table 8.1. Net private capital flows to developing countries (billion US dollars)

Years	Commonwealth of Independent States and Mongolia			Central and Eastern Europe			Africa		
	PPF	PCF	DIN	PPF	PCF	DIN	PPF	PCF	DIN
1980	n.a.	n.a.	n.a.	0	3.601	0.037	-0.443	3.411	0.791
1981	n.a.	n.a.	n.a.	0	4.379	0.151	0.222	10.080	0.352
1982	n.a.	n.a.	n.a.	0	-0.919	0.086	0.902	8.169	1.380
1983	n.a.	n.a.	n.a.	0	-2.950	0.086	-0.291	4.176	0.898
1984	n.a.	n.a.	n.a.	0	-0.411	0.155	1.034	2.495	0.670
1985	n.a.	n.a.	n.a.	0	1.178	0.132	0.057	0.224	0.202
1986	n.a.	n.a.	n.a.	0.146	-2.438	0.141	-0.348	3.898	1.411
1987	n.a.	n.a.	n.a.	0.282	0.969	0.129	-0.328	-1.380	1.472
1988	n.a.	n.a.	n.a.	1.178	3.233	0.377	-0.172	7.454	1.714
1989	n.a.	n.a.	n.a.	1.328	3.514	0.958	-0.009	-0.392	2.495
1990	n.a.	n.a.	n.a.	0.545	6.587	1.173	-0.191	1.679	1.935
1991	n.a.	n.a.	n.a.	0.378	-12.710	3.194	0.729	2.296	2.670
1992	0	2.762	1.024	2.253	5.165	4.010	2.509	-2.497	0.345

Years	Latin America			Middle East including selected advanced economies			Developing Asia including selected advanced economies		
	PPF	PCF	DIN	PPF	PCF	DIN	PPF	PCF	DIN
1980	0.985	36.470	5.621	-0.025	-41.020	-1.439	0.285	19.590	2.999
1981	2.483	45.960	8.442	-1.381	-25.070	0.249	1.340	23.390	4.311
1982	4.443	15.940	6.278	0.326	-15.570	-0.232	1.093	20.340	3.706
1983	0.769	-9.362	5.025	8.100	7.233	0.635	1.104	18.860	4.250
1984	0.489	-1.693	4.285	2.720	-12.000	1.181	0.336	7.348	4.196
1985	-0.897	-2.000	5.879	3.527	0.698	1.392	5.890	12.890	3.066
1986	-0.219	0.839	3.978	2.351	4.217	1.047	1.148	13.970	4.240
1987	0.038	9.885	5.718	6.379	7.232	-0.694	1.128	7.285	6.628
1988	1.354	3.968	8.797	1.565	1.442	-0.151	-1.560	-3.284	7.278
1989	5.175	1.604	7.339	11.630	10.440	-0.577	-0.051	7.601	5.666
1990	-2.636	12.220	6.632	-0.085	15.370	2.391	-1.632	12.030	9.500
1991	17.900	22.720	11.300	-2.178	45.570	1.218	2.111	37.390	17.740
1992	25.700	54.060	13.270	-2.191	18.160	1.413	12.890	25.500	17.880

Table 8.1. (cont.)

Years	Commonwealth of Independent States and Mongolia			Central and Eastern Europe			Africa		
	PPF	PCF	DIN	PPF	PCF	DIN	PPF	PCF	DIN
1993	3.774	8.976	1.758	8.592	12.720	4.897	1.213	0.033	1.794
1994	-11.650	-8.639	1.369	4.045	-14.800	4.412	3.842	6.828	2.095
1995	-11.250	9.692	3.252	6.134	28.660	12.980	3.605	5.827	1.661
1996	-0.086	-3.544	4.886	1.904	22.960	10.400	3.242	-2.986	3.113
1997	17.590	19.860	5.936	5.404	20.230	11.590	7.425	14.250	7.918
1998	7.716	6.721	5.338	-1.394	27.220	19.240	4.273	10.840	6.617
1999	-3.075	-6.401	4.217	5.654	36.700	22.620	9.117	11.460	8.951
2000	-6.063	-12.990	2.432	3.079	39.120	23.890	-1.759	-1.655	8.043
2001	-9.238	-1.813	4.625	0.456	12.230	24.220	-7.655	7.557	22.960
2002	-8.211	-9.529	3.945	1.439	55.310	25.140	-0.877	6.914	14.820
2003	-4.786	16.370	5.250	7.102	51.980	15.080	0.425	12.260	14.590
2004	-1.147	2.873	7.719	24.930	60.630	22.090	3.947	11.370	15.400
2005	-10.810	-6.437	8.626	22.410	65.810	29.530	2.679	15.560	16.720
2006	-2.840	2.671	9.376	19.110	57.670	29.010	3.095	13.460	16.600

154

Years	Latin America			Middle East including selected advanced economies			Developing Asia including selected advanced economies		
	PPF	PCF	DIN	PPF	PCF	DIN	PPF	PCF	DIN
1993	49.570	58.940	8.699	-2.970	15.640	4.575	25.880	49.470	32.510
1994	70.270	45.960	23.320	-2.023	11.360	4.657	20.850	68.270	44.500
1995	3.751	29.220	24.760	-2.129	0.927	3.785	22.900	96.270	53.880
1996	48.190	64.440	39.600	0.340	2.121	3.440	32.030	119.600	53.410
1997	29.910	99.570	57.700	-6.753	7.915	8.306	6.826	36.550	55.720
1998	25.510	70.820	61.980	-2.322	19.070	10.070	8.710	-49.920	56.580
1999	0.953	38.720	65.940	0.681	-3.124	4.507	55.810	11.790	67.110
2000	1.270	40.540	69.330	3.899	-2.246	3.504	20.050	-1.955	67.150
2001	-9.972	27.770	71.310	-2.900	4.478	6.836	-57.570	10.690	54.760
2002	-15.500	3.286	43.770	-4.893	-4.019	4.221	-61.990	23.850	52.500
2003	-10.120	15.170	34.750	-5.099	-2.428	11.650	2.538	56.120	70.580
2004	-14.180	12.660	45.370	-10.530	-21.030	8.833	25.820	130.100	86.990
2005	-8.230	22.400	48.710	-15.000	-31.160	9.545	11.210	108.900	104.300
2006	-0.085	30.260	50.360	-12.340	-25.130	11.170	9.099	115.000	105.800

Notes: n.a. not available; PPF private portfolio flows, net; PCF private capital flows, net; DIN direct investment, net.

Source: International Monetary Fund, *World Economic Outlook* database (April 2005).

Table 8.2. Net private capital flows to developing countries (as a % of GDP)

Years	Commonwealth of Independent States and Mongolia			Central and Eastern Europe			Africa		
	PPF	PCF	DIN	PPF	PCF	DIN	PPF	PCF	DIN
1980	n.a.	n.a.	n.a.	0	0.995	0.010	-0.126	0.969	0.225
1981	n.a.	n.a.	n.a.	0	1.170	0.040	0.062	2.823	0.099
1982	n.a.	n.a.	n.a.	0	-0.237	0.022	0.264	2.388	0.403
1983	n.a.	n.a.	n.a.	0	-0.771	0.022	-0.090	1.295	0.279
1984	n.a.	n.a.	n.a.	0	-0.113	0.043	0.353	0.852	0.229
1985	n.a.	n.a.	n.a.	0	0.316	0.035	0.020	0.079	0.071
1986	n.a.	n.a.	n.a.	0.035	-0.585	0.034	-0.115	1.286	0.465
1987	n.a.	n.a.	n.a.	0.062	0.214	0.028	-0.098	-0.412	0.440
1988	n.a.	n.a.	n.a.	0.244	0.670	0.078	-0.050	2.155	0.495
1989	n.a.	n.a.	n.a.	0.263	0.696	0.190	-0.003	-0.109	0.694
1990	n.a.	n.a.	n.a.	0.106	1.278	0.228	-0.048	0.422	0.487
1991	n.a.	n.a.	n.a.	0.073	-2.461	0.618	0.179	0.562	0.654
1992	0	2.006	0.744	0.572	1.312	1.019	0.628	-0.625	0.086

Years	Latin America			Middle East including selected advanced economies			Developing Asia including selected advanced economies		
	PPF	PCF	DIN	PPF	PCF	DIN	PPF	PCF	DIN
1980	0.123	4.572	0.705	-0.004	-6.810	-0.239	0.014	0.986	0.151
1981	0.288	5.335	0.980	-0.069	-1.246	0.012	0.066	1.151	0.212
1982	0.633	2.272	0.895	0.006	-0.301	-0.004	0.055	1.015	0.185
1983	0.120	-1.458	0.782	0.103	0.092	0.008	0.055	0.946	0.213
1984	0.073	-0.253	0.641	0.070	-0.309	0.030	0.017	0.373	0.213
1985	-0.123	-0.273	0.803	0.051	0.010	0.020	0.296	0.648	0.154
1986	-0.030	0.114	0.542	0.091	0.162	0.040	0.057	0.698	0.212
1987	0.005	1.280	0.740	0.092	0.105	-0.010	0.056	0.364	0.331
1988	0.155	0.453	1.005	0.063	0.058	-0.006	-0.078	-0.164	0.364
1989	0.524	0.162	0.743	0.058	0.052	-0.003	-0.003	0.377	0.281
1990	-0.237	1.099	0.596	0.002	-0.350	-0.054	-0.080	0.591	0.466
1991	1.512	1.919	0.954	-0.010	0.214	0.006	0.102	1.803	0.856
1992	1.995	4.197	1.030	-0.004	0.035	0.003	0.615	1.217	0.853

Table 8.2. (cont.)

Years	Commonwealth of Independent States and Mongolia			Central and Eastern Europe			Africa		
	PPF	PCF	DIN	PPF	PCF	DIN	PPF	PCF	DIN
1993	1.688	4.014	0.786	1.976	2.925	1.126	0.317	0.009	0.468
1994	-3.489	-2.587	0.410	0.951	-3.480	1.037	1.049	1.864	0.572
1995	-0.028	0.024	0.008	1.131	5.284	2.393	0.882	1.425	0.406
1996	-0.017	-0.706	0.973	0.332	4.000	1.812	0.747	-0.688	0.718
1997	3.359	3.793	1.134	0.927	3.468	1.988	1.674	3.213	1.785
1998	2.014	1.755	1.393	-0.219	4.280	3.025	1.002	2.541	1.551
1999	-1.056	-2.199	1.449	0.918	5.960	3.674	2.126	2.672	2.087
2000	-1.706	-3.655	0.684	0.499	6.345	3.875	-0.399	-0.376	1.826
2001	-2.233	-0.438	1.118	0.076	2.026	4.012	-1.744	1.722	5.231
2002	-1.775	-2.060	0.853	0.209	8.036	3.653	-0.189	1.490	3.193
2003	-0.842	2.879	0.923	0.843	6.168	1.790	0.076	2.183	2.599
2004	-0.151	0.379	1.019	2.455	5.972	2.176	0.581	1.672	2.265
2005	-1.113	-0.663	0.889	1.895	5.565	2.497	0.346	2.012	2.162
2006	-0.253	0.238	0.836	1.502	4.532	2.280	0.376	1.633	2.014

Years	Latin America			Middle East including selected advanced economies			Developing Asia including selected advanced economies		
	PPF	PCF	DIN	PPF	PCF	DIN	PPF	PCF	DIN
1993	3.537	4.205	0.621	−0.002	0.013	0.004	1.210	2.313	1.520
1994	4.398	2.877	1.460	−0.002	0.009	0.004	0.991	3.246	2.116
1995	0.222	1.732	1.468	−0.005	0.002	0.009	1.057	4.446	2.488
1996	2.627	3.513	2.159	0.000	0.001	0.002	1.457	5.442	2.429
1997	1.493	4.970	2.880	−0.005	0.006	0.007	0.311	1.665	2.538
1998	1.271	3.530	3.089	−0.003	0.024	0.013	0.418	−2.397	2.717
1999	0.054	2.190	3.730	0.000	−0.002	0.003	2.673	0.565	3.214
2000	0.064	2.057	3.517	0.009	−0.005	0.008	0.973	−0.095	3.258
2001	−0.521	1.451	3.725	0.001	−0.002	−0.003	−2.792	0.519	2.656
2002	−0.915	0.194	2.585	0.002	0.002	−0.002	−2.983	1.148	2.527
2003	−0.576	0.864	1.979	0.019	0.009	−0.042	0.118	2.607	3.279
2004	−0.710	0.634	2.270	−0.012	−0.023	0.010	1.173	5.913	3.953
2005	−0.367	0.999	2.171	−0.188	−0.391	0.120	0.514	4.997	4.784
2006	−0.004	1.273	2.119	−0.020	−0.040	0.018	0.414	5.228	4.807

Notes: n.a. not available; PPF private portfolio flows, net; PCF private capital flows, net; DIN direct investment, net.

Source: International Monetary Fund, *World Economic Outlook* database (April 2005).

This threshold level cannot be interpreted exclusively in terms of the level of economic activity (usually measured by per capita GDP), but rather in terms of the level of institutional development. The basic idea here is that the level of economic activity and the rates of economic growth are not only determined by the endowment of productive factors and the growth of productivity – usually determined by technological aspects – but also by the institutional framework in which both agents and markets operate. Only the countries with sound institutions would benefit from a potentially higher capital flow resulting from capital account liberalization.

Increasingly, most recent studies on the consequences of financial liberalization conclude that these effects are contingent upon the institutional environment in which the capital account liberalization is adopted or capital controls operate. As Klein (2005, p. 2) states:

> an open capital account could, under the right circumstances, contribute to economic growth. The conditional nature of this last statement reflects the theoretical and empirical results presented here that show that institutional quality affects the link between capital account liberalization and economic growth.

In this sense, the circumstances that must exist, according to empirical studies, in a country to benefit from financial liberalization are as follows:

- low level of corruption (De Gregorio et al., 2000; Prasad et al., 2003, 2004);
- institutional development (Forbes, 2004);
- strength and depth of the domestic financial system (Eichengreen, 2001; Eichengreen and Leblang, 2003; Forbes, 2004);
- well-regulated and well-supervised financial and banking systems (Eichengreen, 2001; Eichengreen and Leblang, 2003);
- quality of corporate governance (Eichengreen, 2001; Forbes, 2004);
- flexible exchange rate regimes (Prasad et al., 2003, 2004; Edwards, 2004);
- government reputation (Edison et al., 2002);
- strengthened corporate governance and creditor rights (Eichengreen, 2001; Prasad et al., 2003, 2004);
- transparent auditing and accounting standards (Eichengreen, 2001);
- equitable bankruptcy and insolvency procedures (Eichengreen, 2001);
- macroeconomic stability (Prasad et al., 2004); and
- fiscal discipline (Prasad et al., 2003, 2004).

It is evident that some developed countries satisfy these prerequisites and that therefore these countries benefit the most from capital account liberalization.

An important fact is that developed economies reap most of capital inflows and that, with the exception of the crisis of the European Monetary System in the early 1990s, since the late 1980s all the currency and financial crises have affected developing and emerging countries. This would be a sound proof of the importance of a high-quality institutional environment for capital account liberalization to have any hope of not producing devastating crises of the kind witnessed over the last 30 years or so.

Indeed, the institutional determinant can help to understand the existence and importance of the threshold effects mentioned above. These threshold effects make the relationship between financial liberalization and growth a not-linear relationship (Prasad et al., 2003, 2004; Forbes, 2004). Even a non-monotonic relationship (an inverted U-shaped curve) may very well result, where the maximum effect of capital account liberalization is found at intermediate levels of institutional quality (Klein, 2005). Below a certain level of institutional quality (q^*), a level corresponding to that observed in LDCs, capital account liberalization has poor positive consequences in terms of stability and volume of capital flows. For these economies, the costs of capital account liberalization (in terms of higher probability of financial and currency crises) are higher than the benefits. Consequently, international capital mobility can exert a negative impact on economic growth. In the case of developed economies, once these countries have reached a certain level of institutional quality that maximizes the benefits from capital account liberalization (q^{**}), further measures to liberalize capital flows will have a nil, or even a negative, net effect on growth. Those economies that have the minimum level of institutional quality ($q > q^*$, where $q^* < q < q^{**}$) may benefit from international mobility if the financial liberalization comes with measures to improve their institutional framework.

One problem with the studies on the relationship between international capital mobility and growth, however, is that they assume that capital account liberalization is exogenous to the growth process. As Edison et al. (2002, pp. 20–21) state, 'while capital account liberalization is often treated as exogenous to the growth process, in practice countries with particular growth experiences or at particular levels of development may be more prone to liberalize their capital accounts, implying the potential for reverse causality'. Therefore, countries with a robust long-term growth may engage in financial liberalization even if this process does not have a significant positive effect on growth, or even if the latter effect is negative (Prasad et al., 2003, 2004). Obviously, the problem of reverse causality can also affect the implementation of capital controls: countries suffering from macroeconomic imbalances and with the highest probabilities of suffering a currency and/or a financial crisis will be more prone to restrain international capital mobility (Eichengreen, 2001).

Another problem with the translation of the positive outcomes to the normative field is the problem related to the timing of the structural and institutional reforms that must come with the capital account liberalization (Eichengreen, 2001). In the most optimistic analysis the capital account liberalization is a necessary and sufficient condition for growth, since this financial liberalization will promote and lead to the implementation of the reforms needed to get the expected benefits from international capital mobility. Most analysts, though, do not share such an optimistic view. The latter analysts would argue that the reforms must precede capital account liberalization or be simultaneous with the process of financial liberalization. As Eichengreen (2001, p. 359), for example, argues:

> Capital account liberalization can be counter productive, to be sure, if it takes place before severe policy-related distortions have been removed and before domestic markets, institutions, and the administrative capacity of the prudential authorities have developed enough to generate confidence that foreign finance will be channeled in productive directions.

In these studies, full benefits of capital account liberalization are only reaped when the process of institutional reform is fulfilled. Therefore, during the 'transition' process, financial liberalization can have negative economic consequences. This opens the door to a progressive and a step-by-step dismantlement of capital controls. Capital controls must be maintained whilst the process of institutional reforms lasts. In as much as the process of institutional reforms is a long-lasting one, capital controls cannot be fast removed. The duration of capital controls will be longer for those countries whose level of institutional quality is lower, below or close to the minimum level required for any benefits from capital account liberalization ($q*$) to materialize, if at all.

However, another question arises about the relationship between capital account liberalization and growth, related to the difficulty of isolating the impact of removing capital controls (Forbes, 2004). If capital account liberalization benefits growth when the former comes with a proper set of structural and institutional reforms, is the positive effect on growth generated by financial liberalization or by the reforms adopted? According to the above statement by Eichengreen (2001), financial liberalization only generates net positive effects on growth in the long run, once the process of institutional reform has been successfully completed. Implicitly, during the transition process, financial liberalization can generate negative consequences by increasing the probability of suffering financial and/or banking crises with their disruptive consequences on economic growth (Mishkin, 2001; Eichengreen and Leblang, 2003; Eichengreen and Voth, 2003; Prasad et al., 2003, 2004; Forbes, 2004). Therefore, a conflict exists between the long-run (positive) and the short-run (negative) effects of capital account liberalization. There is always, of course, the puzzle of how long is the long run. Perhaps we are all 'dead' in some long-run situation.

SUMMARY AND CONCLUSIONS

Recent experience shows that the expected positive consequences on growth from the mass and generalized financial liberalization have not materialized. Only a reduced number of economies, namely, developed countries and some emerging economies, have benefited from the higher capital flows generated by capital account liberalization. Developing economies, to wit, those countries that potentially should have benefited the most from liberalization, have not experienced the expected net capital inflows. Furthermore, capital account liberalization has increased the possibility of currency and financial crises. Therefore, for developing economies the consequences of that liberalization process on their growth path has been negative.

According to the most optimistic studies, opening the capital account was a sufficient condition to get its benefit and accelerate economic growth. Less optimistic analyses argued that the opening of capital accounts should come within a framework of macroeconomic stability in the form of stable and low rates of inflation, and low public deficits and debt. However, there is an increasing consensus on the need for deeper structural and institutional reforms, if a country wishes to benefit from capital account liberalization.

The process of structural and institutional reforms becomes a necessary condition in order to benefit from international capital mobility. Nonetheless, this process is not without problems. First, the process is a long-run one, so that the benefits from capital account liberalization are only evident in the long run. Secondly, as experience has shown, once the capital account has been liberalized, even if not fully, the probability of currency and financial crises increases during this transition period.

Therefore, and paradoxically, in the process of capital account liberalization there is a role to be played by capital controls. They must be maintained as long as the process of institutional reforms has not been completed. Although capital controls cannot avoid currency and financial crises generated by domestic circumstances, they can help avoid the problems that an inefficient working of international capital markets can generate in the form of systemic risks and contagion effects. At the end of the day, though, the conclusion would have to be that capital controls have a significant role to play even in the new 'globalized' world. We might add, especially in this new global environment.

NOTES

1. For general surveys and studies about the consequences of capital account liberalization on economic growth and development, see Edison et al. (2002), and Prasad et al. (2003, 2004).
2. In the case of Edwards (2004), the outcome that financial openness reduces the probability of suffering a current account reversal (whose effects on growth are negative) is only significant for the whole set of countries analysed. This outcome, though, is not statistically significant for developing countries.
3. For the concentration of FDI inflows in a small number of developing countries, see Ferreiro et al. (2005).
4. If we measured these figures in terms of nominal flows per capita, the outcome would be even more revealing. In 1970, FDI inflows per capita amounted to 14 US dollars in developed countries and to 2 dollars in developing countries; in 1990, they amounted to 197 dollars in developed countries and to 9 dollars in developing countries; and in 2003, they amounted to 400 dollars in developed countries and to 33 dollars in developing countries (Ferreiro et al., 2005).
5. A few examples can help to make the point: in Africa, private net capital flows fell from 2.672 per cent of GDP in 1999 to 1.672 per cent of GDP in 2004; in Central and Eastern Europe they fell from 8.036 per cent of GDP in 2002 to 5.972 per cent of GDP in 2004; in the Community of Independent States (CIS) and Mongolia they fell from 3.793 per cent of GDP in 1997 to 0.379 per cent of GDP in 2004; in the Middle East they fell from 0.035 per cent of GDP in 1992 to −0.023 per cent of GDP in 2004; and in Latin America they fell from 4.970 per cent of GDP in 1997 to 0.634 per cent of GDP in 2004.

REFERENCES

Arestis, P. (2006), 'Financial liberalization and the relationship between finance and growth', in P. Arestis and M. Sawyer (eds), *Handbook of Alternative Monetary Economics*, Cheltenham, UK and Northampton, MA, USA: Edward Elgar, forthcoming.
Ariyoshi, A., K. Habermeier, B. Laurens, I. Otker-Robe, J.I. Canales-Kriljenko and A. Kirilenko (2000), 'Capital controls: country experiences with their use and liberalization', *International Monetary Fund Occasional Paper*, no. 190.
Asiedu, E. and D. Lien (2004), 'Capital controls and foreign direct investment', *World Development*, **32** (3), 479–90.
Carkovic, M. and R. Levine (2002), 'Does foreign direct investment accelerate economic growth?', Minneapolis: University of Minnesota, mimeo.
Chinn, M.D. and H. Ito (2002), 'Capital account liberalization, institutions and financial development: cross-country evidence', *National Bureau of Economic Research Working Paper*, no. 8967.

Cordella, T. (2003), 'Can short-term capital controls promote capital inflows?', *Journal of International Money and Finance*, **22** (5), 737–45.

De Gregorio, J., S. Edwards and R.O. Valdés (2000), 'Controls on capital inflows: do they work?', *National Bureau of Economic Research Working Paper*, no. 7645.

Dell'Ariccia, G., E. Detragiache and R. Rajan (2005), 'The real effect of banking crises', *International Monetary Fund Working Paper*, WP/05/63.

DeLong, J.B. (2004), 'Should we support untrammeled international capital mobility? Or are capital controls less evil than we once believed?', *The Economists' Voice*, **1** (1), article 1, available at http://www.bepress.com/ev/vol1/iss1/art1.

Economic Commission for Latin America and the Caribbean (2004), *Foreign Investment in Latin America and the Caribbean 2003*, Santiago de Chile: Economic Commission for Latin America and the Caribbean.

Edison, H.J., M. Klein, L. Ricci and T. Sløk (2002), 'Capital account liberalization and economic performance: survey and synthesis', *International Monetary Fund Working Paper*, WP/02/120.

Edwards, S. (2001), 'Capital mobility and economic performance: are emerging economies different?', *National Bureau of Economic Research Working Paper*, no. 8076.

Edwards, S. (2004), 'Financial openness, sudden stops and current account reversals', *National Bureau of Economic Research Working Paper*, no. 10277.

Eichengreen, B. (2001), 'Capital account liberalization: what do cross-country studies tell us?', *The World Bank Economic Review*, **15** (3), 341–65.

Eichengreen, B. and D. Leblang (2003), 'Capital account liberalization and growth: was Mr. Mahathir right?', *International Journal of Finance and Economics*, **8** (3), 205–24.

Eichengreen, B. and H.J. Voth (2003), 'Symposium on capital controls', *International Journal of Finance and Economics*, **8** (3), 185–287.

Ferreiro, J., C. Gómez and C. Rodríguez (2005), 'The pattern of inward FDI geographical distribution: can developing countries base their development on those flows?', in P. Arestis, J. Ferreiro and F. Serrano (eds), *Financial Developments in National and International Markets*, Basingstoke: Palgrave Macmillan, forthcoming.

Forbes, K.J. (2004), 'Capital controls: mud in the wheels of market discipline', *National Bureau of Economic Research Working Paper*, no. 10284.

Gallego, F.A. and F.L. Hernandez (2003), 'Microeconomic effects of capital controls: the Chilean experience during the 1990s', *International Journal of Finance and Economics*, **8** (3), 225–53.

Klein, M.W. (2005), 'Capital account liberalization, institutional quality and economic growth: theory and evidence', *National Bureau of Economic Research Working Paper*, no. 11112.

Klein, M.W. and G. Olivei (2000), 'Capital account liberalization, financial depth and economic growth', Boston: Fletcher School of Law and Diplomacy, Tufts University, unpublished.

Krueger, A. (2000), 'Conflicting demands on the International Monetary Fund', *American Economic Review*, **90** (2), 38–42.

Mishkin, F.S. (2001), 'Financial policies and the prevention of financial crises in emerging market economies', *World Bank Policy Research Working Paper*, no. 2683.

Navaretti, G.B. and A.J. Venables (2004), *Multinational Firms in the World Economy*, Princeton: Princeton University Press.

Prasad, E., K. Rogoff, S.-J. Wei and M.A. Kose (2003), 'Effects of financial globalization on developing countries: some empirical evidence', *International Monetary Fund Occasional Paper*, no. 220.

Prasad, E., K. Rogoff, S.-J. Wei and M.A. Kose (2004), 'Financial globalization, growth and volatility in developing countries', *National Bureau of Economic Research Working Paper*, no. 10942.

Reinhart, C.M. and R.T. Smith (2002), 'Temporary controls on capital inflows', *Journal of International Economics*, **57** (2), 327–51.

Xiaoying, L. and L. Xiaming (2005), 'Foreign direct investment and economic growth: an increasingly endogenous relationship', *World Development*, **33** (3), 393–407.

9. Liberalization or Regulating International Capital Flows?

Paul Davidson

INTRODUCTION

How one interprets financial market activity and chooses a policy stance regarding the either liberalizing or regulating activity on financial markets depends on the underlying economic theory that one explicitly, or implicitly, utilizes to explain the role of financial markets in an entrepreneurial economy. There are two major alternative theories of financial markets: (1) the classical efficient market theory (hereafter EMT), and (2) Keynes's liquidity preference theory (hereafter LPT). Each theory produces a different set of policy prescriptions. The former theory suggests liberalization is a desirable social objective. The latter suggests the need for an understandable publically known set of rules and regulations.

EMT is the backbone of conventional economic wisdom. The mantra of EMT is that 'the market knows best' how to optimally allocate scarce capital resources and promote maximum economic growth. This EMT view was succinctly epitomized in former US Deputy Treasury Lawrence Summers's statement that 'the ultimate social functions [of financial markets are] spreading risks, guiding the investment of scarce capital, and processing and disseminating the information possessed by diverse traders ... prices will always reflect fundamental values. ... The logic of efficient markets is compelling' (Summers and Summers, 1989, p. 166).

In contrast, the logic of Keynes's LPT indicates that the primary function of financial markets is to provide liquidity. Financial markets do not necessarily produce an efficient allocation of capital resources. Since a liquid market requires orderliness, for financial markets to operate continuously there must be some institutional arrangement to guarantee that financial market activity is orderly no matter how chaotic the real world becomes. If

Keynes's LPT of orderly financial markets is relevant, then the world's international capital markets can never deliver, in either the short run or the long run, the results claimed by EMT.

Peter L. Bernstein is the author of the best-selling book entitled *Against the Gods* (1996), which is a treatise on risk management, probability theory and financial markets. Bernstein argues that the LPT, and not EMT, is the relevant theory for financial markets that operate in the world in which we live. The pragmatic Bernstein (1998b, p. 132, emphasis in original) indicates that 'the fatal flaw in the efficient market hypothesis is that *there is no such thing as an [efficient] equilibrium price. . . .* [and] a market can never be efficient unless equilibrium prices exist and are known' (see also Bernstein, 1998a). In other words, in Bernstein's view, EMT is not applicable to real world financial markets since an efficient general equilibrium price vector cannot exist.

If EMT is not applicable to the real world then, as we argue in the fifth section of this chapter, there is an important role for some degree of international capital flow regulation as a necessary but not sufficient condition to produce a golden age of economic development for the global economy of the twenty-first century. Accordingly, in the sixth section, there are some suggestions for reforming the international payments mechanism based on Keynes's liquidity preference analysis in his *General Theory*.

Since the 1970s, however, Summers's 'compelling' efficient market logic has provided the justification for nations to dismantle most of the ubiquitous post-war capital regulations of financial markets. The argument for this 'liberalization' of financial markets was that it would produce lower real costs of capital and higher output and productivity growth rates compared to the growth rates experienced between World War II and 1973, when international capital flow controls were practised by most countries of the world, including the United States.[1]

What are the facts, and do they support this EMT argument for financial liberalization? The next section provides evidence showing that the post-1973 period of capital market liberalization has not delivered what prestigious efficient market theorists (including Nobel Prize winners) claimed it would. The third, fourth, and fifth sections explain why, if we use Keynes's LPT instead of EMT for understanding real world financial markets, this evidence should not surprise us.

THE FACTS

Writing in the 1930s, Keynes (1936, p. 159) noted that '[i]t is enterprise which builds and improves the world's possessions. . . . Speculators may do no harm as bubbles on the steady stream of enterprise. But the position is serious when enterprise becomes the bubbles on a whirlpool of speculation'. Comparing the pre-1973 and post-1973 economic record indicates that, since 1973, enterprise has slowly become enmeshed in an ever-increasing whirlpool of speculation. The years 1950 to 1973, on the other hand, were an era of unsurpassed economic global prosperity that Adelman (1991, p. 15) characterized as a 'Golden Age of Economic Development . . . an era of unprecedented sustained economic growth in both developed and developing countries'.

Table 9.1 provides the statistical evidence (augmented by more recent data) that Adelman used in reaching her golden age conclusion. Adelman (1991, p. 15) found that the *average* annual growth rate of OECD real GDP per capita from 1950 till 1973 was 'almost precisely double the previous *peak* growth rate of the industrial revolution period. Productivity growth in OECD countries was more than triple (3.75 times) that of the industrial revolution era'.

The resulting prosperity of the industrialized world was transmitted to the less developed countries (LDCs) through world trade, aid, and direct foreign investment. From 1950 to 1973, *average* growth in per capita GDP for *all* LDCs was 3.3 per cent, almost triple the *average* growth rate experienced by the industrializing nations during the industrial revolution. Aggregate GDP of the LDCs increased at almost the same rate as that of the developed nations, 5.5 per cent and 5.9 per cent respectively. The higher population growth of the LDCs caused the lower per capita income growth.

By 1973, however, Keynes's analytical vision of how to improve the operations of a market oriented, money-using, entrepreneurial system had been lost by politicians, their economic advisors, and most academic economists. As a result, Keynes's policy prescriptions fell from grace.

Since 1973, OECD economic growth has been slightly better than half of the growth rate during the golden age of 1950–73, and not much better than the experience of industrialized nations in the nineteenth and early twentieth century. Although experiencing slower growth rates than in the 1950–73 period, LDCs on average did better than OECD nations since 1990, in no small measure owing to the now-ended 'economic miracle' of South-East Asia and, since the end of the 1990s, the opening of China to world trade.

Table 9.1. Real GDP (annualized growth rate)

Years	Real GDP per capita (%)		
	World	OECD nations	Developing nations
1700–1820	n/a	0.2	n/a
1820–1913	n/a	1.2	n/a
1919–1940	n/a	1.9	n/a
1950–1973	n/a	4.9	3.3
1973–1981	n/a	1.3	n/a
1981–1990	1.2	2.2	1.2
1991–1993	–0.4	0.6	2.6
1994–2003	2.8	2.3	3.0
1995–2005*	2.9	2.2	3.7

Years	Total real GDP (%)		
	World	OECD nations	Developing nations
1950–1973	n/a	5.9	5.5
1966–1973	5.1	4.8	6.9
1974–1980	3.4	2.9	5.0
1981–1990	2.6	2.9	2.4
1991–1997	2.2	1.9	5.0
1993–2003	3.3	2.7	4.7
1995–2005*	3.8	2.8	5.1

* IMF estimates for 2005.

Source: Adelman (1991) and International Monetary Fund's *World Economic Outlook* (various issues).

What can we conclude from these facts? First, financial liberalization since 1973 has not produced the achievements its advocates claimed it would. The historical record clearly shows that the 1950–73 fixed exchange rate system was associated with better global economic performance than the liberalized exchange rate system that we have experienced since 1973. Secondly, during the post-war period, until 1973, global economic performance was nothing short of spectacular despite fixed exchange rates, widespread capital controls, increasing rigidities in national labour markets, and the growth of social safety nets. Thirdly, since 1973, global economic performance has been comparatively worse. The global economy has stumbled from one economic crisis to another; for instance, stagflation in the 1970s, the Latin American and African debt problems of the 1980s, and the international financial market crises of the 1990s.

In the last decade of the twentieth century, the global economy suffered a major financial crisis every two to three years, that is, the 1992 European Monetary System currency crisis, the 1994–95 Mexican peso crisis, and the 1997–98 Asian and Russian crisis. At the end of the next section, we will explain why the introduction of the euro has the potential to cause a new major global economic crisis in the next few years. Economics has once more become the dismal science.

In the Spring 2003 Internet issue of the *Harvard Relations Council International Review*, Nobel Prize winner Joseph Stiglitz (2003) stated what by now should be obvious to all: 'Something is wrong with the global financial system . . . international financial crises or near crises have become regular events.'

Noting that there have been almost 100 currency crises in the last 30 years, Stiglitz (2003) states that 'the question is not whether there will be another crisis, but where it will be'. According to Stiglitz (2003), '[t]his much is clear: the International Monetary Fund (IMF), whose responsibility is to ensure the stability of the global financial system, has failed miserably in its mission to stabilize international financial flows, arguably making matters worse.'

Thirty years before 2003, however, marked the breakdown of the most successful international financial system in the history of mankind, that is, the Bretton Woods system.[2] Unfortunately, this fact did not stimulate Stiglitz to raise the following questions:

1. Despite the existence of the same IMF during the quarter century after World War II, why did the Bretton Woods financial system tend to, in general, avoid international financial crises?
2. What was it about the international financial system during the Bretton Woods period that encouraged (or at least did not hinder) year-after-year of unparalleled rates of increase in the real GDP per capita for every nation on this side of the Iron Curtain?[3]
3. Why was there such unparalleled growth rates even though every major nation, including the United States, instituted some form of international

capital flow restrictions during the Bretton Woods period?

Stiglitz (2003) focuses instead on the argument that, under the current international financial system, international capital flows are a primary cause of these recurrent international payments crises as every prudent nation (except the United States) strives to maintain a surplus of exports over imports, that is, tries to obtain a net positive financial savings position from its annual internationally earned income. Any net financial savings obtained are added to the nation's foreign reserves. Since 1973 the global economy is, in essence, on a 'dollar standard'. Consequently, additions to a nation's foreign reserves are held primarily in the form of US Treasuries.

Mainstream EMT advocates might respond that the 30-year-old currency crisis disease described by Stiglitz occurs because:

- national governments have been profligate and do not exercise the necessary fiscal discipline, while simultaneously
- governments have permitted, or even encouraged, fixities (rigidities) in labour and product markets and
- governments have insisted that the nations utilize a managed fixed exchange rate that does not represent what liberalized foreign exchange markets would develop.

Yet, during the Bretton Woods period, there was historically unprecedented real economic growth per capita in all capitalist nations, despite the fact that governments often ran deficits without fear, labour union growth was encouraged, legislation specifying minimum wage payments and safe working conditions was enacted, the social safety net including social security for retirees, national health policies and so on, flourished, and fixed exchange rates were the rule.

What advocates of the EMT fail to recognize is that since the global economy is a closed economy, there is an obvious connection between:

- the ubiquitous desire of all nations (except the United States) to oversave on their international earned income by pursuing an export-led growth policy for the primary purpose of accumulating additional reserves, and
- the existence of a large overhang of international debt by other nations, whose exports markets have not grown fast enough to permit them to service their rising debt obligations.

The successful pursuit of international oversaving propensities by countries like China and Japan creates persistent high rates of involuntary unemployment elsewhere and liquidity problems for the global economy – and *this is true whether the global economy is on either a fixed or a flexible exchange rate system.* In other words, in a global economy context, non-liberalized labour, product, and foreign exchange markets, and persistent government deficits, are neither a necessary nor a sufficient condition for the global economic system to have a depressionary bias that can lead to liquidity (currency) crises and debt defaults.

EXPLAINING THE FACTS

Until 1973, the international payments system was, in large measure, shaped by Keynes's thesis that flexible exchange rates and free international capital mobility are incompatible with global full employment and rapid economic growth in an era of multilateral free trade (Felix, 1997–98). Operating until 1973 under an international payments system, with the help of the Marshall plan and the United States's foreign aid and military expenditures, the global market system kept Keynes's 'incompatibility thesis' in abeyance. Instead, the global economy experienced unparalleled economic growth and prosperity despite widespread capital controls and increasing labour markets rigidities and the growth of the welfare state. This occurred when a fixed exchange rate and capital controls system was combined with a civilizing principle that Keynes had emphasized in his writing in the 1940s, namely, that creditor nations must accept a major responsibility for solving persistent international payments imbalances.

Unfortunately the essence of Keynes's *General Theory* analysis of a money-using, market-oriented, entrepreneurial economy was never incorporated into orthodox economic theory. Accordingly, by the 1960s, mainstream classical economists were developing closed and open economy models based on three classical axioms that Keynes had overthrown in developing his *General Theory* analysis.[4] Using these axioms that Keynes had discarded, classical (supply-side) models were propagated that 'demonstrated' that Keynes's incompatibility thesis was wrong. Instead, these classical models 'proved' that free trade and optimum global economic growth required a *laissez-faire* approach with flexible exchange rates, free international capital mobility, and flexible, liberalized domestic labour markets. In these orthodox classical models, regulations to limit financial flows (either cross-border capital flows or within a nation) imposed huge costs on society. Free the banking system and all financial markets from 'onerous' government oversight and regulation, permit unregulated off-shore banking and, policy makers were assured, a world of heavenly economic bliss would envelop the planet.[5]

Those who called themselves Neoclassical Synthesis Keynesians had already adopted microfoundations for their models that required these three (neo)classical axioms that Keynes rejected (Davidson, 1984). This unfortunate marriage of microeconomic classical axioms with Keynesian macro policies was dubbed 'Bastard Keynesianism' by Joan Robinson. Their logical inconsistencies made these 'Keynesians' easy prey for the classical counter-revolution. Nevertheless, this successful academic resurrection of the classical system might not have been sufficient to alter the policy mix if it were not for events of the 1970s.

The 1973 oil price shock created huge international payments imbalances and unleashed inflationary forces in oil consuming nations. Politicians found irresistible the allure of the Panglossian siren song that 'all is for the best in the best of all possible worlds provided we let well enough alone'. Without having to admit that they did not know what to do, policy makers used the conclusions of the 1960s classical counter-revolutionary theories to justify their abandonment of Keynes's international policy prescriptions to constrain 'hot money' international capital flows and to maintain fixed, but adjustable,' exchange rates. Instead, a 'leave it to the efficient marketplace' philosophy was adopted. Then if anything went wrong, policy makers could suggest that they could not be blamed – for, after all, the market 'knows' best as Nobel Prize winners Friedman, Lucas, Merton, and Scholes continually assured us.[6]

The resulting new international world of finance made the exchange rate itself an object of speculation. Utilizing new computer technology, financial capital could speed around the globe at the speed of light. Since the mid-1970s, international financial transactions have grown 30 times as fast as the growth in international trade (Felix, 1997–98). International financial flows now dominate trade payments. Exchange rate movements reflect changes in speculative positions rather than changes in patterns of trade.

Significant exchange rate movements affect the international competitive position of domestic vis-à-vis foreign industries, and therefore tend to depress the inducement to invest in large projects with irreversible sunk costs.[7] In an uncertain (non-ergodic) world, where the future cannot be reliably predicted from past and present price signals, volatile exchange rates undermine entrepreneurs' confidence in their ability to appraise the potential profitability of any large investment project. Every exchange rate increase not only threatens domestic industries with significant loss of export-market share, but also home-market share losses as imports become less expensive.

Managers realize that any upward blip in the exchange rate during the lifetime of any contemplated investment project can saddle their enterprises with irreversible costly idle capacity. Consequently, the marginal efficiency of investment is reduced. The greater the uncertainty regarding future exchange rates, the less investment globally – just as Keynes's (1936, Ch. 17) analysis of liquidity preference and investment predicted. As a result, trade and real investment spending in open economies have become the tail wagged by the international speculative exchange rate dog.

It is not surprising, therefore, that when the free world changed from a fixed to a flexible exchange rate system, the annual growth rate in investment in plant and equipment in OECD nations fell from 6 per cent (before 1973) to less than 3 per cent (since 1973). Less investment growth means a slower economic growth rate in OECD nations (from 5.9 to 2.8 per cent) while labour productivity growth declined even more dramatically (from 4.6 to less than 2 per cent).

Instead of producing the utopian promises of greater stability and more rapid economic growth promised by classical economists, liberalization of capital flow regulations has been associated with exchange rate instability, slower real growth, higher unemployment, volatility in bond rates, and so on. Liberalization drove the final nail into the coffin of the golden age of economic development.

The post-1973 international payments system has not served the emerging global economy well. The *Financial Times* of London and *The Economist*, both early strong advocates of the post-1973 floating rate system, acknowledged that this system is a failure and was sold to the public and the politicians under false advertising claims.[8] In its 26 September 1998 (p. 80) issue, *The Economist* concluded that either a pure floating rate or a dirty (semi-fixed) floating exchange rate was of 'no use'.

Keynes's (1936, p. 158) aphorism according to which '[w]orldly wisdom teaches that it is better for reputation to fail conventionally than succeed unconventionally' rules the day for politicians. There is no national leader willing to challenge conventional economic analysis and call for a *complete* and *thorough* overhaul of an international payments system that is far worse than the system the major nations of the world abandoned in 1973. Instead, there are calls for patches on the current payments system in terms of a marginal transactions tax here and/or a marginally larger lender of last resort there, or marginally higher capital adequacy ratios for banks as part of a package for more 'transparency'. In the last years of the 1990s, while Japan was suffering from a decade-long recessionary period and the United States seemed to be doing well economically (despite large current account deficits), mainstream economists had inconsistent calls for Keynesian spending in Japan while lauding public budget surpluses in the United States and reducing government deficits in the European Union.

There is no one with significant media visibility who has the courage to speak out in public forums and suggest that the classical economic philosophy that has rationalized our macroeconomic affairs in recent decades is a formula for potential economic disaster at worst, and modest global economic growth at best, that is likely to be accompanied by increasing income inequalities domestically as well as among nations.

Until we reform the world's international payments system, it will be impossible for any individual nation to undertake national macro policies to maintain high levels of aggregate demand internally without fear of a balance of payments constraint and resultant exchange rate collapse. As long as the US dollar is the main form of foreign reserves, however, only the United States does not have to worry about a balance of payments constraint. Accordingly, since 1981, the United States has run large trade deficits with impunity. Because of the United States's large trade deficit in 2004, for example, the effective demand of the global economy was almost 600 billion dollars higher and the global economy was better off than it would have been if the United States were constrained by its huge current account deficit, as some conventional economists would desire. Without the huge trade deficit of the United States in recent years, the economic miracle in China since the turn of the century would not be possible, nor would the economic miracle of the paper tigers of South-East Asia observed between 1985 and 1997.

With the introduction of the euro in 1999, however, if international liquidity holders were to suddenly reveal a preference for the euro over the dollar as an international liquid store of value, then Gresham's Law will come into play, and the global stimulus that has been coming from the United States's current account deficits could readily disappear in the early years of the twenty-first century. The result will be an additional deflationary force unleashed on the global economy. And yet, it is only through a significant stimulus to global effective demand that we can restore a golden age of economic growth for the twenty-first century similar to what the global economy experienced for almost a quarter of a century between 1950 and 1973.

This post-Keynesian message is contrary to the conventional wisdom of mainstream economic theory that attributes the cause of persistently high unemployment to labour market rigidities (in closed economy models) and, in an open economy context, government interference in (1) exchange rates, (2) capital flows, and (3) investments (via crony capitalism). Since the late

1960s, the conventional wisdom of economists has been to advocate micro-policies to free-up, that is, liberalize, both labour and capital markets.

I call this belief in a policy to loosen labour and capital movements as 'the laxative theory to economic bliss'. If such purgative capital and labour movement market medicines succeed in increasing employment and growth in any one country, it does so only by exporting some of its unemployment to its trading partners. The pursuit of these purgatory prescriptions in many nations simultaneously invokes a negative-sum game that unleashes deflationary forces around the globe.

UNDERLYING THEORY: KEYNES VERSUS CLASSICAL MICROFOUNDATIONS

Samuelson (1969, p. 184) has made the acceptance of a basic classical postulate, the ergodic axiom, the *sine que non* of economics as a science. Following Samuelson's ergodic edict, Lucas and Sargent (1981, pp. xi–xvi) made the ergodic axiom not only a necessary and sufficient condition for forming rational expectations but also a necessity for developing economics as an empirically based science.[9] In an ergodic system, estimates of today's objective probabilities calculated from an observed data set provide (statistically) reliable information about the conditional probability function that will govern future outcomes. Accordingly, the future is merely the statistical shadow of the past.

This ergodic axiom is the twentieth century stochastic process equivalent of the perfect certainty assumption of the nineteenth century deterministic classical model. This axiom assures that the future long-run equilibrium path of the economy is immutably preprogrammed and embodied in today's 'fundamentals'. In such a predetermined system, the market will necessarily optimally allocate capital among projects so long as self-interested agents are free to make market decisions based on statistically *reliable* current information about future rates of return.

The ergodic axiom is one of three axioms that Keynes rejected[10] when he emphasized the uncertainty that surrounds future outcomes. Keynes's description of uncertainty matches technically what mathematical statisticians call a nonergodic stochastic system. In Keynes's 'general theory' (1936, pp. 161–3), the explanation of the long-run persistent existence of self-interested speculators[11] in financial markets makes sense only if one assumes that market participants 'know' that it is impossible to calculate any reliable mathematical-based expectation of gain calculated in accordance with existing objective probabilities. Today's (presumed to exist) objective probability conditional distribution is not a reliable actuarial guide to the future. Had Scholes and Merton understood the *General Theory* before they won their Nobel Prize, then, in 1998, they and their partners in the Long Term Capital Management hedge fund would not have been threatened with bankruptcy and required the intervention of the Federal Reserve to prevent a financial market meltdown.

In 1937, Keynes emphasized this difference between his 'general theory' and the classical orthodoxy embodied in EMT. In classical theory, Keynes (1937/1973, pp. 112–5) wrote:

> Facts and expectations were assumed to be given in a definite form; and risks . . . were supposed to be capable of an exact actuarial computation. The calculus of probability . . . was supposed capable of reducing uncertainty to the same calculable state as that of certainty itself. . . . I accuse the classical economic theory of being itself one of these pretty, polite techniques which tries to deal with the present by abstracting from the fact that we know very little about the future. . . . [A classical economist] has overlooked the precise nature of the difference which his abstraction makes between theory and practice, and the character of the fallacies into which he is likely to be lead.

In Keynes's *General Theory* (1936, p. 159) money is never neutral, and therefore dealings in liquid financial assets can affect real economic outcomes. In a world of non-ergodic uncertainty, *the primary function of organized financial markets is to provide liquidity*. Liquidity involves the ability to buy and resell assets in a well-organized, *orderly* market in order to obtain *the medium of contractual settlement* (that is, money) to meet one's nominal contractual liabilities when they come due or when there is fear of an asset bubble collapse. An orderly financial market requires a method for limiting market movements by controlling the net cash flows into and out of the market; just as a theatre owner, to control crowd inflows, will not sell more tickets than permitted by government regulations specifying a maximum occupancy for a performance of a Broadway hit, while laws preventing shouting fire in a crowded theatre encourage an orderly crowd outflow – rather than encouraging everyone to make a fast and disorderly exit through the doors.

The ability to maintain one's liquidity is important to people in the real world, but it would not be an important social function if, as orthodox theory presumes, efficient market ubiquitously prevailed. If one presumes markets are efficient, then logical consistency requires the presumption that individuals can plan their future spending on goods and services efficiently by buying and selling financial assets whose maturity date exactly matches the individual's life-cycle spending pattern stream vis-à-vis the individual's income pattern stream (for instance, as assumed in overlapping generation models). Sudden liquidity needs to meet uncertain, unpredictable future contractual obligations when they come due have no role to play in EMT.

If, however, agents in one's model believe their world is uncertain (non-ergodic), as Keynes and later Hicks (1977, p. vii) claim, then decision makers 'know' that what others call today's 'fundamentals' do not provide a statistically reliable guide to future market valuations. Although in his published papers using non-stochastic modeling Hicks (1979, p. 113) associated uncertainty and Keynes's liquidity analysis with a violation of the ordering axiom, in a private letter to me, he indicated that he should have labeled his 'own point of view as non-ergodic'.[12]

Financial markets provide liquidity as long as market participants accept the convention 'that the existing state of affairs will continue indefinitely, except as we have specific reasons to expect a change' (Keynes, 1936, p. 152). Accordingly:

> a practical theory of the future [market valuation is] ... based on a flimsy foundation. It is subject to sudden and violent changes. The practice of calmness and immobility, of certainty and security, suddenly breaks down. New fears and hopes will, without warning, take charge of human conduct. The forces of disillusion may suddenly impose a new conventional basis of valuation (Keynes, 1937/1973, pp. 114–15).

In the real world, protecting the value of one's portfolio of liquid (resalable) financial assets against unforeseen and unforeseeable changes in financial market values becomes an important economic activity. Every portfolio fund manager must, in an instant, conjecture how other market players will interpret a news event occurring anywhere in the world. With instant global communications, any event occurring in the world can set off rapid changes in subjective evaluation of the market value of one's portfolio. Speculation about the psychology of other market players can result in lemming-like behaviour that can become self-reinforcing and self-justifying. In a non-ergodic system, if enough agents possess the same 'incorrect' expectations (to use a Stiglitz (1989) phrase), the result can be that these faulty expectations actually create future outcomes (see Arestis and Sawyer, 1998, pp. 188–9). The first 'irrational' lemmings to hit the ocean of liquidity may not drown. They may survive to make more mistakes and lead more leaps into liquidity in the future.

THE NEED FOR MARKET ORDERLINESS

Financial markets furnish liquidity by providing an orderly, well-organized environment where financial assets can be readily resold for cash – while the essential properties of the underlying real capital assets prevent them from producing the attribute of liquidity.[13] Market orderliness requires a private or a public institution that regulates the net flows into and out of the market. Orderly liquid financial markets, however, encourage each investor to believe they can have a fast *'exit strategy for the moments when they are dissatisfied with the way matters are developing*. Without liquidity, the risk of making an investment as a minority owner would be intolerable' (Bernstein, 1998a, p. 18). This fast exit strategy potential is inherent in any well-organized financial market, and therefore it promotes the separation of ownership and management (Keynes, 1936, pp. 150–51; see also Davidson, 1972, and Bernstein, 1998). With a liquid capital market, owners have no legal or moral commitment to stick around long enough to make sure their capital is used efficiently.

In the absence of a liquid financial market, '[t]here is no object in frequently attempting to revalue an investment to which we are committed' (Keynes, 1936, p. 151), for there can be no fast exit strategy. If capital markets were completely illiquid, then there would be no separation of ownership and control. Once some volume of capital was committed, the owners would have an incentive to use the existing facilities in the best possible way, no matter what unforeseen circumstances might arise. Perhaps then capital markets might behave more like the efficient markets of mainstream theory. Bernstein's (1998a, p. 23) homily that 'an efficient market is a market without liquidity' is a lesson that policy makers must be taught. Judicious use of capital controls can promote efficiency by constraining any sudden change in the demand for liquidity that would adversely affect the real economy.

If financial markets are primarily organized to provide liquidity, then when bullish sentiment about the uncertain future dominates financial markets, rising capital market prices encourage savers to readily provide the funding that induces entrepreneurial investors to spend sums on new investment projects that (i) far exceed their current incomes and (ii) induce exuberant expectations of future returns. The result is an investment boom. If, some time in the future, doubts suddenly arise concerning the reliability of these euphoric expectations, then bearish sentiment will come to the fore and the investment boom will turn into a bust.

When the bearish view of the future becomes overriding, an excessive demand for liquidity can develop that will impede the production of new investment capital even when real resources are idle and therefore readily available to produce new real capital goods. The basic message of Keynes's *General Theory* is that too great a demand for liquidity can prevent 'saved' (that is, unutilized) real resources from being employed in the production of investment goods. These resources will be involuntarily unemployed.

Unlike Old and New Keynesians, Keynes explicitly recognized that the introduction of sand in the wheels of liquidity-providing financial markets via a transactions tax is a double-edged sword. Keynes (1936, p. 160) noted that a financial transactions tax 'brings us up against a dilemma, and shows us how the liquidity of investment markets often facilitates, though it sometimes impedes, the course of new investment'.

In the absence of concerted intervention by a market maker, what market conditions will create non-volatile movements of prices in real world financial markets?

> It is interesting that the stability of the [financial] system and its sensitiveness . . . should be so dependent on the existence of a variety of opinion about what is uncertain. Best of all that we should know the future. But if not, then, if we are to control the activity of the economic system . . . it is important that opinions differ (Keynes, 1936, p. 172).

In other words, an ergodic system would provide the 'best of all' possible worlds for financial market stability. Then the future can be reduced to actuarial certainty, that is, 'we should know the future'. Market efficiency would be assured as long as agents operated in their actuarially known self-interest. There would be no need for a fast exit strategy.

If the system is non-ergodic, however, then actuarial certainty and the possibility of rational probabilistic risk spreading – which, according to Lawrence Summers, is an essential function of efficient markets – is impossible. Consequently, a second best solution is to encourage substantial numbers of market participants to hold continuously differing expectations about the future so that any small upward change in the market price brings about a significant bear reaction, while any slight downturn induces a bullish reaction. The result will be to maintain spot financial market (resale) price orderliness over time and therefore a high degree of liquidity.[14]

If, however, there is a sudden shift in the private-sector's bull–bear disposition, what I call a bandwagon effect, then price stability requires capital regulations to prevent the bears from liquidating their position too quickly (or the bulls from rushing in) and overcoming any single agent (private or public) who has taken on the responsible task of market maker to promote 'orderliness'. Capital controls serve the same function as laws that make it a crime to yell fire in a crowded theatre. In the absence of such social constraints on free speech, the resulting rush to the exit may inflict more damage than any potential fire.

Despite their willingness to accept the 'compelling logic' of EMT, the common sense of Tobin and his New Keynesian followers regarding real world financial markets cannot help but break into their logical models – with injury to their logical consistency. Thus to solve today's international monetary problems, some 'Keynesians' advocate a Tobin tax. Since 1974, Tobin (1974) has warned that free international financial markets with flexible exchange rates create volatile international financial markets that can have a 'devastating impact on specific industries and whole economies' (Eichengreen et al., 1995, p. 164). Tobin recommended that government could limit market volatility by increasing the transactions costs on all international payments via a small 'Tobin tax'. Unfortunately, though Tobin's assessment of the problem is correct, the empirical evidence is that any increase in the transactions costs significantly increases rather than decreases measured market volatility (Davidson, 1998). Moreover, a Tobin tax does not create a greater disincentive for short-term speculators as Tobin has claimed (Davidson, 1997). Hence, the 'Tobin tax' solution is the wrong tool to solve the growing international financial speculative market problem.

Since the Mexican peso crisis of 1994, pragmatic policy makers have advocated a lender of last resort (LOLR) to stop international financial market liquidity hemorrhaging and to 'bail out' the international investors. In 1994, US Treasury Secretary Rubin encouraged President Clinton to play this LOLR role. With Clinton's liquidity facilities exhausted, the IMF stepped into this lender role when the Asian crisis of 1997 and the Russian debt default occurred in 1998.

When, in 1999, it appeared that the IMF may soon reach the end of its liquidity rope, then IMF Director Stanley Fischer suggested that the G7 nations take over the LOLR function. Fischer's cry for a G7 LOLR collaboration is equivalent to recruiting a volunteer fire department to douse the flames after someone has cried fire in a crowded theatre. Even if the fire is ultimately extinguished, there will be a lot of innocent casualties. Moreover, every new currency fire requires the LOLR to pour more liquidity into the market to put out the flames. The goal should be to produce a permanent fire prevention solution, not to rely on organizing larger and larger volunteer fire fighting companies after each new currency fire breaks out.

Finally, the man who 'broke the Bank of England', George Soros, as well as the economist Rudiger Dornbusch, recommended a currency board solution. A currency board fixes the exchange rate so that the domestic money supply does not exceed the amount of foreign reserves a nation possesses.[15] Thus, if and when investors panic and rush to exit from a nation, the currency board maintains the exchange rate by selling foreign reserves and reducing the domestic money supply by an equivalent sum. A currency board solution, therefore, is equivalent to the blood letting prescribed by seventeenth century doctors to cure a fever. Enough blood loss can, of course, always reduce the fever but often at a terrible cost to the body of the patient. Similarly, a currency board may douse the flames of a currency crisis but the result will be a moribund economy. The recent dreadful experience of Argentina with a currency board illustrates this problem dramatically.

Jeffrey Sachs, Milton Friedman, and others have suggested a return to completely freely flexible exchange rates. Unfortunately, whenever there is a persistent international payments imbalance, free market exchange rates flexibility can make the situation worse. For example, if a nation is suffering a tendency towards international current account deficits, then free market advocates argue that a decline in the market price of the currency will end the deficit. If, however, the Marshall–Lerner condition does not apply, then a declining market exchange rate worsens the situation by increasing the magnitude of the payments deficit.[16] For example, for the United States, the dollar has declined more than 25 per cent since January 2002. Nevertheless, the current account deficit has increased from 20 billion dollars per month in January 2002 to over 50 billion dollars per month in December 2004.[17]

If the payments imbalance is due to capital flows, there is a similar perverse effect. If, for example, country A is attracting a rapid net inflow of capital because investors in the rest of the world think the profit rate is higher in A, then the exchange rate will rise. This rising exchange rate creates even higher profits for foreign investors and contrarily will encourage others to rush in with additional capital flows pushing the exchange rate even higher. If then suddenly there is a change in sentiment (often touched off by some ephemeral event), then a fast exit bandwagon will ensue pushing the exchange rate perversely down.

WHERE DO WE GO FROM HERE?

The function of capital flow regulations (or controls) is to prevent sharp changes in the bull–bear sentiment from overwhelming market makers and inducing rapid changes in price trends, for such volatility can have devastating real consequences.

There is a spectrum of different capital controls available. At one end of the spectrum are controls that primarily impose administrative constraints either on a case-by-case basis or expenditure category basis. These controls include administrative oversight and control of individual transactions for payments to foreign residents (or banks) often via oversight of international transactions by banks or their customers. Mayer (1998, pp. 29–30) has argued that the Asian problem was due to the interbank market that created the whirlpool of speculation and that what is needed is 'a system for identifying ... and policing interbank lending' *and* banks' contingent liabilities resulting from dealing in derivatives. Echoing our non-ergodic theme, Mayer (1998, p. 31) declares that '[t]he mathematical models of price movements and covariance underlying the construction of these [contingent] liabilities simply collapsed as actual prices departed so far from "normal" probabilities'.

Other capital controls include (a) policies that make foreign exchange available but at different exchange rates for different types of transactions, and (b) the imposition of taxes (or other opportunity costs) on specific international payments, for instance, the Tobin Tax or the 1960s United States Interest Equalization Tax. Finally, there can be many forms of monetary policy decisions undertaken to affect international payment flows, for example, raising the interest rate to slow capital outflows, raising bank reserve ratios, limiting the ability of banks to finance purchases of foreign securities, and regulating interbank activity as suggested by Mayer (1998).

The recent experience of the IMF, as lender of last resort imposing the same conditions on all nations requiring international liquidity loans, should have taught us that in policy prescriptions one size does not fit all situations. Accordingly, the type of capital regulations a nation should choose from the spectrum of tools available at any time will differ depending on the specific circumstances involved. In the limits of this chapter it would be presumptuous of me to catalogue what capital regulations should be imposed for any nation under any given circumstances. Nevertheless, it should be stressed that regulating capital movements is a necessary but not sufficient condition for promoting global prosperity.

Elsewhere (Davidson, 1992–93, 1997, 2002) I have developed in detail a proposal for reforming the entire international payments system via an international clearing union that provides for capital controls and other necessary and sufficient conditions to permit the establishment of a golden age in the twenty-first century. The main provisos of my proposal are:

1. The unit of account and ultimate reserve asset for international liquidity is the International Money Clearing Unit (IMCU). All IMCU's are held *only*

by central banks, not by the public.

2. Each nation's central bank is committed to guarantee one way convertibility from IMCU deposits at the clearing union to its domestic money. Each central bank will set its own rules regarding making available foreign monies (through IMCU clearing transactions) to its own bankers and private sector residents.[18] Ultimately, all major private international transactions clear between central banks' accounts in the books of the international clearing institution.

3. The exchange rate between the domestic currency and the IMCU is set *initially* by each nation – just as it would be if one instituted an international gold standard.

4. Contracts between private individuals will continue to be denominated into whatever domestic currency permitted by local laws and agreed upon by the contracting parties.

5. An overdraft system will make available short-term unused creditor balances at the clearing house to finance the productive international transactions of others who need short-term credit. The terms will be determined by the *pro bono* clearing managers.

6. A trigger mechanism will encourage a creditor nation to spend what is deemed (in advance) by agreement of the international community to be *'excessive' credit balances accumulated by running current account surpluses*. These excessive credits can be spent in three ways: (1) on the products of any other member of the clearing union, (2) on new direct foreign investment projects, and/or (3) to provide unilateral transfers (foreign aid) to deficit members.

7. A system to stabilize the long-term purchasing power of the IMCU (in terms of each member nation's domestically produced market basket of goods) can be developed. This requires a system of fixed exchange rates between the local currency and the IMCU that changes only to reflect permanent increases in efficiency wages.[19] This assures each central bank that its holdings of IMCUs as the nation's foreign reserves will never lose purchasing power in terms of foreign produced goods, even if a foreign government permits wage–price inflation to occur within its borders.

8. If a country is at *full employment* and still has a tendency towards persistent international deficits on its current account, then this is *prima facie* evidence that it does not possess the productive capacity to maintain its current standard of living. If the deficit nation is poor, then surely there is a case for the richer nations that are in surplus to transfer some of their excess credit balances to support the poor nation.[20] If it is a relatively rich country, then the deficit nation must alter its standard of living by reducing

the relative terms of trade with major trading partners. If the payment deficit persists despite a continuous positive balance of trade in goods and services, then there is evidence that the deficit nation might be carrying too heavy an international debt service obligation. The *pro bono* officials of the clearing union should bring the debtor and creditors into negotiations to reduce annual debt service payments by (1) lengthening the payments period, (2) reducing the interest charges, and/or (3) debt forgiveness.[21]

It should be noted that proviso 2 permits capital controls. Proviso 6 embodies Keynes's innovative idea that whenever there is a persistent (and/or large) imbalance in current account flows – whether owing to capital flight or to a persistent trade imbalance – there must be a built-in mechanism that induces the surplus nation(s) to bear a major responsibility for eliminating the imbalance. The surplus nation must accept this burden, for it has the wherewithal to resolve the problem.

In the absence of proviso 6, under any conventional system, whether it has fixed or flexible exchange rates and/or capital controls, there will ultimately be an international liquidity crisis (as any persistent current account deficit can deplete a nation's foreign reserves) that unleashes global depressionary forces. Thus, proviso 6 is necessary to assure that the international payments system will not have a built-in depressionary bias. Ultimately then it is in the self-interest of the surplus nation to accept this responsibility, for its actions will create conditions for global economic expansion some of which must redound to its own residents. Failure to act, on the other hand, will promote global depressionary forces that will have some negative impact on its own residents.

Some think that my specific clearing union plan, like Keynes's bancor plan a half century earlier, is utopian. In fact, if we start with the defeatist attitude that it is too difficult to change the awkward system in which we are trapped, then no progress will be made. Global depression does not have to happen again if our policy makers have sufficient vision to develop this post-Keynesian approach. The health of the world's economic system will simply not permit us to muddle through.

NOTES

1. In July 1963, the United States introduced the Interest Equalization Tax (IET) on purchases by residents of foreign (other than Canadian) fixed-rate securities. The tax rate varied from zero to 150 basis points depending on maturity. In August 1971 the dollar convertibility was suspended, and in 1973 Nixon closed the gold window. In 1974 the IET was formally abolished.
2. The Bretton Woods system was successful in the sense that, under it, the average annual real growth per capita was almost double the peak growth rate of developed nations during the period of the industrial revolution, while the average real growth rate of developing nations equalled or exceeded the industrial revolution growth rate (see Davidson, 2002, p. 2).
3. See Davidson (2002, pp. 1–2) for the relevant figures, and Davidson (2002, pp. 225–8) for an explanation.
4. These classical axioms are the neutrality of money axiom, the gross substitution axiom, and the ergodic axiom. See Davidson (1984).
5. Only the supply side limitations of available resources and the level of technical progress would prevent the immediate achievement of a Garden of Eden on Earth.
6. In an article in the *Wall Street Journal*, Friedman (1998) argues that with market determined exchange rates, exchange rate pressures will always be dissipated, despite the long-known argument that, in the absence of the Marshall–Lerner condition, market forces would exacerbate exchange rate problems. For a further discussion see the fifth section.
7. At the same time, great exchange rate volatility vastly increases the liquidity demands of entrepreneurs, bankers, and ultimately central bankers in terms of foreign reserve holdings. The results are episodes of international liquidity crises.
8. *The Economist* magazine (6 January 1990) indicated that the decade of the 1980s will be noted as one in which 'the experiment with floating currencies failed'. Almost two years earlier (17 February 1987), the *Financial Times* admitted that 'floating exchange rates, it is now clear, were sold on a false prospectus. . . . they held out a quite illusory promise of greater national autonomy. . . . [But] when macro policies are inconsistent and when capital is globally mobile, floating rates cannot be relied upon to keep the current accounts roughly in balance'.
9. Simultaneously, Lucas (1981, p. 563) admits that classical axioms are 'patently artificial'.
10. By not requiring three classical axioms for his 'general' theory, Keynes placed the burden on those who make use of such highly special assumptions to justify them, while those who reject restrictive axioms are not required to prove the general negative (Keynes, 1937/1973, p. 109).
11. Speculators believe they can secure a 'profit from knowing better than the market what the future will bring forth' (Keynes, 1936, p. 170).
12. After reading my paper on rational expectations (Davidson, 1982–83), in a letter (dated 12 February 1983) Hicks wrote: 'I just have just been reading your RE [rational expectations] paper. . . . I do like it very much. I have never been through that RE literature . . . but I had just enough of it to be put off by the smell of it. You have now *rationalized* my suspicions, and have shown me that I missed a chance of labeling my own point of view as *non-ergodic*. One needs a name like that to ram a point home' (italics in original).
13. Keynes (1936, p. 241) argues that the 'attribute of liquidity' of an asset is by no means independent of the presence of two essential properties, namely, that the asset is not reproducible via the employment of labor, and it is not substitutable for the producible output of industry.
14. Only in the non-ergodic world, that is, our entrepreneurial economic system, is it sensible to organize complex and lengthy production and exchange processes via the use of nominal contracts (Davidson, 1994) in order to give entrepreneurs some control of cash flows over an otherwise uncertain future. In such a world, the primary function of organized financial

markets is to provide liquidity by permitting the resale of assets in an orderly market. Only secondarily do modern super-efficient financial markets affect the allocation of new capital amongst industries, and to the extent that it apportions capital, this distribution is not predetermined by some long-run immutable real economic fundamentals.

15. A currency board is the modern equivalent of the gold standard where US dollars are the 'gold'. The gold standard worked only when there was no bandwagon effects. It always failed when there was a bandwagon effect for a fast exit.

16. The Marshall–Lerner condition requires that the sum of the price elasticities for exports and imports exceed unity for a depreciating exchange rate to reduce the payments deficit. The textbook J-curve for a depreciating exchange rate recognizes that in the short run the payments deficit worsens (the downward part of the J-curve). The J-curve ultimately turns upward, because it is *assumed* that in the long run, price elasticities are approximately infinite.

17. These facts do not faze advocates of a flexible exchange rate system (for instance, former World Bank economist Kenneth Rogoff and Fred Bergsten, President of the Institute of International Economics). They merely imply that the dollar decline has been insufficient, and that a fall of at least another 29 to 40 per cent may be necessary to reduce the current account deficit.

18. Correspondent banking will have to operate through the International Clearing Agency, with each central bank regulating the international relations and operations of its domestic banking firms. Small scale smuggling of currency across borders, and so on, can never be completely eliminated. But such movements are merely a flea on a dog's back – a minor, but not debilitating, irritation. If, however, most of the residents of a nation hold and use (in violation of legal tender laws) a foreign currency for domestic transactions and as a store of value (for example, it is estimated that Argentineans hold more than 5 billion US dollars), this is evidence of a lack of confidence in the government and its monetary authority. Unless confidence is restored, all attempts to restore economic prosperity will fail.

19. The efficiency wage is related to the money wage divided by the average product of labour. It is the unit labour cost modified by the profit mark-up in domestic money terms of domestically produced GNP. At this preliminary stage of this proposal, it would serve no useful purpose to decide whether the domestic market basket should include both tradeable and non-tradeable goods and services. (With the growth of tourism, more and more non-tradeable goods become potentially tradeable.) I personally prefer the wider concept of the domestic market basket, but it is not obvious that any essential principle is lost if a tradeable only concept is used, or if some nations use the wider concept while others the narrower one.

20. This is equivalent to a negative income tax for poor fully employed families within a nation.

21. The actual programme adopted for debt service reduction will depend on many parameters including: the relative income and wealth of the debtor vis-à-vis the creditor, the ability of the debtor to increase its per capita real income, and so on.

REFERENCES

Adelman, I. (1991), 'Long term economic development', *California Agricultural Experiment Station Working Paper*, no. 589.

Arestis, P. and M. Sawyer (1998), 'Keynesian economic policies for the new millennium', *Economic Journal*, **108** (446), 181–95.

Bernstein, P.L. (1996), *Against the Gods: The Remarkable Story of Risk*, New York: John Wiley & Sons.

Bernstein, P.L. (1998a), 'Stock market risk in a Post Keynesian world', *Journal of*

Post Keynesian Economics, **21** (1), 15–24.

Bernstein, P.L. (1998b), 'Why efficient markets offer hope to active management', keynote address to the European Federation of Financial Analysts Societies, Brussels, 28 September.

Davidson, P. (1972), *Money and the Real World*, London: Macmillan.

Davidson, P. (1982–83), 'Rational expectations: a fallacious foundation for studying crucial decision-making processes', *Journal of Post Keynesian Economics*, **5** (2), 182–98.

Davidson, P. (1984), 'Reviving Keynes's revolution', *Journal of Post Keynesian Economics*, **6** (4), 561–75.

Davidson, P. (1991), 'Is probability theory relevant for uncertainty? A Post Keynesian perspective', *Journal of Economic Perspectives*, **5** (1), 29–43.

Davidson, P. (1992–93), 'Reforming the world's money', *Journal of Post Keynesian Economics*, **15** (2), 153–79.

Davidson, P. (1994), *Post Keynesian Macroeconomic Theory: A Foundation for Successful Economic Policies for the Twenty-First Century*, Aldershot, UK and Brookfield, USA: Edward Elgar.

Davidson, P. (1997), 'Are grains of sand in the wheels of international finance sufficient to do the job when boulders are often required?', *Economic Journal*, **107** (442), 671–86.

Davidson, P. (1998), 'Volatile financial markets and the speculator', *Economic Issues*, **3** (2), 1–18.

Davidson, P. (2002), *Financial Markets, Money and the Real World*, Cheltenham, UK and Northampton, MA, USA: Edward Elgar.

Eichengreen, B., J. Tobin and C. Wyplosz (1995), 'Two cases for sand in the wheels of international finance', *Economic Journal*, **105** (428), 162–72.

Felix, D. (1997–98), 'On drawing general policy lessons from recent Latin American currency crises', *Journal of Post Keynesian Economics*, **20** (2), 191–221.

Friedman, M. (1998), 'Markets to the rescue', *Wall Street Journal*, 12 October, A22.

Hicks, J.R. (1977), *Economic Perspectives: Further Essays on Money and Growth*, Oxford: Clarendon Press.

Hicks, J.R. (1979), *Causality in Economics*, Oxford: Basil Blackwell.

Keynes, J.M. (1936), *The General Theory of Employment, Interest and Money*, New York: Harcourt Brace.

Keynes, J.M. (1937/1973), 'The general theory of employment', *Quarterly Journal of Economics*, **51** (2), 209–23, in *The Collected Works of John Maynard Keynes*, Vol. XIV, London and Basingstoke: Macmillian.

Lucas, R.E. (1981), 'Tobin and monetarism: a review article', *Journal of Economic Literature*, **19** (2), 558–67.

Lucas, R.E. and T.J. Sargent (1981), *Rational Expectations and Econometric Practices*, Minneapolis: University of Minnesota Press.

Mayer, M. (1998), 'The Asian disease: plausible diagnoses, possible remedies', *Levy Economics Institute Public Policy Brief*, no. 44.

Samuelson, P.A. (1969), 'Classical and neo-classical monetary theory', in R.W. Clower (ed.), *Monetary Theory: Selected Readings*, Harmondsworth: Penguin Books, 170–90.

Stiglitz, J.E. (1989), 'Using tax policy to curb speculative short-term trading', *Journal of Financial Services Research*, **3** (2–3), 101–15.

190   *From Financial Instability to Macroeconomic Performance*

Stiglitz, J.E. (2003), 'Global greenbacks', *Harvard Relations Council International Review*, Spring electronic issue.
Summers, L.H. and V.P. Summers (1989), 'When financial markets work too well: a cautious case for securities transactions tax', *Journal of Financial Services Research*, **3** (2–3), 261–86.
Tobin, J. (1974), *The New Economics, One Decade Older*, Princeton: Princeton University Press.

10. Cross-Border Transactions and Exchange Rate Stability

Sergio Rossi

INTRODUCTION

After the break-up of the Bretton Woods system of fixed exchange rates in 1971–73, the international financial system has undergone a series of modifications that resulted from (and featured) essentially two phenomena: the appraisal of financial innovations, which have given more freedom to international investors, and integration of globalized financial markets. These trends have been seriously amplified over the last ten years or so, which, despite some progress in international cooperation, led to several financial crises such as the Mexican 'tequila crisis' (1994–95, which spread contagiously to Argentina), the East-Asian crisis (1997–98), involving Indonesia, Korea, Malaysia, the Philippines, as well as Thailand – and which was at the root of the Russian (1998) and Brazilian crises (1998–99) – and the more recent crises in Turkey (2001) and Argentina (2002).

According to the taxonomy adopted by the International Monetary Fund (1998, pp. 74–5), there are in fact four main types of financial crises:

1. currency crises (characterized by speculative attacks, ending with a devaluation and/or with massive intervention of monetary authorities on the foreign exchange market);
2. banking crises (featuring an actual or potential bank run, which provokes a suspension of internal convertibility and/or induces government intervention);
3. foreign-debt crises (when either private or public institutions in a country are unable to serve their external debt obligations);
4. balance-of-payment crises (resulting from a structural unbalance between absorption (current account) and sources of financing (capital account)).

These crises are not mutually exclusive. In fact, they may occur simultaneously or even overlap to some extent or somehow feed into each other. Moreover, when important in size or unfortunately combined, they can form a fully-fledged, systemic financial crisis, that is to say, a disruption in settlement systems with large adverse effects on the real economy, mainly in the form of output, growth, and employment losses.[1] Financial crises are today so pervasive that they are sometimes considered as a feature of modern capitalist economies. They are indeed an important part of the evolution, sophistication, and development of capitalism. Suffice it to observe that most of the contemporary financial institutions and best practices – like deposit insurances, lenders of last resort, prudential and regulatory standards, and international financial agreements – are the institutional by-product of these crises.

The constitution of an international monetary and financial architecture that may avoid these crises, and the ensuing financial instability and monetary disorder all around the world, has been debated for at least 60 years now, since the Bretton Woods (1944) conference set up the 'twin institutions', that is, the International Monetary Fund (IMF) and the International Bank for Reconstruction and Development (now called World Bank). A number of key questions that were at stake at the Bretton Woods conference still have to be answered today. To cite only a few of them: can a local currency (the British pound, the US dollar, the yen, the euro, and so on) play the role of international currency essentially? Do we need international money? In the affirmative, which institution should issue it, and how? What are the links between money, credit, and finance at the international level?

This chapter focuses on the need of a structural monetary reform of the international payment system along the lines that Keynes put forward at the Bretton Woods conference, which, once refined, will avoid the occurrence of currency crises and their negative effects on the real economy. The chapter also aims to show that the alleged inconsistency between full international capital mobility, monetary policy autonomy, and stable exchange rates can be disposed of, if Keynes's plan for a new world monetary order is developed considering the financial issues *pari passu* with the monetary ones.

The structure of the chapter is as follows. The next section briefly presents the performance of, and the challenges for, the contemporary international economy, as regards monetary as well as financial instability and the ensuing effects on real magnitudes. The third section elaborates on a proposal for an international monetary reform in the spirit of Keynes, showing in particular how a structurally-improved monetary architecture could be set up to avoid the disruptive effects that currency crises have on our economic systems. The fourth section illustrates the main benefits of such a plan, and discusses some objections that might be raised against it. The last section concludes.

THE INTERNATIONAL ECONOMY: CURRENT PERFORMANCE AND CHALLENGES

Over the last 20 years (1985–2005), but the same might be said for a much longer period of time, cross-border transactions have been unbalanced, and have given rise to economic instability and uncertainty. Current accounts have recorded either important deficits or surplus as a percentage of GDP, thus contributing to the observed volatility on the foreign-exchange market, because of excessive demand for the so-called key currencies as a result of the need to finance trade deficits. Figure 10.1 shows the evolution of current account balances for some of the G7 countries (data are taken from the IMF's *World Economic Outlook*).

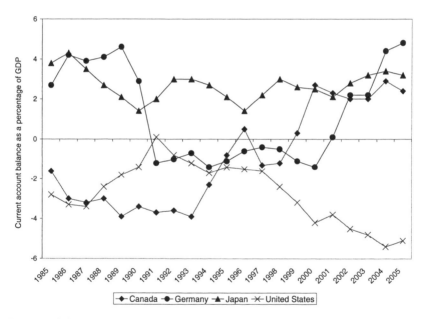

Figure 10.1. Current account balance as a percentage of GDP, 1985–2005

These phenomena, together with speculation on the foreign-exchange market, reduced growth and employment, mainly via interest rate hikes that countries had to implement in order for them to attract capital inflows so as to finance their current account deficits. As a result, domestic investment has been limited on account of the high cost of capital, and capital inflows have been very sensitive to exchange-rate and interest-rate volatility. 'In fact, the volatility of portfolio flows and of other short-term capital flows has been a major cause of the currency and financial crises that have beset many emerging-market countries in recent years' (Kenen and Meade, 2003, p. 9). The ongoing increase in the US policy interest rates may imply that capital flows to emerging-market countries could reverse rapidly, not least since these flows occur largely in the form of volatile portfolio investments and loans (see Bank for International Settlements, 2004, Ch. 3). The same can be said with respect to European Union (EU) countries and participation in the Exchange Rate Mechanism (ERM) of the European Monetary System (EMS). As Begg et al. (2003, pp. 6–7) point out in their review of financial crises in the 1990s, both the inception and the virulence of the 1992–93 ERM crisis was due to the narrow (±2¼ per cent) fluctuation band for EMS currencies, combined with the lifting of capital controls and the related increase in the size and volatility of capital flows as a result of the 1986 European Single Act. All this puts a strong downward pressure on aggregate demand, with its ensuing negative effects on growth and employment, which then impinge also on income distribution both across and within countries. As a striking example of the unwelcome effects that greater integration of trade and fully liberalized finance elicited over the last 20 years or so, Weller et al. (2001, p. 7) note that '[t]he median per-capita income of the world's richest 10% of countries was 76.8 times that of the poorest 10% of countries in 1980 ... and 121.8 times greater in 1999. The ratio of the average per capita incomes shows a similar, yet more dramatic, increase' (for further and more detailed empirical evidence see Svedberg, 2001).[2] These results are in line with those of Quah (1996, 1997), who shows that income distribution among countries is becoming increasingly more unequal.

The promises of more equal income distribution and economic growth all over the world as a result of trade and financial integration have therefore failed to materialize under the current international monetary system. The time has come to reconsider the architecture of the latter system afresh, in order to develop a monetary and financial structure able to provide economic stability and recovery in those countries most in need of them.

THE CREATION AND WORKINGS OF AN INTERNATIONAL SETTLEMENT AGENT

The creation of an international settlement agent for the final payment of cross-border transactions should be at the centre of world monetary reform. In fact, it was already at the core of Keynes's proposals at the Bretton Woods conference, by which he aimed at making sure that international imbalances are finally settled, whilst providing deficit countries with the means to finance their trade imbalances with respect to surplus countries. In Keynes's (1980, p. 169) own words:

> We need a method by which the surplus credit balances arising from international trade, which the recipient does not wish to employ for the time being, can be set to work in the interests of international planning and relief and economic health, without detriment to the liquidity of these balances and to their holder's faculty to employ them himself when he desires to do so.

To this end, Keynes proposed the creation of an international bank money, which he dubbed bancor, to be issued by a world central bank that in his own words 'might become the pivot of the future economic government in the world' (p. 189). In this respect, Keynes pointed out that '[w]e need a central institution, of a purely technical and non-political character, to aid and support other international institutions concerned with the planning and regulation of the world's economic life' (p. 169). Owing to many different economic and political powers, however, Keynes's proposals for the creation of an International Clearing Bank (ICB) were not endorsed by the national delegations at the Bretton Woods conference, which *de facto* gave rise to the dollar standard. This, in fact, comes as no surprise. As Rowley and Hamouda (1989, p. 2) observe with respect to the future of the current international monetary system:

> The attendant complacency restrains our willingness to accept both novel proposals and the revival of older views, previously rejected for adoption in different situations of the world economy, even though such deviations from fashion might provide important ingredients for solutions to our present difficulties.

Let us therefore elaborate on a novel proposal, while reviving Keynes's plan, to add a 'supranational' tier to the two-tier banking structure existing today in each country, in order for the final settlement of international transactions to occur, without creating instability or turmoil on the foreign-exchange market.

Suppose, for instance, that countries A and B participate in a reformed world monetary and financial architecture along Keynes's lines. Suppose also that country A records a trade deficit worth x units of money A, MA, or equivalently z bancor. For expositional ease, let us assume that country A's deficit is country B's surplus, as if the structurally reformed system were composed of two countries only. To refine Keynes's plan, and to make sure that the money-purveying and credit-purveying functions of the ICB are clearly separated, let us introduce a two-department bookkeeping in each national central bank involved (see Schmitt, 1973, for an analogous proposal at the international level). In other words, let any international transaction be recorded by the country's central bank in two separate monies: the Domestic Department of the national central bank enters the payment in local currency, while the External Department enters it in international money, namely, in bancor.[3] This clear-cut, and tight, separation in the books makes sure that the international monetary unit is mechanically out of reach for investors as well as for speculators. In the proposed system, in fact, the bancor is merely a *means* of payment between *nations*, and not an *object* of trade or speculation. The result of the payment of the trade imbalance between countries A and B is shown in Table 10.1 (where we assume that x MA = z bancor = y MB).

If the settlement of the international transaction were stopped here, however, country A would be allowed to pay for its (net) commercial imports without relinquishing an equivalent amount of financial claims. As a result, country A would live beyond its income, because it could pay for its (net) commercial imports without exporting real goods, services, or securities for an equivalent amount. This would certainly not be accepted by the rest of the world, and for a very good reason, namely, equity.

If the intervention of the ICB were to stop at this stage, in fact, a deposit of z bancor would co-exist alongside of a sum of bank deposits in the form of money B worth exactly the same amount (see Table 10.1). In other words, the number of money units that would exist as a result of a single payment would be twice (2x) the value of the items so exchanged (x MA) – recall that in our example x MA = z bancor = y MB. To make sure that the total sum of bank deposits corresponds to the value of the relevant transaction, therefore, the proposed international settlement system has to ensure that either one of the two sums of money worth y MB each – to wit, the deposit in the Domestic Department of country B's central bank and the deposit at the ICB – disappears as soon as it is formed. Only in this case will the intervention of the ICB (which is necessary to finalize any international payment) leave the money–output relationship unaltered worldwide.

Table 10.1. The result of an international payment in bancor for a cross-border transaction on the market for produced goods and services

---

Central bank of country A
Domestic Department

Assets		Liabilities	
Bank B1 (for the importer) +x MA		External Department	+x MA

Central bank of country A
External Department

Assets		Liabilities	
Domestic Department	+z bancor	ICB	+z bancor

International Clearing Bank

Assets		Liabilities	
Central bank of country A (External Department)	+z bancor	Central bank of country B (External Department)	+z bancor

Central bank of country B
Domestic Department

Assets		Liabilities	
External Department	+y MB	Bank B2 (for the exporter)	+y MB

Central bank of country B
External Department

Assets		Liabilities	
ICB	+z bancor	Domestic Department	+z bancor

At this stage, the recent advances made by domestic payment systems (see Rochon and Rossi, 2004) in the management of settlement risks can provide a crucial element to this end. In short, it is possible to link together funds transfers and securities transfers at the international level to make sure that delivery of a financial asset occurs if, and only if, the corresponding final payment occurs, too (this is the delivery-versus-payment mechanism by means of which both actions actually take place at one and the same time; see Committee on Payment and Settlement Systems, 2003, p. 492).

Let us illustrate the working of this mechanism by referring to our stylized example. When the central bank of country B is informed that it is entitled to a deposit in international money at the ICB, it should decide whether to lend this amount directly to a deficit country (that is, a country in the position of country A) or to spend it for buying an amount of interest-bearing securities in the international financial market (see below). If country B lends its bancor deposit to country A voluntarily, this means that country A sells indeed an equivalent amount of financial assets to country B. If so, then the book-entry situation after this financial transaction has taken place, and has been finally settled in bancor, is depicted in Table 10.2 (previous entries are shown in italics, and exchange rates are those of Table 10.1).

Table 10.2 shows that as a result of the international payment in bancor via the ICB's ledger no one country has a monetary imbalance, because all trade imbalances are finally settled by a transfer of eligible assets in a multilateral framework under the aegis of the ICB. To be sure, country A ends up with a net financial outflow, since it sells a number of securities to finance its final payment to country B (via the international settlement agent). In other words, country B spends in the international financial market the deposit in bancor it gets as a result of its trade surplus (worth z bancor). Country A finds thereby in the international financial market the funds it really needs to reimburse the overdraft it obtained at the ISA (see Table 10.1). In the end, international money disappears as the reflux principle indicates (see the ICB balance sheet in Table 10.2), and therefore no inflationary pressure can arise in the market for produced goods: a bank deposit of y MB exists (in country B) as a result of the international settlement of A's trade deficit (B's trade surplus). This bank deposit is backed by an amount of securities (as a collateral) that are transferred from country A to country B with the *monetary* intermediation of the ICB.

> The International Clearing Union [that is, the ICB] would then be a purely formal institution with no influence upon member countries, its function being merely to settle the ultimate outstanding balances between Central Banks. It would not aim at 'equilibrium' of any kind; it would not be concerned with the size of balances to be settled; it would merely keep the big ledger in which is recorded how much some nations owe to others (Kalecki and Schumacher, 1943, p. 30).

Table 10.2. The result of a payment in bancor on the international financial market

Central bank of country A
Domestic Department

Assets		Liabilities	
Bank B1 (for the importer)	*+x MA*	*External Department*	*+x MA*
External Department	+x MA		
Financial assets (sold to country B)	–x MA		
Bank B1 (for the importer)	+x MA		
Financial assets (sold to country B)	–x MA		

Central bank of country A
External Department

Assets		Liabilities	
Domestic Department	*+z bancor*	*ICB*	*+z bancor*
ICB	+z bancor	Domestic Department	+z bancor

International Clearing Bank

Assets		Liabilities	
Central bank of country A (External Department)	*+z bancor*	*Central bank of country B (External Department)*	*+z bancor*
Central bank of country B (External Department)	+z bancor	Central bank of country A (External Department)	+z bancor

Central bank of country B
Domestic Department

Assets		Liabilities	
External Department	+*y MB*	*Bank B2 (for the exporter)*	+*y MB*
Financial assets (bought from country A)	+y MB	External Department	+y MB
Financial assets (bought from country A)	+y MB	Bank B2 (for the exporter)	+y MB

Central bank of country B
External Department

Assets		Liabilities	
ICB	+*z bancor*	*Domestic Department*	+*z bancor*
Domestic Department	+z bancor	ICB	+z bancor

Now, although the most needed purpose of an international clearing agent is that of providing member countries with a means of payment for the orderly working of the international monetary system, it would also certainly be wise to let this agent act also as a *financial* intermediary. The ICB could, notably, lend to deficit countries the amount of bancor deposited by surplus countries. Consider in this respect the ICB balance sheet in Table 10.2. From a circular-flow point of view, the two double-entries in the ICB ledger are the mark of two distinct circuits of international money that occur in one and the same point of time (recall the delivery-versus-payment protocol referred to earlier). The first circuit of bancor concerns the payment of country A's trade deficit. The second circuit of bancor, by way of contrast, concerns the payment of a transaction on the international financial market that has been induced by the former circuit (see above). The second circuit being induced by the first, we may analyse them together (Figure 10.2).

The goods-market circuit of international money, represented anticlockwise in Figure 10.2, is elicited by the money-purveying role of the international settlement agent in connection with foreign trade. Countries need to ask the ICB in order for their commercial transactions to be finally paid (see above). The financial-market circuit of international money, represented clockwise in Figure 10.2, is elicited by the fact that the first (anticlockwise) circuit alone would not be enough for the surplus country to be paid really: the monetary intervention of the ICB would give rise merely to a promise to pay if it were not complemented by a reverse (open-market) operation whereby the newly-created international money is really destroyed in a financial transaction. This reverse operation amounts to a purchase of securities by country B, which in so doing spends the bancor deposit it is entitled to as a result of the goods-market circuit of international money. On the whole, if country B is led to spend on the international financial market the whole amount of international money that it obtains from foreign trade, it contributes to ensure the orderly working of the international payment system, namely, the bancor standard system.

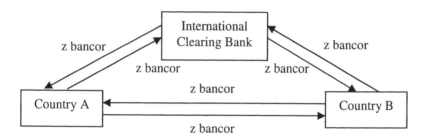

Figure 10.2. The two circuits of international money

What happens, however, if country B does not spend its bancor deposit to buy those financial assets that country A seeks to sell in order for the latter to obtain the funds it needs to finance its foreign trade imbalance? It is at this juncture that the credit-purveying function of the international clearing agent acquires its full meaning and practical purpose. In fact, instead of selling its financial assets to country B, country A may sell them to the ICB, which, in purchasing them, advances a payment that country A will benefit from when exporting real goods or services. If so, there may be two kinds of financial assets behind the entries in Table 10.2: country A's securities sold to the ICB, and the ICB securities sold to country B. In fact, by selling its own securities (or certificates) on the international financial market, the ICB would be able to collect private as well as public capital and invest it in those countries most in need of a recovery, and in which otherwise capital would not flow (see Kalecki and Schumacher, 1943, pp. 30–33, but also Arestis and Sawyer, 1997, pp. 362–3). 'The [ICB] certificates would end up with the countries which are in over-all surplus – which, therefore, would have automatically lent . . . that surplus to the rest of the world' (Stamp, 1963, p. 81).

Of course, the open-market and lending operations that the international clearing agent carries out would have to be rigorously supervised and respect the principles of sound banking as well as international best practices. The ICB's lending facilities are not to be granted *ad libitum*, but some limits must be provided, and an interest rate above market level must be paid by those countries obtaining the ICB's financial assistance. In fact, the main objection against our reform proposal is that it might invite abuse, and that the quality of the securities sold by debtor countries to the ICB (in its acting as long-term purveyor of funds) might not match the quality of the ICB's securities sold to creditor countries, so that the latter quality is likely to deteriorate over time, too. In this respect, the statutes of the international settlement agent will need to provide some limits, say in terms of a percentage of either total foreign trade or GDP (for instance, calculated on a ten-year moving average), beyond which no country is allowed to finance its current account deficit by selling financial assets – namely, when the country's risk is too high to provide sound collateral – and must therefore cut back on its commercial imports and/or increase its exports of real goods and services (not least to pay for debt service, that is, interest on the securities sold either to creditor countries or to the ICB to finance the country's trade deficit).[4] To be sure, creditor countries would suffer from no credit risks under the proposed international settlement system: bancor balances would always be fully, and immediately, convertible into real goods and/or services sold by any member of the system, and also into securities sold either by any other (deficit) country or by the ICB itself, acting as a financial intermediary between member countries. Also, the ICB certificates may be disposed of in settlement of any trade deficits by creditor countries.

In sum, the result of the financial transactions carried out through the ICB shows that the money-purveying and the credit-purveying functions of this international settlement institution will be kept separate explicitly. When the ICB issues a sum of bancor for the final payment between two countries to be made, it does not necessarily enter into a credit operation with any of these countries. It is only when a country does not find in the financial market the funds it needs to clear off its position multilaterally that the ICB intervenes by granting it a credit (through an open-market operation, say, in the form of a repurchase agreement), in order not to jeopardize the smooth working of the international payment system based on the bancor standard. This would be enough, but instrumental, for providing several important economic benefits to participating countries.

SOME MAIN BENEFITS OF AND OBJECTIONS TO AN INTERNATIONAL SETTLEMENT INSTITUTION

The delivery-versus-payment protocol that we propose to put into practice for the new international settlement machinery guarantees that each monetary transaction between any two countries gives rise to both a funds transfer in the ICB ledger and a securities transfer between the countries involved by the final payment in bancor (or whatever the name of the international money will be). If international settlements are carried out through the monetary and financial intermediation of the ICB, then each national currency will be instantaneously exchanged against itself through international money. In the example we analysed in the previous section, for instance, x units of MA are supplied (against z bancor) in the payment of country A's trade deficit, at the same time as x units of MA are demanded (against z bancor) in the payment of the securities sold by country A. Similarly, y units of MB are demanded (against z bancor) in the payment of country B's trade surplus, at the same time as y units of MB are supplied (against z bancor) in the payment of the securities bought by country B. Each currency being simultaneously supplied and demanded against an identical amount of bancor, its exchange rate can never be affected by international transactions – be they on the product or on the financial market (hence speculation cannot alter exchange rates in such a system).

The first benefit of our system would notably consist in introducing a mechanism by which any surplus country spends its positive balances in bancor as soon as it earns them, so that at the end of each settlement day no credit balances at the ICB will be held idle.[5] If the latter balances are not spent by surplus countries for purchasing the financial assets sold by deficit countries, a protocol would make sure that end-of-day bancor balances are automatically spent for the purchase of ICB's securities. Further, and more importantly, in our system any participating currency will have an exchange rate that is stable (though not fixed) with respect to the bancor, hence also in terms of any other participating currency, in a framework of fully liberalized international capital flows[6] – without this being at odds with a higher degree of flexibility in domestic policy making. In fact, the structurally-modified international monetary system that we propose as new world monetary order grants another vital benefit to its participating countries, because it increases their room for manoeuvre when gearing their economic policies (particularly an independent monetary policy) to the needs of their domestic economies, including growth and hence employment. The international settlement system proposed in this chapter would indeed make sure that cross-border payments take place in an orderly framework, that is to say, with no disturbances on the foreign-exchange market that may put in danger the policy goal of exchange rate stability and its ensuing macroeconomic benefits. The age-long conflict between domestic and external goals of a country's monetary policy would thus be resolved definitively, to the benefit of growth, employment, effective demand, and income distribution among trading countries.

A number of questions, however, remain to be addressed and might indeed be raised against our plan. In the system we propose, in fact, and up to some limit (see above):

> no individual member State would be prevented from determining for itself to what extent it wished to allow its Current Account to be unbalanced. . . . Such a country might aim, for instance, at a drastic over-valuation of its own currency, thus being able to pay highly attractive prices for its imports and making its (potential) exports inordinately dear to the foreigner (Kalecki and Schumacher, 1943, p. 30).

If so, then competitive devaluation policies might be deliberately put into practice, in a beggar-thy-neighbour, non-cooperative game whose dynamics might be disruptive for the global economy, so much so that it might lead to pervasive deflationary pressures around the world. To deal with these issues, an intergovernmental conference should be gathered, and write the 'rules of the game' that participating countries will have to abide by under the aegis of the international settlement agent (ICB). As in domestic payment systems, the statutes of the international settlement agent need to provide a regulatory framework, particularly with a system of checks and balances, so that debtor countries must care about their financial position. As already noted by Arestis and Sawyer (1996, pp. 158–9), the international settlement agent may also be given the statutory power to require exchange rate changes, if current account surpluses threaten economic growth in deficit countries, or if overvaluation of a currency's exchange rate threatens financial stability.

Now, provided that misuse of the new international settlement system can be avoided by appropriate regulation, how should a country's policy makers choose the exchange rate of their local currency against the bancor? More precisely, what elements should they consider when determining the rate at which this currency will be exchanged for a given amount of bancor? The answer really depends on the country's economic policy targets, domestic as well as external: a country might decide to have a current account surplus so as to secure employment and to have a positive amount of net investment abroad, or it may decide to have a current account deficit in order to develop its economy through capital inflows. Indeed, as was argued by Kalecki and Schumacher (1943, p. 29):

There is no merit in a general policy aiming at *Current Account equilibrium* for all countries, because different countries are at different stages of economic development, and a regular flow of investment from the more highly developed to the more backward regions of the world may redound to the benefit of all.

In either case, the exchange rate between the local currency and the bancor ought to be fixed at a level that allows the country to hit its external target. Further, a country might have an output/employment target that it may want to attain using (also) the exchange rate instrument: in this case, the exchange rate between the local currency and the bancor should be set at a level compatible with this goal. Any other policy variable might be considered, of course, the important point being that the country concerned will be able to set, and to modify (if necessary),[7] the exchange rate of its currency against the bancor, which would become the standard of the structurally reformed international monetary system (Figure 10.3).

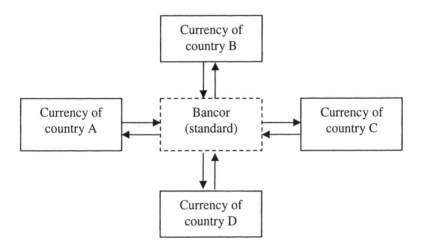

Figure 10.3. The bancor standard as new international monetary system

A further advantage of such a system is that, if a world monetary reform appears to be utopian owing to political reasons, its architecture can easily be put into practice at a regional level – for instance, at the European level in connection with EU enlargement (see Rossi, 2003, 2004) or EU partnerships (see Rossi, 2005). This may then lead to implementing a new world monetary order on regional grounds, without *ipso facto* abolishing national currencies and the monetary room for manoeuvre they offer. Monetary and exchange-rate policy decisions would thereby remain at the national level, in order for any nations to have a larger set of policy tools when addressing the domestic needs of increasingly-open economies – be they emerging, advanced, or in transition. Indeed, 'if policies of a broadly Keynesian type are to be revived at the level of the national economy, some freedom of action over the external value of the currency must be retained' (Smithin and Wolf, 1993, p. 367).

CONCLUSION

The creation of an international settlement institution in the spirit of Keynes would be a crucial step to solve the problem of funding, and finally settling, economic transactions between trading countries without creating the risk of financial instability or affecting the world economy negatively. This chapter shows that a structural–monetary reform of the international payment system is necessary to provide for funding in settlement of cross-border transactions. Analysing international money, credit, and finance with the endogenous-money paradigm, we reach indeed the conclusion that these issues need to be addressed and solved together to set up an institutional system that can avoid world monetary disorder and exchange rate volatility. The structural reform of the international payment system that we propose in this chapter combines the benefits of exchange rate stability with the flexibility offered by an exchange rate that can be adjusted over time by the country concerned – as in the gold standard system – under the aegis of an international settlement agent whose creation would eliminate any instability on the foreign-exchange market by issuing the yardstick that the current international monetary system lacks. Let us hope that the powerful elite of this latter system recognizes the real need for corrective actions, to set up financial institutional arrangements that will be apt 'to limit or avoid deflationary tendencies, to enable correction of trade imbalances without deflationary biases, and to underpin an adequate level of aggregate demand' (Arestis and Sawyer, 1997, p. 356).

ACKNOWLEDGEMENTS

This chapter is the result of research work presented at several conferences and workshops held at the Universities of Bergamo, Bilbao, Leeds, Lugano, and Treviso. The author would like to thank Philip Arestis, Duncan Cameron,

Anna Carabelli, Alvaro Cencini, Eugenia Correa, Paul Davidson, Meghnad Desai, Antony Endres, Korkut Erturk, Nicola Giocoli, Claude Gnos, Harald Hagemann, Omar Hamouda, Geoffrey Harcourt, Jochen Hartwig, John King, Bill Lucarelli, John Maloney, Antonella Picchio, Malcolm Sawyer, Hans-Michael Trautwein, and Domenica Tropeano for their comments. Research assistance by Dante Caprara and Szymon Klimaszewski is also gratefully acknowledged. The usual disclaimer applies.

NOTES

1. For example, Borio and Lowe (2002, p. 43) point out that '[o]ver the last two decades, banking crises have become more frequent and severe in both emerging market and industrial countries. Their cost in terms of output lost has been high, typically double digit percentages of GDP'.
2. The International Bank for Reconstruction and Development (2001, Ch. 3) points out, both theoretically and empirically, that the causal relationship between economic growth and income distribution is actually bi-directional.
3. As explained by Schumacher (1943, p. 150), the settlement of international transactions on real goods and services by way of clearing means that '[t]he importer in country *A* pays for the goods he buys from country *B* by handing over to the Clearing Authority in his own country a sum of *A*-money which is deemed to discharge his debt. The exporter in country *B* receives from the Clearing Authority in his country an equivalent sum of *B*-money which is deemed to satisfy his claim'. Hence multilateral clearing implies that each international transaction has to be finally settled in local currency within the countries concerned, and in an international monetary unit, say bancor, between them.
4. As another likely alternative, the country concerned might have to modify the exchange rate between its currency and the bancor. The bancor standard, to be sure, is not a system of irrevocably fixed exchange rates. Generally speaking, '[c]hanges in parities can take place when money wages and profit margins relative to productivity are permanently out of line, or when countries experience chronic difficulties in their balance of payments for other reasons' (Arestis and Sawyer, 1997, p. 363). The next section expands on this.
5. International hoarding would thus be mechanically impossible.
6. Two-way convertibility between any participating currency and the bancor through the proposed two-department bookkeeping system in the national central banks (see Table 10.2) amounts to free international capital flows. This contrasts with the one-way convertibility mechanism called for in the Davidson proposal (2002, p. 232), which permits each nation to control and regulate international capital flows, but which seems unrealistic in the current framework of full financial liberalization (see also Davidson, this volume). 'The so-called globalization of capital markets, meaning a combination of technical change and deregulation, has greatly increased both the volume and velocity of capital transfers around the world, and has made the textbook assumption [of perfect capital mobility] a much closer approximation to reality' (Smithin, 1999, p. 51). Smithin and Wolf (1999, p. 224) are indeed sceptical about the possibility of limiting international capital mobility in the present conditions, either via a 'Tobin tax' or other methods.
7. The possibility of modifying the exchange rate is necessary to correct it in case of non-attainment of the relevant target (defined with respect to external trade, real growth, inflation, or any other policy variable that the country's policy makers may target).

REFERENCES

Arestis, P. and M. Sawyer (1996), 'European monetary integration: a post Keynesian critique and some proposals', in P. Arestis (ed.), *Keynes, Money and the Open Economy: Essays in Honour of Paul Davidson*, Aldershot, UK and Brookfield, USA: Edward Elgar, vol. I, 144–64.

Arestis, P. and M. Sawyer (1997), 'Unemployment and the independent European system of central banks: prospects and some alternative arrangements', *American Journal of Economics and Sociology*, **56** (3), 353–67.

Bank for International Settlements (2004), *74th Annual Report*, Basle: Bank for International Settlements, June.

Begg, D., B. Eichengreen, L. Halpern, J. von Hagen and C. Wyplosz (2003), 'Sustainable regimes of capital movements in accession countries', *Centre for Economic Policy Research Policy Paper*, no. 10.

Borio, C. and P. Lowe (2002), 'Assessing the risk of banking crises', *Bank for International Settlements Quarterly Review*, December, 43–54.

Committee on Payment and Settlement Systems (2003), *Payment and Settlement Systems in Selected Countries*, Basle: Bank for International Settlements.

Davidson, P. (2002), *Financial Markets, Money and the Real World*, Cheltenham, UK and Northampton, MA, USA: Edward Elgar.

International Bank for Reconstruction and Development (2001), *World Development Report 2000/2001: Attacking Poverty*, Washington, DC: International Bank for Reconstruction and Development.

International Monetary Fund (1998), *World Economic Outlook*, Washington, DC: International Monetary Fund.

Kalecki, M. and E.F. Schumacher (1943), 'International clearing and long-term lending', *Bulletin of the Oxford University Institute of Statistics*, **5** (supplement), 29–33.

Kenen, P.B. and E.E. Meade (2003), 'EU accession and the euro: close together or far apart?', *Institute for International Economics Policy Brief*, no. 03–9.

Keynes, J.M. (1980), *The Collected Writings of John Maynard Keynes* (vol. XXV *Activities 1940–1944. Shaping the Post-War World: The Clearing Union*), London and Basingstoke: Macmillan.

Quah, D. (1996), 'Twin peaks: growth and convergence in models of distribution dynamics', *Economic Journal*, **106** (437), 1045–55.

Quah, D. (1997), 'Empirics for growth and distribution: stratification, polarization, and convergence clubs', *Journal of Economic Growth*, **2** (1), 27–59.

Rochon, L.-P. and S. Rossi (2004), 'Central banking in the monetary circuit', in M. Lavoie and M. Seccareccia (eds), *Central Banking in the Modern World: Alternative Perspectives*, Cheltenham, UK and Northampton, MA, USA: Edward Elgar, 144–63.

Rossi, S. (2003), 'Monetary union and monetary policy in an enlarging EU', in P. Gugler and R. Ratti (eds), *L'espace économique mondial et régional en mutation*, Zurich: Schulthess, 409–28.

Rossi, S. (2004), 'Monetary integration strategies and perspectives of new EU countries', *International Review of Applied Economics*, **18** (4), 443–69.

Rossi, S. (2005), 'The Bretton Woods institutions sixty years later: a "glocal" reform proposal', in P. Arestis, J. Ferreiro and F. Serrano (eds), *Financial Developments in National and International Markets*, Basingstoke: Palgrave Macmillan, 56–76.

Rowley, R. and O.F. Hamouda (1989), 'Disturbance in the world economy', in O.F. Hamouda, R. Rowley and B.M. Wolf (eds), *The Future of the International Monetary System: Change, Coordination or Instability?*, Aldershot, UK and Brookfield, USA: Edward Elgar, 1–3.

Schmitt, B. (1973), *New Proposals for World Monetary Reform*, Albeuve: Castella.

Schumacher, E.F. (1943), 'Multilateral clearing', *Economica*, **10** (38), 150–65.

Smithin, J. (1999), 'Money and national sovereignty in the global economy', *Eastern Economic Journal*, **25** (1), 49–61.

Smithin, J. and B.M. Wolf (1993), 'What would be a "Keynesian" approach to currency and exchange rate issues?', *Review of Political Economy*, **5** (3), 365–83.

Smithin, J. and B.M. Wolf (1999), 'A world central bank?', in J. Michie and J. Grieve Smith (eds), *Global Instability: The Political Economy of World Economic Governance*, London and New York: Routledge, 212–26.

Stamp, M. (1963), 'The Stamp plan – 1962 version', in H.G. Grubel (ed.), *World Monetary Reform: Plans and Issues*, Stanford and London: Stanford University Press and Oxford University Press, 80–9.

Svedberg, P. (2001), 'Income distribution across countries: how is it measured and what do the results show?', *Institute for International Economic Studies Seminar Paper*, no. 698.

Weller, C.E., R.E. Scott and A.S. Hersh (2001), 'The unremarkable record of liberalized trade: after 20 years of global economic deregulation, poverty and inequality are as pervasive as ever', *Economic Policy Institute Briefing Paper*, October.

11. To Fix or to Float: Theoretical and Pragmatic Considerations

L. Randall Wray

INTRODUCTION

This chapter will begin by contrasting the orthodox view of 'money' – both at the national and at the international levels – with the heterodox, post-Keynesian conception of money. In the orthodox view, money is primarily a medium of exchange that facilitates the circulation of goods either domestically or internationally. Accordingly, monetary policy should be concerned primarily with maintaining domestic and international values of money with respect to goods and services. Hence, policy ought to minimize inflation (as normally defined). We next examine the post-Keynesian view of money, according to which money is first and foremost a unit of account. This helps to clarify the nature of various manifestations of money: credit money, commodity money, and reserve (or 'fiat', or 'state', or 'high-powered' – HPM) money. We can then move to an informed understanding of the functioning of the modern international financial system. Finally, this chapter will examine alternative proposals for reformation of the international financial system: a fixed (but adjustable) exchange rate regime along the lines of Keynes's famous bancor proposal versus a floating rate system.

THE ORTHODOX VIEW OF DOMESTIC AND INTERNATIONAL MONEY

The orthodox story begins with a barter economy, which discovers that money can be used to lubricate the market mechanism. While the first monies are sea shells, huge stone 'wheels', or even wives, it is eventually discovered that precious metals serve as better media of exchange (owing to their relative scarcity and physical characteristics – portability, easily divisible, high value relative to carrying cost). Transactions costs are further reduced when the goldsmith accepts deposits of gold, discovering the 'deposit expansion process' as he issues paper money backed by gold reserves, the quantity of which closely governs the amount of paper money issued, ensuring redeemability. Eventually, government fiat money becomes the reserve held by banks against deposits, with the quantity of privately issued money determined by HPM reserves. Since the central bank determines the quantity of reserves, it controls the money supply. If it supplies too many reserves, the money supply increases too fast, causing inflation. Thus, according to orthodoxy, monetary policy should control reserves in order to control inflation: the primary domestic responsibility of the central bank is to stabilize domestic prices. Of course, in recent years doubts have grown about the ability of the central bank to target reserves or the money supply (owing, apparently, to financial innovations that make 'money demand' unpredictable). Hence, the overnight interest rate is the tool used to tighten or loosen monetary policy in order to achieve price stability.

The orthodox view of international money is similarly based on the barter paradigm. As Hahn (1991, p. 1) argues, '[t]he pure theory of International Trade pays no regard to financial matters and deals with non-mediated exchange of regions'. In a simple, moneyless, model, the addition of 'foreign countries' does not complicate the analysis; each country is treated as an optimizing agent such that an equilibrium vector of relative prices emerges from barter. If production is added, countries specialize according to the Ricardian Law of comparative advantage, with each taking advantage of its unique national environment (Davidson, 1992, p. 116). *Tâtonnement* generates an equilibrium vector of relative prices in accordance with technologies and tastes. All trades are executed at an instant of logical time, as each purchase of a time-dated commodity by country A is offset by a time-dated commodity sale by country A. A trade deficit is impossible, as '[e]ach region is at all times taken to be in Walrasian equilibrium' (Hahn, 1991, p. 1).

Things become more complicated once we allow for the use of money as a medium of exchange, because we must specify whether our international economy operates with a unified money system (UMS) or with a non-unified money system (NUMS) (Davidson, 1992). A unified money system is one in which all nations either use the same monetary unit, or one in which different monetary units are used but exchange rates are stable. (It is not necessary for the exchange rates to be fixed, but only that their movements are perfectly foreseen.) A non-unified money system is one in which a number of monetary units are used with exchange rates that are not necessarily expected to be stable. A trade deficit is now possible: country A can import more commodities than it exports, leading to an outflow of the currency of A. However, assuming that currency A will not be accepted as legal tender in country B, then the agents of B will hold A's currency only on the expectation that it will be used later to buy the exports of A. Alternatively, the currency of A will have to be converted into the currency of B; this might be accomplished by profit-seeking agents specializing in currency exchange (who charge a small fee for the service). These currency 'converters' would have to keep reserves of a variety of currencies in order to accomplish conversions for a variety of trading partners; these 'capital' reserves would have to earn a normal return obtained through the fees. In general equilibrium theory, a gold standard is often assumed. Gold can operate as the single reserve, reducing the required reserves of the currency converters, resulting in efficiency gains. Alternatively, the currency of the dominant economy could be used as an international reserve, again reducing transactions costs.

As Hahn (1991, p. 1) argues, addition of (UMS) money under a gold standard to general equilibrium theory leads to 'no changes in the "real" equilibrium conditions, that is, the equilibrium terms of trade'. Just as money is neutral in the domestic economy, it is neutral in the international economy. The specie-flow mechanism is supposed to quickly rectify a trade imbalance through price level adjustments. No country could maintain a trade deficit indefinitely, for the simple reason that it would eventually run out of gold reserves. Before this point is reached, the country would have to depreciate its currency, making imports more expensive and exports cheaper.

Given these considerations, many neoclassical economists call specifically for fixed exchange rates. Some, like Jude Wanniski (and Alan Greenspan, although he has been silent on this issue since becoming head of the Fed) would like to return to the gold standard. On the other hand, Milton Friedman argues that while a rigorously applied gold standard would be preferable, the problem is that history shows that nations 'cheat', setting off competitive devaluations as they try to gain trade advantages. Hence, he prefers a system of floating exchange rates (Davidson's NUMS), and, indeed, argued that floating rates would push countries toward balanced trade. Furthermore, according to Hahn (1991, p. 6), a 'variable exchange rate is an ideal (although imperfect) substitute' to perfectly flexible domestic prices. For example, assume that wages and prices are rigid in an economy experiencing a negative productivity shock. If exchange rates are fixed, this economy can adjust to the shock only by lowering employment and real income; if exchange rates are flexible, however, adjustment is made through depreciation that lowers domestic prices relative to foreign prices. Thus, the flexible exchange rate regime allows adjustment to shocks without adverse employment effects, even if domestic prices are not flexible. In this sense, flexible exchange rates are seen as a substitute for flexible domestic prices, and thus increase flexibility of a market economy to speed adjustment to equilibrium. While a flexible exchange rate system generates uncertainty about the exchange rate, Hahn argues this replaces 'uncertainty' over employment levels – because the fixed exchange rate system would use unemployment as the method for adapting to rigid wages. He thus argues that a flexible exchange rate system is preferred over a fixed exchange rate system in the 'real world' where wages are not perfectly flexible.

Finally, other neoclassical economists (and at least one post-Keynesian, Moore (2004), who favours a 'bottom-up' creation of 'dollarized' and 'euroized' zones) have followed Mundell (1961) in advocating 'optimal currency areas' (OCAs) as a better alternative. This essentially combines the advantages of fixed exchange rates in promoting certainty within OCAs, while allowing flexible exchange rates across OCAs. Briefly, Mundell had recognized that if money developed primarily as a medium of exchange, then there is no reason to suppose that the optimal region within which a particular currency ought to be adopted should coincide with nation states. Instead, an optimal region should be defined as one within which labour is mobile. He provided an example in which the eastern United States and eastern Canada formed an 'optimal' region, with highly mobile labour and similar production characteristics, while the western United States and western Canada formed another 'optimal' region with production based on natural resource exploitation. In this case, it is not optimal to have a US dollar and a Canadian dollar; rather, there should be an eastern dollar and a western dollar. When applied to Europe, it could be argued that the individual nation states within Europe did not represent optimal currency areas but rather had issued currencies based on arbitrary political boundaries. Hence, formation of the European Monetary Union (EMU) based on the euro could be promoted as an application of Mundell's OCA theory. Certainly, not all orthodox theorists would agree that the EMU is the appropriate OCA. However, what is important for our purposes is the belief that it is not necessary to link a currency with a nation state (Goodhart, 1998). In a similar vein, many orthodox economists (as well as Moore (2004)) have applauded the creation of currency boards in (mainly) less developed countries, on the argument that abandonment of monetary sovereignty by explicitly tying a nation's (weak) currency to another nation's (strong) currency helps to discipline profligate governments. Rather than adopting fixed exchange rates across the entire world, the globe would be divided among a small number of huge trading blocks, with each adopting a strong currency (the dollar for the Americas, the euro for Europe, the yen for Asia) that would fluctuate relative to the small number of other strong currencies. So long as labour is mobile within each OCA, full employment would be ensured, with flexible exchange rates between OCAs balancing trade across regions (where labour would not be mobile).

In sum, orthodox economists variously accept an international gold standard in which the specie-flow mechanism leads to movement toward trade balance, or a flexible exchange rate system in which fluctuating values of currencies rectify trade imbalances, or Mundell's OCA approach that combines the two. In any case, the focus is on real variables, with money mostly lubricating the market system. Money is neutral (at least in the long run), and freely flexible prices (including the 'price' of the domestic currency in terms of foreign currencies) lead to a general equilibrium. Domestic policy is reduced to maintaining price stability to avoid (temporary) deviations from equilibrium that could be caused by unanticipated nominal price movements. International policy either pegs the currency (to gold, or to a dominant currency) or floats it. These conclusions follow on from two key hypotheses: a) there is no critical link between nation states and a currency; and b) money is mostly about market exchange.

A POST-KEYNESIAN VIEW OF MONEY

As discussed, the orthodox view of money (whether national or international) begins with barter into which money lubricating trade as a medium of exchange is injected. While it is true that all orthodox economists would also admit a role for money as a store of value, as Keynes remarked, only a lunatic would hold money for such purposes in the neoclassical world, because uncertainty of the Keynesian variety is ruled out by neoclassical assumptions. Hence, post-Keynesians have long insisted on the importance of the store of value and unit of account functions of money in an uncertain world. Further, some have revived the 'state money' approach of Knapp (1924) (favourably reviewed by Keynes) and the 'functional finance' approach of Lerner (Wray, 1998, 2004; Goodhart, 1998). This leads to an additional important consideration of the role played by money: to move resources to the state sector. If this is the case, then there is an important connection between 'currencies' and nation states that must be taken into account when considering the international financial system.

According to what has been called the 'neo-chartalist' view, based on the state money approach, the money of account could not have originated in the hypothesized transaction-cost minimizing search by individual utility-maximizing barterers. Rather, the money of account was socially created to measure obligations. We need not repeat a detailed history here (see Wray, 2004, for several accounts), as it is sufficient to summarize the main argument. The money of account evolved as the unit in which payments would be made to an authority (fees, fines, tithes, tribute, and eventually taxes). The authority would impose an obligation in a unit of account, and then identify what could be delivered in payment. On this view, prices did not spring from barter, but rather were imposed by the authority. At some stage, the authority recognized that it could issue 'money things' denominated in the money of account to 'buy' the goods and services required. Markets would then develop, at the prices set by the authority in the 'state money' of account. Hence, the revised sequence runs from a unit of account to a medium of exchange, and from (tax) obligations and established prices to markets. Private credits and debits and private 'money things' follow on from this logic. A 'functional finance' approach to fiscal policy is indicated, because the state issues money to purchase what it needs, while the citizenry uses state (high-powered) money things to meet tax obligations. Hence, taxes do not really 'pay for' state spending, which means there is no necessary relation between state expenditures and tax receipts. Nor, as we briefly describe below, does a state need to 'borrow' its own money in order to 'deficit spend'.

Following Keynes, many post-Keynesians view the capitalist economy as something more than market-based exchange, but rather as a 'monetary production economy' (Wray, 1990). In a monetary economy of production, production occurs not to satisfy 'needs', but to satisfy the desire to accumulate wealth in money form. Unlike production in, say, a tribal society, capitalist production always involves money. The capitalist must hire workers to produce the goods that will be sold on markets. As production takes time, the capitalist must pay wages now, before sales receipts are realized. There is thus a logical sequence: spend money now on the expectation of receiving more money later. Often this involves 'borrowing' by the firm: the issue of liabilities to obtain (more liquid) bank liabilities that can be used to pay wages. Because the future is uncertain, sales receipts are uncertain. This means that interest must be paid on the firm's liabilities and that capitalist production is only undertaken on the expectation of making profits. Thus, capitalist production always involves 'money now, for more money later'. Since forward money contracts include interest, and because such contracts are of the nature of 'money now for more money later', this means that monetary contracts will grow over time at a rate determined in part by the rate of interest (see Wray, 1993). This generates a logic of accumulation: all monetary economies must grow. If they do not, accumulation falters and nominal contracts cannot be met. The logic of monetary production, then, requires nominal economic growth. It cannot be constrained by a fixed money supply, nor by a commodity money whose quantity expands only upon new discoveries. This means that private money supply is determined in the private contracts between debtors and creditors. This leads directly to what is called the endogenous money approach: money must be endogenous in a monetary economy of production, with its quantity determined in debt contracts denominated in money terms (or in the unit of account). The same principles hold regardless of the money unit of account chosen (whether it is the dollar or the yen), and regardless of the medium of exchange used (bank notes or bank deposits), which would be denominated in the money of account.

In order to enhance the ability of privately created money to circulate, money-denominated IOUs would be 'accepted' by trustworthy individuals or institutions, through an endorsement that guaranteed the IOU. In ancient times, this role was played by the temples, but later, a wide variety of institutions and individuals could perform the role, ranging from governments to merchants, to respected and usually wealthy individuals, and to banks. Clearly, not all liabilities that serve to fulfil certain functions associated with 'money' fulfil all functions. Some serve as general media of exchange; others serve as means of payment only for those lower in the debt pyramid. Over time, there has been a continual narrowing of the types of liabilities that will circulate, to those in the highest reaches of the pyramid. Thus, the financial system has evolved from one in which a wide variety of types of liabilities circulated to one in which HPM and the liabilities of banks comprise the vast majority of the circulating 'money supply'. Similarly, there has been a narrowing of the liabilities that are accepted as means of payment that discharge liabilities, although this narrowing has not been as pronounced as that for media of exchange.

The first central banks were created to provide government finance (more below on the relation between high-powered money and 'state finance'). In fact, the Bank of England was founded because the Crown could not borrow from private lenders to finance a war with France, as it had recently seized gold that had been deposited for safe-keeping, defaulting on its tallies. Thus, central banks were created to buy government debt as they issued their own notes. This development allowed the government to create fiat money without doing so directly: central bank notes could be denominated in pounds

– just as any private bank notes were denominated in pounds – and issued to 'finance' treasury spending. For a number of reasons, central banks gradually took a position at the apex of the pyramid of liabilities – with their liabilities sitting at or near the top of the pyramid, used for clearing. Most capitalist countries eventually developed mono-reserve systems, with the liabilities of the central bank acting as the reserve. Under the gold standard, the central bank liabilities would be made convertible into gold at the price established by the central bank. However, with the abandonment of the gold standard, the central bank liabilities served the purpose of ultimate (external) clearing without guaranteeing any convertibility. (Of course, private banks could also operate clearing systems – debiting and crediting reserves of banks and requiring the services of the central bank only for external, net, clearing – with the state, with banks outside the private clearing system, or in foreign currency.)

Meantime, European states (re-)discovered that imposition of a tax made payable in terms of the state's own liabilities would generate a demand for government 'fiat' money to be used in paying taxes. To be sure, there was a long history of issue by government of 'debt' (in Europe, largely in the form of wooden tallies) that would be accepted by government in payment of taxes. Indeed, it has been argued that this was always the true purpose of coins, which were issued by governments to 'soldiers and sailors' as a convenient means of paying taxes (Wray, 1998, 2004). Government-issued currency operated as the 'ultimate' means of payment and medium of exchange. At this point, the government could purchase merely by issuing its own liabilities, gladly accepted by the population as the means with which taxes could be paid. Perhaps because the implications were not fully recognized, states continued to maintain a sort of fiction – 'selling bonds' to the central bank, which then increased central bank liabilities (reserves and notes). (In modern America, it is even more convoluted as the Treasury first sells bonds to special types of banks that are permitted to buy them without having their reserves debited; this essentially amounts to the same thing as direct sales of bonds to the Fed.) While it would have been easier to dispense with the central bank, this might have made matters too transparent – the government can always obtain anything for sale in the domestic money of account merely by offering fiat money. Rather than providing finance for government spending, taxes simply ensure a demand for this fiat money. Indeed, according to at least some post-Keynesian histories of money, money originated as a means of moving resources to the 'government' (early temple and palace communities that evolved to monarchies) (see Wray, 1998, 2004). Hence, rather than seeing the state as a 'recent' interloper into the monetary system, the fundamental role of the state in creating and enforcing a unit of account is acknowledged.

Importantly, over the nineteenth century central banks gradually discovered that their position at the apex gave them the ability to function as lenders of last resort – historically, the second major function of central banking (a policy promulgated by Bagehot) (Wray, 1990). As they could essentially provide reserves without limit merely by discounting the assets of other banks, they could always stop a run. However, such behaviour required that the central bank abandon narrow self-interest, a development that took nearly two centuries after the establishment of the Bank of England to come to pass. This greatly increased the stability of the capitalist system, for it solves the primary problem of a commodity reserve system: the supply of reserves becomes elastic at precisely the moment that reserves are needed, maintaining orderly markets. But under a gold standard, even the central bank is ultimately limited by its gold reserves, so its ability to stop a crisis is limited. This is why countries invariably went off the gold standard whenever there was a crisis, and this is why a gold standard (or any other fixed exchange rate system with anything less than fully elastic supply of the reserve) is not consistent with stabilization of the capitalist economy. Abandoning the gold standard as well as fixed exchange rates was a major innovation, because it made the supply of reserves completely elastic.

In short, the current system, based on central bank reserves and flexible exchange rates, did not evolve out of a commodity money system that discovered a deposit multiplier. While a commodity reserve system with fixed exchange rates is possible, it is far more unstable than a central bank reserve system operating on a floating rate. Rather than attempting to constrain the central bank so that its liabilities are supplied as if we had a commodity money reserve system, it is far better to maintain the current accommodative reserve with flexible exchange rates. This requires a perfectly elastic supply of reserves that can guarantee parity of bank (and perhaps other) liabilities against HPM. This is effectively a domestically fixed exchange rate (UMS). As we shall see, some post-Keynesians argue that a similar arrangement is required for the international economy. In the absence of an international equivalent to a treasury and a central bank, however, fixed exchange rate systems internationally entail insurmountable costs for most nations.

IMPLICATIONS FOR THE INTERNATIONAL FINANCIAL SYSTEM

Some post-Keynesians argue that 'free' market determination of exchange rates in a 'freely' floating regime faces problems similar to those faced by domestic use of monies that do not trade at par. Speculative runs into/out of a currency can easily swamp flows of a currency arising from its medium of exchange function. For this reason, speculation can, at times, dominate over 'fundamentals' having to do with the current account balance. Free marketers had argued that flexible exchange rates would make adjustment to a balance on current account rapid, because a deficit nation would face loss of reserves and depreciation of the currency. In reality, many countries in Latin America as well as the United Kingdom and the United States have run persistent deficits after exchange rates became more flexible. Orthodox economists had also argued that flexible exchange rates would increase the independence of countries to pursue domestic monetary and fiscal policy. This was based on the belief that floating exchange rates could eliminate trade imbalances without necessitating domestic austerity programmes. In reality, austerity has been used as the major adjustment mechanism for most trade deficit nations (excluding the United States). Rather than allowing greater independence of nations to pursue policy, flexible exchange rates appear to have increased the synchronization of economic policies among countries.

For this reason, some post-Keynesians have returned to the 'Keynes plan' for reformation of the international financial system. Keynes called for the creation of an International Clearing Union (ICU) based on a bancor unit of account. The bancor in turn would be fixed in value relative to gold, and then all the currencies of all countries participating in the ICU would be fixed in value relative to the bancor. The bancor would be used only for clearing purposes among countries; countries could buy bancor balances from the ICU using gold, but bancor could not be redeemed for gold. In this way, bancor reserves could never leave the system, eliminating any possibility of a run on bancor. The initial quantity of bancor reserves would be allocated among countries based on their previous levels of imports and exports. Countries which then ran trade surpluses would accumulate further bancor reserves, while deficit countries would lose reserves. The ICU would provide overdraft facilities to those countries that exhausted their reserves. Since reserves could not leave the system, the ICU could always expand the supply of bancor reserves merely by making advances to deficit countries. In addition, surplus countries could use bancor reserves to make loans to, investments in, or unilateral grants to deficit countries. The ICU would adopt rules regarding sanctions to be placed on such debtors and on countries that ran persistent surpluses (thus, accumulated bancor reserves). Keynes called for a charge on excessive overdrafts and on excessive reserve balances of one or two percentage points in order to encourage balanced trade. Other possible actions to be taken in the case of deficit countries would include: currency devaluation, capital controls, seizure of gold reserves, and domestic policy 'which may appear to be appropriate to restore the equilibrium of its international balance' (Keynes, 1980, p. 462). Actions to be taken in the case of surplus countries include: measures to expand domestic demand, appreciation of the currency, reduction of tariffs and other trade barriers, and encouragement of international development loans (p. 463). Finally, the ICU could use its power to encourage economic development through the use of overdrafts for relief work, for development of buffer stocks of commodities to provide 'ever-normal granaries', for the establishment of an International Investment Corporation, and to help stabilize prices (p. 190).

Similarly, Davidson (1992) has proposed the use of an international clearing money unit (ICMU) as an international reserve used only by central banks in an international UMS. Each country would continue to use its unique money of account for domestic purposes; private agents could choose any of these monies of account for international purposes. Exchange rates among the international monies of account would be fixed (with allowance made for adjustments under specified conditions). Clearing among central banks would then take place on the books of an international central bank, kept in ICMUs. The ICMUs would be used only for clearing purposes among central banks. As in Keynes's scheme, sanctions would be placed on countries that continually faced clearing drains, and would also be placed on those countries that continually accumulated reserves of ICMUs. As Davidson (2002) explains, this allows creditor nations to share the burden of adjustment with deficit nations. This has three justifications: i) creditor nations can 'afford' to bear the costs of adjustment; ii) creditor nations may share the 'blame' for the deficits of others; iii) placing the full burden of adjustment on deficit countries contributes to worldwide stagnation, if it forces them to use austerity. Under the Keynes–Davidson scheme, the creditor nations will lose their ICMU reserves if they do not use them. These nations would then have an incentive to stimulate their economies so that the ICMU reserves would be used to support greater imports or greater foreign investment. Alternatively, excess ICMUs could be given as grants.

If the creation of the ICMU were accompanied by the creation of an international central bank, this institution would act as lender of last resort for deficit countries once they have lost their ICMU reserves. This intervention, however, would come with strings attached, comprised of a combination of rules and discretionary actions taken by the international central bank. Because the creditor nations would be similarly forced to rectify their balance sheet flows, adjustment by the deficit nations would not be so difficult – they would be trying to increase exports precisely when the creditors are trying to increase imports. Since the ICMU reserves could always be expanded without limit by the international central bank, this institution could always maintain fixed exchange rates among international units of account by purchasing the liabilities of the central bank of any nation facing pressure to depreciate. Essentially, the international central banker would operate with its ICMU at the very top of the debt pyramid.

The argument used by Keynes to promote his ICU seems to be based on a view of money as medium of exchange that is consistent with neither his unit of account approach to money, nor with his endorsement of the Knapp state money approach. He began by noting that his goal is to design an international currency system so that the currency exchange will be made to operate as if countries were 'trading goods against goods' (Keynes, 1980, p. 12). 'The principal object can be explained in a single sentence: to provide that money earned by selling goods to one country can be spent on purchasing the products of any other country' (p. 270). The operation of the ICU would be designed to ensure that bancor reserves would not be lost to idle hoards. Rather, the reserves of one country would form the basis of overdrafts of another. Keynes argued that his proposal would merely 'generalise the essential principle of banking as it is exhibited within any closed system' (p. 44). In Keynes's own words (1980, p. 177):

> This will substitute an expansionist tendency in place of a stagnationist tendency. In short, the analogy with a national banking system is complete. No depositor in a local bank suffers because the balances, which he leaves idle, are employed to finance the business of someone else. Just as the development of national banking systems served to offset a deflationary pressure which would have prevented otherwise the development of modern industry, so by extending the same principle into the international field we may hope to offset the contractionist pressure which might otherwise overwhelm in social disorder and disappointment the good hopes of our modern world. The substitution of a credit mechanism in place of hoarding would have repeated in the international field the same miracle, already performed in the domestic field, of turning a stone into bread.

This is because hoarded reserves lower world aggregate demand and employment. If instead reserves form the basis of loans, world demand and employment would be higher. Davidson's justification for his proposal is similar.

According to the perspective adopted above, however, there is a problem with Keynes's argument. An international monetary system cannot be designed as if trade were 'goods against goods'. The fundamental activity of any capitalist economy consists of position-taking in assets that are expected to generate gross money income. So long as foreign ownership of assets is permitted, the international monetary system must be designed with this in mind. To be sure, the goal of Keynes's ICU or Davidson's ICMU is not to limit trade to 'goods against goods', but to eliminate speculation against currencies that supposedly arises from floating exchange rates. In other words, the goal is to remove expected currency appreciation/depreciation as a component of the expected returns that foreign assets can deliver. Further, Keynes's banking analogy is confused. While he is correct in his assertion that prohibiting conversion of bancor to gold will eliminate the possibility of a run developing on bancor, his argument that the existence of the ICU ensures that bancor reserves will necessarily form the basis of loans is flawed. The Keynes–Davidson plan is not expansionist merely because reserves remain in the system, but because the supply of reserves can be elastic. The sanctions put on creditor nations are expansionist, because they might encourage surplus nations to stimulate their economies. So long as bancor reserves are elastic at the aggregate level, hoarding of reserves is really not a problem. If creditor nations can be encouraged to increase domestic demand for the output of deficit nations, or to employ labour in deficit nations in order to generate foreign investment, then Keynes's plan will indeed be expansionist. The form in which the creditor nation chooses to hold its wealth depends, of course, on the state of liquidity preference. The fixed exchange rate system is expected to lower the return to liquidity that will be required in order to raise the expected returns $(q - c + l + a)$ from capital investment sufficiently to stimulate world demand.

Keynes offered the bancor plan as a pragmatic policy proposal that would replace the gold standard. What we actually got was a fixed-but-adjustable exchange rate system based on a dollar–gold standard. This worked reasonably well at first, because the dollar was operated as an elastic international reserve, but it broke down precisely because of the link to gold when the United States floated to protect its reserves. Since the demise of the Bretton Woods system, most of the major nations have operated with 'dirty float' systems, while the developing world has mostly operated with highly unstable 'dirty fixed' exchange rate systems. To protect their pegged rates, developing countries have adopted modern mercantilist policies designed to allow accumulation of hard currency reserves. As Davidson (2002) describes accurately, this creates a deflationary bias; and Davidson offers the ICMU as an alternative to the stagnationist tendencies of the current system. However, while Keynes's bancor plan was offered as a pragmatic compromise, there is very little political will today to return to a fixed exchange rate system and certainly even less support for the creation of an international central bank – or even for an internationally coordinated fiscal policy. Hence, the Keynes–Davidson plan is highly unpragmatic.

Further, one of the lessons to be learned from crises in Asia and Latin America in recent years (Asian Tigers, Tequila crises, Argentina's currency board fiasco) is that 'go-it-alone' fixed exchange rate systems are disastrous except in a few special cases – those modern mercantilist nations that can accumulate overwhelming reserves of dollars. Further, nations that adopt pegs lose control of domestic fiscal and monetary policy so that mercantilism is the only policy response to domestic stagnation. Ironically, the pegs are often adopted on the argument that this will lower interest rates and increase access to 'international capital'. Sadly, nations that fix exchange rates on the belief that this will lower domestic interest rates only find that exchange rate uncertainty is transformed into default risk. The peg usually worsens trade balances, increasing trade deficits that threaten reserves. The nearly inevitable defaults then trigger exchange rate crises.

While it is true that exchange rates have become more unstable and that financial crises have become more frequent since 1973, it is possible that some post-Keynesians have laid too much blame on flexible exchange rate regimes for these outcomes. In a perceptive analysis, Kregel (2004) argued that the real problem is the transformation of developing country finances to Ponzi positions – something that can happen on either fixed or floating exchange rates. In the Bretton Woods era, developing countries with insufficient current account earnings to cover payment commitments and to keep exchange rates fixed had to rely on official lending by multilateral lenders (the International Monetary Fund or World Bank). These imposed a deflationary bias on the borrowing nations that effectively curtailed the propensity to move to deeply Ponzi positions. However, since the break-up of Bretton Woods and with the evolution to 'free' international capital markets, such nations are able to use private capital markets to cover payment commitments. Further, the movement to flexible exchange rates encouraged borrowing in foreign currencies to eliminate exchange rate risk. This promoted evolution from speculative to Ponzi positions, as foreign currency borrowing increased payment commitments without increasing foreign exchange earnings. Indeed, so long as interest rates on foreign currency denominated debt exceeds a country's growth rate (which is almost always the case), deterioration to Ponzi finance is virtually inevitable. Developing countries find themselves in a position in which the positive net lending by developed countries is accompanied by a negative current account balance in the developing country, meaning that the debt service on the accumulating stock of foreign-held debt must be covered by external borrowing (Kregel, 2004, p. 579). A debt crisis is virtually ensured, with the multilateral lenders intervening post-crisis to impose the 'Washington consensus' to salvage exchange rates. Hence, the problem is not simply one of flexible exchange rates, but rather one of private capital flows denominated in foreign currencies and resulting debt crises. While flexible exchange rates might play a secondary role in this phenomenon, the real problem is the free flow of private capital denominated in foreign currencies that allows creation of Ponzi positions that in turn lead to highly unstable exchange rate systems. A solution must look toward limits to developing country borrowing so that payment commitments are more closely tied to increased ability to pay resulting from development. Capital controls could be a part of the solution.

The most interesting application of a policy similar to Davidson's proposal is the EMU, in which member nations adopted fixed exchange rates against an ICMU, the euro. There is some elasticity of the supply of euro reserves, and there is limited redistribution of euro reserves among member nations. Further, sanctions are imposed on chronic 'abusers' – those that run budget deficits exceeding Maastricht norms – that are supposed to deflate. (Importantly, one of Davidson's key proposals – a penalty on surplus nations – is notably absent.) However, Euroland has, if anything, become even more aggressive in its beggar-thy-neighbour mercantilist stance, as the individual nations as well as Euroland as a whole see trade surpluses as the only real solution to domestic stagnationist pressures. Individual nations have completely ceded monetary policy to the European Central Bank, and many (especially the biggest economies) have little fiscal policy discretion because of budget deficits that already near or exceed Maastricht limits. There is some evidence that financial markets are beginning to price default risk into national borrowing rates, as they have come to recognize that adoption of the euro meant abandonment of currency sovereignty (Goodhart, 1998; Bell, 2003). To be sure, the EMU did not adopt all components of the Davidson plan, and we do not know how Euroland will evolve, but the experiment at this point appears highly risky.

Goodhart (1998) argues that the EMU was actually based on Mundell's optimal currency area approach. (Moore (2004) is a post-Keynesian who has explicitly advocated adoption of fixed exchange rates within trading blocks.) Again, the notion is that there should be no necessary correlation between use of a currency and national borders. Fiscal and monetary policy sovereignty is seen by Mundell (1961) as actually undesirable. (Moore (2004) argues that adoption of a strong currency will allow weak countries to borrow at the interest rates enjoyed by the issuer of the strong currency. This appears to discount transformation of currency risk to default risk.) In the modern context, the world would be divided among large trading blocks, with each adopting one of the major currencies – the euro, the dollar, and perhaps the yen. In this way, markets would discipline nations, ensuring that government policy would be subject to market forces as interest rates would be market-determined, and government spending would be limited to tax revenue plus the market's willingness to lend to government. In short, the EMU–OCA approach seems to be based on a medium of exchange–market view that is quite incomplete when applied to modern capitalist nations.

AN ALTERNATIVE VIEW AND PROPOSAL

There is an alternative to fixed exchange rate regimes, whether of the go-it-alone variety advocated by Mundell (1961) and Moore (2004), or of the politically infeasible bancor/ICMU type adopted by Keynes, Davidson, and many other post-Keynesians. The alternative is based on a synthesis of the endogenous money–exogenous interest rate approach adopted by almost all post-Keynesians, plus the state money–chartalist approach favoured by Keynes. This would allow currencies to float, taking advantage of the policy independence this provides to sovereign nations that adopt their own currencies. However, it is critical that sovereign nations avoid the temptation to directly (or indirectly) take on foreign currency-denominated debt. In this way, they avoid the Ponzi financing trap examined by Kregel (2004).

In modern economies, the banking system operates as an agent of the government, as almost all government payments and tax receipts flow through banks. In a floating rate regime, the government that issues the currency spends by crediting bank accounts. Tax payments result in debits to bank accounts, so deficit spending by government takes the form of net credits to bank accounts. Those receiving net payments from government hold banking system liabilities, while banks hold reserves in the form of central bank liabilities (we can ignore leakages from deposits – and reserves – into cash held by the non-bank public as a simple complication). Further, there are fairly complicated coordinating activities between the central bank and the treasury that essentially subvert prohibitions on central bank purchase of treasury debt – allowing, for example, private banks to buy bonds without a debit of reserves. We will leave these issues to the side, and simply proceed from the logical point that deficit spending by the treasury results in net credits to banking system reserves (see Wray, 1998; Bell and Wray, 2002–03; Bell, 2003).

If these net credits by the government lead to excess reserve positions, overnight interest rates will be bid down by banks offering the excess in the overnight interbank lending market. Unless the central bank is operating with a zero interest rate target, declining overnight rates trigger open market bond sales to drain excess reserves. Hence, on a day-to-day basis, the central bank intervenes to offset undesired impacts of fiscal policy on reserves that would cause the overnight rate to miss the target. The process operates in reverse when the treasury runs a surplus, which results in net debits of reserves from the banking system and puts upward pressure on overnight rates – relieved by open market purchases. If fiscal policy were biased to run deficits (or surpluses) on a sustained basis, the central bank would eventually run out of bonds to sell (or would accumulate too many bonds, offset on its balance sheet by a treasury deposit exceeding operating limits). Hence, policy is coordinated between the central bank and the treasury, to ensure that the treasury will begin to issue new securities as it runs deficits (or retire old issues in the case of a budget surplus). Again, these coordinating activities can be varied and complicated, but they are not important to our analysis here. Ultimately, a budget deficit that creates excess reserves leads to bond sales by the central bank (open market) and the treasury (new issues) to drain all excess reserves. A budget surplus causes the reverse to take place, when the banking system is short of reserves.

Bond sales (or purchases) by the treasury and central bank are, then, triggered by deviation of reserves from the position desired (or required) by the banking system, which causes the overnight rate to move away from target (if it is above zero). Bond sales by either the central bank or the treasury are really part of monetary policy designed to allow the central bank to hit its exogenous interest rate target 'administered' by the central bank. Obviously, the central bank sets its target as a result of its belief about the impact of this rate on a range of economic variables that are included in its policy objectives. In other words, setting this rate 'exogenously' does not imply that the central bank is oblivious to economic and political constraints it believes to reign (whether these constraints and relationships actually exist is a different matter).

This discussion applies only to nations in which the government issues a currency in a floating exchange rate system. A country that pegs its currency to a foreign currency or to precious metal operates differently, with constraints on both fiscal and monetary policy. If a government promises to redeem its currency for another, or for a precious metal, at a fixed rate, it must retain sufficient reserves of that currency or metal to meet all conceivable requests for conversion. This could require reserves equal to, or even greater than, the total stock of domestic HPM plus outstanding government bonds. Government budget deficits threaten the peg, unless a trade surplus can keep the foreign currencies, or precious metals, flowing into official reserves. In addition, interest rates become endogenous, in the sense that monetary policy must discourage redemption of domestic currency assets for foreign currency or precious metal. Further, a looser fiscal policy might have to be offset by a tighter monetary policy (higher rate target), unless the country enjoys a sufficient trade surplus. Hence, both fiscal and monetary policies become constrained. If private banks offer convertible accounts, they also must retain sufficient reserves to meet conversions. Note also that central bank policy will tighten in crisis, just as the Bank of England used to raise rates and call in loans whenever there was a run on private banks during the nineteenth century – and as the Fed did in the Great Depression. Accommodative behaviour of the central bank operating in a fixed exchange rate regime is dangerous, because it places the country's reserves of foreign currency or metal at risk.

Much of the 'conventional wisdom' about fiscal policy applies only in the case of a fixed exchange rate regime. In such a regime, rising deficits will increase interest rates, not simply because government borrowing 'competes' with private borrowing, but because the central bank will raise its target rate to protect reserves on a fixed exchange rate regime. The government faces an apparent 'government budget constraint': its spending is constrained by the sum of new debt issues, new money creation, and tax revenues. Taxes result in a currency drain that reduces leverage ratios on reserves of foreign currency or precious metal. While taxes do not really 'pay for' government spending, they loosen the reserve constraint on spending. Issues of bonds also drain currency, substituting an interest-earning government liability for non-earning reserves. At best, they simply push possible conversion of domestic currency to the reserve into the future. Hence, new issues will likely cause the central bank to raise interest rates to protect reserves. Finally, government spending financed by money emission increases leverage ratios on reserves; so it will likely cause the central bank to raise rates for reasons just discussed. Thus, there is a reason to focus on the 'constraint' that governments face on fixed exchange rate regimes, and reason to believe that deficits tend to raise interest rates (even if there is some discretion) and threaten the value of the currency. If the deficit causes exchange rates to depreciate, inflation would be a possible result. Thus government deficits are more or less correctly 'fought' by higher interest rates to protect reserves of foreign currency or metals, and to maintain stable currency values domestically and internationally.

By contrast, a sovereign government that issues a non-convertible currency on a floating exchange rate faces a much different situation. The 'government budget constraint' is nothing but an *ex post* identity that in no way constrains government spending. Government spends by crediting bank accounts. Taxes drain bank accounts; deficits mean net credits to accounts. Even in this case, one can think of these net credits to bank accounts as a 'leverage' of reserves. However, because the government does not promise to convert HPM reserves to foreign currencies or metals, it can always supply domestic currency reserves 'horizontally' on demand. Bonds are still issued to drain excess reserves, but the interest rate target is exogenously set, and this target rate need not be raised by the central bank in response to government deficits.

The floating rate provides a 'degree of freedom' within which domestic policy can operate. Because the interest rate is exogenous and because budget deficits do not threaten a peg, domestic policy is freer to pursue other goals such as full employment. To be sure, if exchange rates float, there can be exchange rate implications of setting a low domestic overnight rate, or of running budget deficits to stimulate the economy to lower unemployment rates. The government might also choose to keep labour markets slack, in the belief that this will keep exchange rates high (more below). However, with a fixed exchange rate regime, the imperative of operating policy to ensure exchange rate rigidity becomes overriding – the central bank simply cannot ignore forces that threaten the peg. Monetary policy must focus on the exchange rate, so that the interest rate target can be considered to be endogenous – determined by what is thought necessary to protect reserves of foreign currency and metals. A central bank operating in a floating exchange rate regime might choose to raise target rates in response to treasury deficits, and it might even believe that this policy protects the exchange rate, but this behaviour is not required in such a regime. The floating rate provides additional policy discretion that is not available in a fixed exchange rate system.

A floating rate with a sovereign currency and domestic policy independence may not be the best of all imaginable worlds. It is, however, a clearly superior choice for most countries in the absence of a thorough reform of the international monetary system along the Keynes–Davidson plan – a reform that appears to be politically infeasible. Unless a country has accumulated huge reserves of the international reserve currency, pegging exchange rates, adopting currency boards, or even joining monetary unions (without creation of a centralized fiscal authority for the monetary union that would approach the scope of the US Treasury) is far too costly in terms of constraints placed on domestic policy. Further, the loss of policy independence makes it highly likely that the country will not be able to hold the peg should market forces and speculators turn against it. In other words, for most countries, a pegged exchange rate is necessarily temporary – the peg will be abandoned when crisis hits.

Neither a world central bank nor an internationally coordinated fiscal policy is pragmatic. Fixed exchange rates without such international coordination implies loss of ability to use domestic fiscal and monetary policy. An alternative to the current stagnationist tendency is to float the currency but use domestic fiscal and monetary policy to achieve full employment with adequate economic growth. So long as the government of such a country pursues 'functional finance' as well as 'horizontalism' with 'exogenous interest rates', it can avoid evolution to Ponzi finance. This is for two reasons. First, it can control its interest 'borrowing' rate. Secondly, all of its commitments will be in its own sovereign currency.

CONCLUSION

Many post-Keynesians have offered a justification for fixed exchange rates. Unlike the neoclassical approach, in the post-Keynesian approach exchange rates are not merely seen as relative prices that emerge from trade, but as ratios of the units of account in which monetary contracts are written. Fixing these ratios as part of a comprehensive reformation of the international financial system would seem to apply at the international level the step taken in every developed country at the national level. In the domestic sphere, capitalist countries moved from non-par money to 'par money' based on gold reserves, and finally to 'par money' based on central bank 'fiat' reserves. In summary, establishing fixed exchange rates, a bancor or an ICMU, and an international central bank would appear to have the following benefits:

1. Expected appreciation/depreciation of a currency no longer plays a role in determining asset prices.
2. Use of forward contracts is encouraged because uncertainty over exchange rates is removed.
3. Speculation in currencies is eliminated.
4. The volume of reserves (of gold and foreign currencies) that must be held (for speculative and precautionary purposes) by national central banks and

private agents is reduced.
5. A method of dealing with trade imbalances is created that does not rely on austerity. This carries over to the international sphere practices that are frequently adopted domestically. (A nation normally does not force austerity onto a region that runs a trade deficit with the rest of the nation.)

The bancor or IMCU plan is believed to eliminate stagnationist tendencies in world economies, recognizing that capitalist economies require accumulation of money-denominated wealth. The problem is that trying to fix exchange rates in the absence of creation of international institutions that can perform the functions of a treasury and a central bank leads to a cure that is worse than the disease. Fixing an exchange rate eliminates an important degree of freedom for domestic monetary and fiscal policy. If there is an international institution that can fill the role, operating in the interest of the nation that fixes exchange rates, this may not be a problem. However, it is hard to imagine creation of such an institution – or of widespread willingness of nation states to submit to the authority of such an institution if it could be created. (Indeed, as post-Keynesians are frequent critics of central bankers, it is somewhat surprising that they are willing to submit control of domestic policy to an international central banker even more divorced from domestic – political-democratic – pressure.) This means that any nation that pegs its currency is effectively 'going it alone', surrendering a substantial degree of policy discretion to keep exchange rates fixed.

Except in unusual circumstances (in which a few countries are able to accumulate massive quantities of foreign exchange reserves), countries cannot actually peg exchange rates, because speculative pressures build to break the peg. Further, the conditions that allow accumulation of foreign exchange reserves – required for successful pegging of exchange rates – are exactly those that lead to stagnation pressures that both the bancor and ICMU plans are designed to relieve. Nations unable to accumulate such reserves will be forced to deflate their economies to protect their exchange rates. In practice, a very large part of the world is already trying to 'go it alone', pegging to major currencies. If the issuers of those international reserve currencies (and most importantly, the United States) joined the bandwagon in an effort to fix exchange rates, worldwide deflationary pressures would only be higher. Even if an international agreement to create a bancor or ICMU system headed by an international institution (operating in the interests of all members) is the best of all possible proposals, such appears to be exceedingly unlikely at present.

The best of the feasible alternatives is a floating exchange rate system with a sovereign-issued currency and independent fiscal and monetary policy. This allows a nation to exogenously set its overnight rate as desired, and to pursue fiscal policy directed toward achieving full employment. Any nation that does so can set interest rates at the level it desires, and can 'afford' full employment. The obstacle to be overcome is that most policy makers do not recognize the policy independence that a floating sovereign currency gives to them.

REFERENCES

Bell, S.A. (2003), 'Neglected costs of monetary union: the loss of sovereignty in the sphere of public policy', in S.A. Bell and E.J. Nell (eds), *The State, the Market and the Euro: Chartalism versus Metallism in the Theory of Money*, Cheltenham, UK and Northampton, MA, USA: Edward Elgar, 160–83.

Bell, S.A. and L.R. Wray (2002–03), 'Fiscal effects on reserves and the independence of the Fed', *Journal of Post Keynesian Economics*, **25** (2), 263–71.

Davidson, P. (1992), *International Money and the Real World*, London and New York: Macmillan and St. Martin's Press, second edition.

Davidson, P. (2002), *Financial Markets, Money and the Real World*, Cheltenham, UK and Northampton, MA, USA: Edward Elgar.

Goodhart, C.A.E. (1998), 'The two concepts of money: implications for the analysis of optimal currency areas', *European Journal of Political Economy*, **14** (3), 407–32.

Hahn, F. (1991), 'Policy seminar', Banca d'Italia, December, mimeo.

Keynes, J.M. (1980), *The Collected Writings of John Maynard Keynes* (vol. XXV *Activities 1940–1944. Shaping the Post-War World: The Clearing Union*), London and New York: Macmillan and Cambridge University Press.

Knapp, G.F. (1924), *The State Theory of Money*, abridged edition translated by H.M. Lucas and J. Bonar, London: Macmillan (first German edition 1905).

Kregel, J.A. (2004), 'Can we create a stable international financial environment that ensures net resource transfers to developing countries?', *Journal of Post Keynesian Economics*, **26** (4), 573–90.

Moore, B.J. (2004), 'A global currency for a global economy', *Journal of Post Keynesian Economics*, **26** (4), 631–53.

Mundell, R.A. (1961), 'A theory of optimum currency areas', *American Economic Review*, **51** (4), 657–65.

Wray, L.R. (1990), *Money and Credit in Capitalist Economies: The Endogenous Money Approach*, Aldershot, UK and Brookfield, MA, USA: Edward Elgar.

Wray, L.R. (1993), 'Money, interest rates, and monetarist policy: some more unpleasant monetarist arithmetic?', *Journal of Post Keynesian Economics*, **15** (4), 541–69.

Wray, L.R. (1998), *Understanding Modern Money: The Key to Full Employment and Price Stability*, Cheltenham, UK and Northampton, MA, USA: Edward Elgar.

Wray, L.R. (ed.) (2004), *Credit and State Theories of Money: The Contributions of A. Mitchell Innes*, Cheltenham, UK and Northampton, MA, USA: Edward Elgar.

12. Exchange Rate Arrangements and EU Enlargement

Jesper Jespersen

INTRODUCTION

The exchange rate has always been a highly sensitive political concern, because it is one of the country's windows abroad. In this sense, devaluations or depreciations are considered a defeat of economic policy and an erosion of national governments' credibility. Furthermore, when the exchange rate finally adjusts, the trading partners are, for good reasons, fearing that a 'beggar-your-neighbour' development will ensue. And even if a regime of fixed exchange rates is well designed, it may suffer in practice from a number of built-in weaknesses, which lead to these seemingly inevitable economic crises where high rates of interest and financial bankruptcies cause unemployment. The history of exchange rate arrangements is paved with such financial crises. The more recent and spectacular examples were the breakdowns of the European Monetary System in 1992–93, the South-East Asian crises in 1998, followed by the Russian, Brazilian, Turkish, and Argentinean crises. Indeed, the list seems endless.

One of the major conclusions of this chapter is that even within the European Union (EU), currency and financial crises remain a current threat. The economic performances of the 25 countries in the Union are dissonant, with balance-of-payments imbalances building up, rates of inflation rising, and unemployment rates diverging among member countries. Hence, in that perspective we will argue that it is difficult to imagine future financial crises being avoided, especially for the new EU member countries (EU-10) that are still in transition from a planned economic system to a full-scale market economy. An additional disturbing matter is that these countries are undertaking this transition under the severe Stability and Growth Pact (SGP), which forces all EU countries into a considerable fiscal and monetary straightjacket. Moreover, the ten new EU countries have been asked to make their macroeconomic development conform to the EMU convergence criterion of low inflation, and to prepare themselves for participation to the fixed exchange rate mechanism (ERM2), in which the euro is the anchor currency.

The overall objective of this chapter is to discuss the possible exchange rate regimes that the ten new EU countries (especially the former Eastern European countries) could choose for the future. Before moving on, however, we should keep in mind that these ten countries, except Poland, are all considered 'small and open economies' with respect to foreign trade. Even though the population of these countries reach 80 million citizens, their total GDP is only a little more than 5 per cent of the EU-15's total GDP. Moreover, the average income per capita in these countries is less than a third of the EU-15's. Hence, in terms of living standards and macroeconomic impact we are considering two separate worlds. If these two worlds should grow more equal, then the poorest countries could embark on an export-led growth path (as Ireland did in the early 1990s) without changing the economic development in the EU-15 in any significant way.

The structure of this chapter is as follows. The next section gives a brief overview of two distinct (and competing) macroeconomic theories: the new consensus economics (which is a merge of neoclassical and new-Keynesian equilibrium economics), and post-Keynesian macroeconomics.[1] In the third section we evaluate the different monetary and exchange rate arrangements and balance-of-payments constraints within the EU from a post-Keynesian point of view. In the fourth section we discuss how the exchange rate arrangements existing within the EU fit the overall growth strategy of the EU-10 countries. We conclude arguing that the new EU-10 countries should be allowed to follow an individually adapted exchange rate policy, which could mirror the differences among the countries and the fragile structures of the transitional economies.

TWO DIFFERENT VIEWS ON GROWTH, EMPLOYMENT, AND ECONOMIC POLICY

Although the political sensitivity towards unemployment within the EU (new as well as old member countries) has decreased, high unemployment is still a matter of concern. In this section we argue that, in countries with high unemployment, demand management and the exchange rate regime are important factors explaining the development of employment. Germany, as well as France, Poland, and Sweden are cases in point.

For instance, an unemployment rate close to 10 per cent is still a political liability in Germany in 2005. The government of Gerhard Schröder failed to improve on employment during its term in office. Of course, many reasons have been put forward for the disastrous employment record. Conventional neoclassical equilibrium theory is blaming inflexible and sclerotic labour market structures. Post-Keynesian theorists, on the other hand, put more emphasis on the lack of effective demand for labour in countries where unemployment is substantial.

New-Consensus Macroeconomics

Within the neoclassical/new-Keynesian (today the so-called new consensus) macroeconomics, sustained levels of high unemployment are caused by structural factors in the labour market and are hardly, if at all, affected by aggregate demand factors. This strand of thought argues that unemployment is due to a lack of real wage flexibility, which is caused by exaggerated labour protective legislation, generous unemployment benefits, trade unions, and incentive-reducing wage and income taxes (for a textbook presentation, see Sørensen and Whitta-Jacobsen, 2004).

Saint-Paul (2004) goes one step further, and combines the new consensus macroeconomic theory with political theory. He gives a revealing example of this 'changed ideology' (to use his own expression) within the so-called new consensus *political economy*. According to Saint-Paul (2004, p. 63), financial crises are necessary events that, by short-term hardship, prepare the public opinion for much needed labour market reforms. Hence, an external shock would rather have a (longer-term) beneficial effect by creating an increased *political* pressure for the, according to Saint-Paul (2004), *objectively* needed labour market flexibility and welfare reforms to improve employment.[2]

New consensus political economists would further argue that a sustained public sector deficit is further evidence of an excessive fiscal policy and of labour market rigidities. If the labour market was made sufficiently flexible, and if politicians were made responsible for matching public expenses with current income, the structural budget will be self-balancing. Hence, within this theoretical perspective, a sustained public deficit is a sign of unsound public finances and/or labour market rigidities. In both cases a fiscal crisis unveils the needed labour market reforms and fiscal consolidation. A balanced budget is a remedy (together with labour market reforms), and solves the fiscal crisis and reduces involuntary unemployment as well.

This new political and economic consensus is the official theoretical argument underpinning current EU strategies for growth and employment. Hence, unemployment cannot be addressed by macroeconomic policies, but is a matter of labour market organization, together with national structural programmes and welfare reforms. In this theoretical setting, unemployment has become a matter of national policies, where exchange rate arrangements are of a second-order concern.

Macroeconomic policies and exchange rate arrangements are mainly directed towards monetary stability. Price stability becomes the overarching macroeconomic goal. Hence, an inflation target-oriented monetary policy and irrevocably fixed exchange rates are considered suitable for this stability, which promotes the EU ambition of high economic growth.

Post-Keynesian Considerations

If we consider the German case, the new-consensus macroeconomics fails to explain the development in employment. In fact, the number of jobs *expanded* by nearly two million during the period 1998–2000 without any structural reforms.[3] This expansion was brought to a stop by the international downturn in 2001–03, when the German economy was hit by weak foreign (and domestic) demand. Then rising unemployment brought the German government's budget into conflict with the 3 per cent limit of the SGP, and the government was forced once again to tighten fiscal policy to avoid political and economic punishment from the other EU countries.

Furthermore, the employment prospects seemed to have deteriorated even in spite of the 2004–05 labour market reforms, which were mainly directed towards a reduction of social welfare for unemployed citizens. During the spring of 2005 the number of registered unemployed citizens breached the 5 million benchmark.

This development of expanding and contracting employment is fully consistent with post-Keynesian theory, where fluctuations in effective demand for goods and services are a main (but of course not the only) factor causing changes in growth rates and employment (see for instance Arestis and Sawyer, 2003).

In short, post-Keynesian macroeconomics stipulates that expanding effective demand is a necessary, but in many cases not a sufficient, factor to improve employment. Effective demand, it is argued, is affected by private sector behaviour toward consumption and real investment, economic policies and international competitiveness. In that theoretical perspective, the public, private, and foreign sectors are interrelated, and it is hardly meaningful to specify a target for the public sector budget independently of the development in the other two sectors.

With these fundamental theoretical divergences and political priorities in mind, we are better equipped to understand and to evaluate the challenges the EU-10 countries are confronted with when they have to choose a future strategy for their exchange rate arrangement within the EU.

MACROECONOMIC STABILITY AND EXCHANGE RATE ARRANGEMENTS IN A POST-KEYNESIAN PERSPECTIVE

In the post-Keynesian perspective, macroeconomic stability can be disrupted by a lack of effective demand. In this section we discuss how the balance of payments interferes with macroeconomic stability, and how the design of the exchange rate arrangement transmits effective demand through external relationships.

There are two major constraints on domestic growth emanating from the balance of payments: *a lack of foreign effective demand* (net exports and foreign direct investment), and *a lack of foreign reserves* (which holds back domestic expansion). These are explained in turn below.

The current account, together with the inflow of foreign direct investment, measures the foreign net effect on effective demand, which is crucial for growth and employment. By contrast, a purely domestic expansion may run into a lack of foreign reserves constraint as the current account deteriorates and foreign long-term capital inflows dry up.

The exchange rate is a macroeconomic price that has a major impact on international competitiveness. When one of the balance-of-payments constraints is binding, the exchange rate could be a useful instrument: in a freely floating exchange rate regime, the government has no formal exchange rate commitment. In this case, the 'lack of foreign reserves' constraint ceases to be binding, because the exchange rate is solely determined by the aggregate effect of private transactions in the current and capital accounts. Movements of the exchange rate have an impact on effective demand, as we mentioned above. Hence, the constraint of the foreign effective demand is also present in a floating exchange rate regime, and expected changes of the exchange rate play an important role as a borrowing cost on foreign loans.

Foreign Effective Demand Constraint

In the post-Keynesian perspective, effective demand for goods and services is given highest priority when dealing with growth and unemployment. Of course, there is no one-to-one relationship between balance-of-payments transactions and effective demand. Nonetheless, there will be a rather close link between the transactions recorded in the current account and effective demand. Exports of goods and services have an immediate effect on production and employment, whereas imports are a substitute for domestic production, which reduces effective demand at home (and increases it abroad). When analysing the impact of balance-of-payments transactions on effective demand, we should also add (at least a part of) foreign direct investments. Indeed, when such direct investments are made real, in the sense of setting up new factories, renovating old plants, or building houses, they increase effective demand like any other real investment, and should be analysed as such. On the other hand, foreign direct investments consisting of buying shares in existing firms, with no explicit purpose of making real investments, are more like financial portfolio investments and do not add to effective demand.

As long as countries have separate currencies, they should keep in mind Thirlwall's theory of balance-of-payments constrained growth (McCombie, 2003), because in that case the domestic growth process could at any time be hindered or impeded by a lack of foreign effective demand or by a lack of foreign exchange causing indeed a financial crisis. Hence, the exchange rate arrangement plays a crucial role for countries that are in a vulnerable process of catching up with more mature economies, such as the EU-10 in respect of the EU-15.

Foreign-Exchange-Reserves Constraint

The growth process may also be constrained by a lack of foreign liquidity, when the stock of foreign reserves is low. In that case, a financial crisis can occur if the deficit in the foreign exchange market is not reduced through credible economic policies. In this sense, the foreign exchange market can be disrupted by speculative short-term financial flows. Foreign exchange reserves are a protection against this source of disturbance. Keynes as well as post-Keynesian economists (Davidson, 1997) favour a ban on speculative international transactions, which more often than not put the international financial system under stress (see also Rochon and Vernengo, 2000). The foreign-exchange-reserves constraint can be handled in a more orderly way in a system without financial flows generated by currency speculation. Unfortunately, in practice it is difficult to separate serious long-term capital movements from speculative financial transactions. In fact, the EU Treaty requires free cross-border capital flows, and does not distinguish between sound and unsound financial capital movements.

The most important institutional change within international finance over the last two decades has been the elimination of border controls on financial capital movements within the OECD area. As a consequence, the citizens of the EU countries are free to borrow from any country abroad. Private banks and larger firms, therefore, cannot be liquidity constrained as long as they are able to pay the market rate of interest (and have the required creditworthiness). Those governments that have committed themselves to keep a fixed exchange rate, however, might become foreign-reserve constrained. Hence, in a fixed exchange rate regime there is always a risk that foreign reserves may be drained more quickly than the government is able to provide new and sufficient quantities of them. Paradoxically, free capital movements imply that governments have to stock an even larger foreign-exchange reserve than within a system where capital controls prevail.

Fixed Exchange Rate Regimes

In a fixed exchange rate regime without international capital controls, the central bank has to sell or buy whatever amount of foreign exchange the private sector requires. The central bank needs to have sufficient foreign reserves (and credit lines) to satisfy existing demand. Substantial capital outflows reduce the privately held amount of central bank money (M0), which then puts some upward pressure on money market interest rates. If the day-to-day rate of interest goes beyond, say, 100 per cent (per annum), the politicians (and with them the public opinion) are prepared for a substantial devaluation of the exchange rate.

A fixed exchange rate regime is biased against the deficit country, because the surplus countries can just leave the rate of interest at a level that best fits their domestic economy. When the central bank of the deficit country experiences a foreign-reserves constraint, something has to give in. On the other hand, there is no mechanism, except for international political pressure, that can prevent a central bank of a surplus country from going on accumulating foreign reserves. In fact, a 'strong currency' is an undervalued currency, which generates a substantial surplus in the current account. A strong currency position leaves more room for directing monetary and fiscal policies towards addressing domestic imbalances.

On the other hand, foreign reserves are somewhat costly to accumulate, because the central bank will only obtain a yield on its reserves equal to the interest rate on the anchor currency. Hence, any country – except for the anchor-currency country – that takes part in a fixed exchange rate system has to pay a participation fee, which amounts to the difference between the domestic and the foreign rate of interest times the average size of the foreign reserves. One could also call it a 'currency discount'. The mechanism is the following: the larger the accumulated deficits of the current account (with a negative effect on effective demand), the larger the spread between the domestic and the foreign interest rate. As mentioned above, an *under*valued currency means in practice a *strong* currency with a smaller interest premium. Countries with the largest surplus on the current account of the balance of payments (together with a reliable political system) have the lowest interest rate spread, which, in case of a substantial surplus, might even become negative.

The reason behind international capital controls in the years following the Second World War was to give countries participating in the Bretton Woods system the ability to pursue a more independent monetary policy.[4] This was, of course, of primary interest to those countries that were constrained by effective demand but had sufficient foreign exchange reserves. During the 1960s, it became increasingly difficult to prevent the private sector from circumventing international capital regulations. Hence, the beneficial effects of capital controls were undermined, and participation in a fixed exchange rate regime required an increasingly larger stock of foreign exchange reserves.

Floating Exchange Rate Regimes

Within a floating exchange rate regime, the central bank has no obligation to peg the exchange rate. The foreign payments undertaken by the private sector have to add up to zero. The exchange rate will adjust in such a way that realized demand and supply of foreign exchange equalize.

A floating exchange rate regime removes the foreign reserve constraint on macroeconomic policy. Hence, monetary policy can be directed also towards addressing domestic imbalances.

Without international capital controls, purely financial transactions dominate the foreign exchange market and the exchange rate. Unfortunately, however, financial markets need an anchor so they do not go astray; but within a floating exchange rate regime there is no such anchor. Misguided expectations can make the exchange rate be adrift for years, which might then harm the foreign competing sectors considerably (see for instance Harvey, 1999).

If governments want to pursue a stabilization (full-employment) policy, then a domestic-oriented demand management policy may countervail the disturbances to effective demand caused by an over- or undervalued exchange rate within a floating exchange rate regime. In fact, recent research has shown that pre-announced exchange rate targets defined with reference to macroeconomic fundamentals, that is, a purchasing power index, may have a stabilizing effect in a world of imperfect knowledge (Frydman and Goldberg, 2004). In that case, the central bank has to intervene in the foreign exchange market, not in order to defend a specific exchange rate, but rather to market a signalling effect that might give to market participants a kind of guidance with regard to fundamentals. The development of the euro–dollar exchange rate is an illustrative example, where limited interventions could have had an effect without the European Central Bank risking being foreign-reserves constrained.

Another more structural-oriented aspect related to a floating exchange rate regime is price stability. Economies in transition may need an external anchor for the domestic process of inflation. Speedy and far-reaching structural changes within the real economy might fuel an internal process of inflation, which needs some brakes. Depending on the transmission mechanism a floating exchange rate will reduce the impact of this external brake. As a consequence monetary policy in a floating exchange rate system, following the advice of the new-consensus theory, is directed towards a specific inflation target. But, in practice, the impact of monetary policy on price developments is uncertain. It has to pass through the formation of expectations in a world of imperfect knowledge. This is not the place to discuss inflation theory in a post-Keynesian perspective. One could only note that the balance of powers in the labour market, the welfare systems, and the level of unemployment are equally important factors (see Arestis, 1992).

Summing Up

There is no simple theoretical conclusion with regard to making a robust design of the exchange rate arrangement with reference to the EU-10 countries. In this section we identified four different systems, which are presented in Table 12.1. The right choice depends on the priorities of the overall macroeconomic stability, and even more importantly on the economic theory lying behind the evaluation. Furthermore, the best design depends on what kind of shocks are the most likely: internal or external; real or nominal.

Taking into consideration that the EU-10 countries are small economies, shocks are mainly expected to be caused by internal factors. (External shocks are expected to be rather symmetric and handled at the EU level.)

Table 12.1. Different exchange rate arrangements

	Macroeconomic target	
	Employment (demand management)	Inflation (foreign anchor)
Floating exchange rate	++	–
Fixed, but adjustable exchange rate[a]	+++	+
Fixed exchange rate (ERM2)	+	++
Monetary union[b]	–	+++

Notes: the number of + indicates the ability of the exchange rate arrangement to cope with internal real (employment) or nominal (inflation) shocks; [a]adjustable with regard to securing a sustainable surplus in the current account; [b]with binding requirements on national fiscal policy.

One can sum up the arguments concerning macroeconomic stability in the following way. Employment is affected by effective demand (and structural policies). If effective demand is constrained, real stability is at risk. In addition, the internal process of inflation is difficult to manage through macroeconomic policies: it is often a consequence of structural imbalances and uncoordinated struggles over income shares running out of control. A fixed exchange rate regime may give a nominal guideline on price formation, but no guarantee that inflation is at bay.

Hence, in transition economies, a floating exchange rate arrangement may remove the 'foreign-reserve constraint', but at a price of forsaking the inflation anchor. Conversely, a fixed exchange rate arrangement *à la* ERM2 introduces a kind of nominal anchor, but leaves the country vulnerable to effective demand shocks.

A well-designed (that is, fixed but adjustable) exchange rate regime could support full-employment policies, especially if adjustments were coordinated at a regional level to prevent beggar-your-neighbour policies. In that case capital control is not really an issue, because it does not make sense to speculate against a 'healthy' currency. By way of contrast, a badly-designed fixed exchange rate arrangement causes real uncertainty, which, furthermore, can be reinforced by waves of speculative financial flows (see Davidson, 2002b).

A monetary union removes the foreign-reserve constraint definitively and provides a nominal anchor (defined by the average rate of inflation) for the participating countries, but leaves especially small and open economies vulnerable to effective demand shocks and fiscal crises if they are out of tune with the major countries.

DO THE EU-10 COUNTRIES FIT THE EUROPEAN MONETARY UNION?

This section evaluates the likely impact of the EU-10 countries embarking on the route to the EMU. Before we go into a more detailed analysis, from Table 12.2 it is obvious that there is a dividing line between the six smallest countries[5] (Cyprus, Estonia, Latvia, Lithuania, Malta, and Slovenia) and the somewhat larger countries (the Czech Republic, Hungary, Poland, and Slovakia) of the EU-10.

Table 12.2. Exchange rate arrangements of the EU-10 countries as of May 2005

Joined ERM2 in June 2004

    Estonia (unilaterally decided to maintain a currency board)
    Lithuania (unilaterally decided to maintain a currency board)
    Slovenia

Joined ERM2 in May 2005

    Cyprus
    Latvia (unilaterally reduced fluctuation band to ±1 per cent)
    Malta

Floating exchange rate arrangements

    Czech Republic
    Hungary
    Poland
    Slovakia

The smaller countries seem to have a politically-defined goal of joining the EMU as quickly as possible, leaving the real macroeconomic considerations aside, whereas the larger countries have taken a more contemplative attitude, before they lock their currency up in the formal ERM2 arrangement.

According to the EU Treaty, new member countries are committed to pursue an economic policy that makes them qualified to a membership of the EMU without any unduly delays. The convergence criteria of the EMU consist of requirements related to low inflation, low rates of interest, a public budget deficit not exceeding 3 per cent of GDP, a public debt below 60 per cent of GDP, and participation in the ERM2 for at least two years without tensions within the band defined as ±15 per cent around the central exchange rate against the euro.

Why a European Monetary Union?

The EU had (and still has) the ambition of being an economic (and political) heavy weight on the world stage that could match the two – at that time – superpowers: the United States and the Soviet Union. For that purpose, a single European currency was considered important. Furthermore, it was argued that the economic counterpart of 'one Europe' would be 'one money', which could reduce the costs of cross-border transactions (in goods, services, tourism) and increase transparency and competition.

On the other hand, obtaining macroeconomic benefits from the use of a single currency is less obvious. In that case, participating countries have to be economically well integrated and quite similar with respect to their vulnerability to internal and external shocks (as suggested by the theory of 'optimal currency areas', OCAs; see De Grauwe, 2005, for a textbook presentation of the costs and benefits of OCAs).

Plans for such a monetary union were put forward as far back as 1969 – the so-called Werner Plan. But it was not before the late 1980s that an elaborate and realistic plan leading to a European Monetary Union was designed. At that time, the overarching goal was political unification. For that purpose, a single currency was seen as a useful instrument. To give the euro a status of a strong international currency, it was considered necessary to keep inflation low in all participating countries. The design of the EMU was directed towards this goal by strengthening the nominal anchor. The main instrument was an independent central bank only responsible for price stability, and narrowly defined strings on the fiscal policy conducted by the member countries.

The deliberate political intention (and a requirement by the German government before giving up the Deutschmark) was to give the monetary union a deflationary bias, to ensure that the nominal stability of the new currency was not put at risk. In practice, it has been showed that the EMU has a strong deflationary bias (see Arestis and Sawyer, 1999). Indeed, as a consequence of the substantial budget consolidations required during the 1990s, economic growth within the euro area was at its lowest since the Second World War, and unemployment at its highest.

After the spring of 1998, when the formal decision was taken regarding which countries would form the monetary union, there was a brief period of relief over fiscal policy. As a result, growth resumed, as in the German case. This expansion only lasted a few years. Then, the requirements of the SGP forced a number of countries, which found themselves in conflict with the 3 per cent rule (deficit to GDP ratio), to restrict their fiscal policy. Furthermore, the European Central Bank (ECB) was tough on monetary policy, because the rate of inflation was continuously above the self-declared target of 2 per cent. When the international boom ended in 2001, a number of EMU countries realized that they could not keep the budget deficit within the narrow limit of 3 per cent of GDP. The automatic stabilizers were much too strong, which initially prevented the recession from deepening too much. But the requirements of the SGP caused the EU countries to reduce their cyclically-adjusted budget deficits. Unless something unforeseeable happens in the international arena, the EMU countries could remain for an extended period in this low growth trap, which, in fact, had destabilized the political process within the EU (Bini Smaghi, 2004, p. 173).[6]

For this very reason, three of the 'old' EU member countries (the United Kingdom, Sweden, and Denmark) have chosen to stay outside the EMU – although they all fulfil the formal convergence criteria. These countries do not need an external nominal anchor, and they consider the restrictions on effective demand much too narrow. It is remarkable that on the issue of joining the EMU, the popular vote was significantly different from the recommendation of the political leadership in Sweden and Denmark (and polls suggest that the same will happen in the United Kingdom if a referendum is called on substituting the pound with the euro). There are no simple explanations for this divide between the people and the politicians, but the divide seems to indicate that Danish and Swedish voters weighted macroeconomic stability with low rates of unemployment, an extended welfare state, and decentralized decision-making higher than to take part in a European currency area with the aim of matching the dollar in the global arena (Jespersen, 2004). The outcome of the 2005 referenda in France and the

Netherlands may be interpreted in the same direction, showing that the population is more worried about securing the welfare systems than to go on improving economic efficiency at any costs.

These are a number of background considerations upon which the EU-10 countries have to decide their future exchange rate arrangements.

The Road Ahead for the EU-10 Countries[7]

The EU was enlarged by 10 countries in May 2004.[8] These countries have 75 millions of inhabitants, which equals 20–25 per cent of the population of the EU-15. Economically, these Eastern and Central European countries are minuscule. Together, they only account for 5 per cent of the EU-15's GDP (with Poland counting for approximately one third of the EU-10's GDP, see Table 12.3). This means that if measured at the actual exchange rates, the average level of income (per capita) is only around 30 per cent of the 'old' member countries (the EU-15). If measured in purchasing-power-adjusted exchange rates, however, the difference in income levels comes closer to 50 per cent (on average). In fact, the income level varies from 77 per cent of the EU-15 level in Cyprus to 40 per cent in the Baltic countries. Although growth rates have been quite impressive in recent years in a number of the new member countries of the EU, unemployment is still very high in them. Countries that are among the worst hit are Poland and Slovakia, which have close to 20 per cent registered unemployed. The Czech Republic and Hungary are doing better regarding unemployment, but have on the other hand huge current account deficits as well as substantial fiscal deficits (see Table 12.3).[9]

Although the EU-10 countries have chosen two different sorts of exchange rate arrangements, all of them are characterized by a substantial deficit on the current account and high unemployment rates (see Table 12.3). These macroeconomic imbalances indicate unambiguously that the exchange rates are overvalued – even in those countries with a free floating exchange rate. This is due in part to a strong inflow of foreign direct investments, but also to the fact that factors other than relative prices matter when currency traders form their expectations.

Poland has had an increasing rate of unemployment and a substantial balance-of-payments deficit for more than ten years. Until 2001, the deficit in the current account was around 5 per cent of GDP, then the exchange rate was made free floating. This gave rise to a subsequent fall of more than 30 per cent in the real effective exchange rate (see Table 12.4) and to an improvement of the current account.

Table 12.3. Key statistics of the new EU member countries

	1. %	2. %	3. %	4. %	5. %/GDP	6. %/GDP
Fixed exchange rate (ERM2) members						
Cyprus	77.5	2.0	4.4	4.0	−4.4	−6.2
Estonia	41.2	4.8	10.0	1.4	−13.7	2.4
Latvia	37.1	7.5	10.5	2.9	−9.1	−1.9
Lithuania	42.7	8.9	12.7	−1.1	−6.1	−1.8
Malta	64.7	0.4	8.2	1.3	−3.4	−9.7
Slovenia	71.3	2.3	6.5	5.7	0.2	−1.9
Floating exchange rate members						
Czech Republic	63.8	4.1	8.3	−0.1	−4.8	−13.0
Hungary	55.1	3.6	6.3	4.7	−7.3	−6.0
Poland	42.7	4.2	18.2	0.7	−1.3	−4.0
Slovakia	48.3	4.8	17.9	8.5	−5.7	−3.7
EU-15	100.0	1.2	9.0	2.0	0.1	−2.4

Notes: 1. national income (PPP) per capita compared to the EU-15 average; 2. real GDP growth rate; 3. unemployment rate; 4. inflation rate; 5. balance of payments, current account; 6. public sector budget deficit. The figures for the smaller countries refer to 2003, those for the larger countries and the EU-15 are OECD projections for 2005 (except national income per capita).

Sources: Danmarks Nationalbank (2004), Table 1 and Figure 3 (based on 'European Commission spring economic forecast 2004-05'); Organisation for Economic Cooperation and Development (2004, 2005).

Slovakia has also adopted a floating exchange rate, but employment is suffering from a highly overvalued currency. It needs a macroeconomic adjustment, probably an experience similar to Poland with a substantial drop in the exchange rate. This seems unavoidable, because the inflow of foreign direct investments has forced the local currency to appreciate much above a sustainable level. Then it is a matter of robustness in the financial sector to prevent this drop to lead to a genuine financial crisis.

In fact, in the Slovakian case it is obvious that a fixed, but adjustable exchange rate regime would have been preferred from a stability point of view (see Table 12.1).

Table 12.4. Development of the effective, real exchange rate

Country	1993	1994	1995	1996	1997	1998
Czech Republic	90.4	98.4	100.0	106.9	104.7	114.4
Hungary	122.9	121.6	100.0	92.0	91.8	84.2
Poland	87.9	93.7	100.0	102.4	102.2	107.5
Slovakia	82.6	89.6	100.0	108.9	127.3	134.0
EU	101.0	97.5	100.0	100.8	91.0	93.8

Country	1999	2000	2001	2002	2003	2004
Czech Republic	116.9	115.0	117.8	125.1	122.4	117.6
Hungary	85.0	77.5	84.8	97.0	101.5	105.7
Poland	101.3	101.1	104.6	94.5	77.6	69.1
Slovakia	131.1	141.0	135.9	138.6	148.0	158.3
EU	92.8	84.0	85.2	89.9	101.1	106.0

Source: Organisation for Economic Cooperation and Development (2004), *Economic Outlook*, December, Table 44.

For the EU-10 countries the effective, real exchange rate is of special importance, since these countries are (except for Poland) highly dependent on foreign trade. Imports and exports account for a larger share of GDP in these countries than they do for the EU-15. Exports are determined by international competitiveness and foreign effective demand. Unfortunately, the effective demand from the EU-15 is held back by low growth, caused by a restrictive fiscal policy (SGP) and a monetary policy directed towards price stability. The new member countries do not benefit from any kind of 'Marshall Aid' like the Western European countries did 50 years ago. They have to rely upon their competitive abilities and on access to the EU market (which has 450 million consumers).

The economic performance of the EU-10 countries is highly exposed to external imbalances. A successful growth path has to build on exchange rate arrangements, where they have gotten rid of external constraints imposed by balance-of-payments imbalances. Otherwise, their foreign debt will pile up, and make interest and dividend payments abroad become a millstone around their necks.

To be true, when the new EU members signed the EU Treaty, they accepted the political goals of the SGP and gave a high priority to full membership in the EMU and the single European currency. This means that they are asked to conform to the convergence criteria. One of these criteria is to join the ERM2 and then not to devaluate the currency at any time in the future. To make these requirements successful, it is important that any country running a persistent deficit in the current account is allowed to make a pre-entry adjustment of the exchange rate to a sustainable level in a long-run perspective.

A sustainable exchange rate should notably take account of:

- the needed structural adjustments,
- an unavoidable excess inflation as a part of the transition process,
- the correction of the actual balance-of-payments deficit,
- any over-valuation due to net inflows of foreign direct investments, and
- slow growth of the EU-15 countries.

Unfortunately, it is rather likely that the ECB will insist on fixing the ERM2 exchange rate at the existing level without considerations to future developments. Using the actual exchange rate (which in fact was the case with the six smaller new EU countries both in June 2004 and May 2005) means eliciting adjustment problems in the future. One could just look at the recent experiences within the EMU, where for instance Greece and Portugal are struggling with unemployment and balance-of-payments deficits. Hence, a strong competitive position within the EU is a necessary condition for these newly industrialized countries to keep growth rates high, especially when the increasing global competitive pressure is taken into consideration.

Ironically, there is a real risk that the earlier the EU-10 countries embark on the road to EMU membership, the more likely it will happen at a long-run unsustainable exchange rate, which might damage the needed structural adjustments owing to increasing balance-of-payments constraints. A lack of effective demand is a recipe for economic and political crises. It is a matter of dispute to what extent the negative outcome of the referendum in France and the Netherlands (in spring 2005) can be referred to the unsuccessful economic development during the EMU period.

One more complicating factor is that the slow economic growth of the EMU countries caused by the SGP has made the balance of payments of the new EU member countries deteriorate even further in 2004–05.

Instability in a Period of Transition

Within any fiat-money economic system, there is a risk of run away inflation. When a government wants to reap a short-term benefit independently of the longer-term costs, borrowing from the banking system at a 'special' rate of interest is a temptation. Avoiding inflation requires a firm hand when the economy is in a process of political transition. The clearing of structural imbalances might be facilitated through changes in relative prices, with the risk of causing the overall price level to move upward more quickly than productivity gains.

In fact, transition economies have some structural similarities with a post-war economy. Relative prices have not adjusted for a long period of time; a number of traditional market institutions are missing – especially in the financial sector. There is a risk that inflation will emerge and build into the market system through a wage–price–wage spiral, fuelled by loose monetary and fiscal policies and not checked by foreign competition. This was the case in Latin America for quite a number of years. It could have been the case of Eastern and Central Europe. The prospect of becoming a member of the EU, however, gave support to the viewpoint that monetary stability should, at least temporarily, be given an overarching priority.

From a post-Keynesian perspective, it makes more sense to aim at balance in the labour market (full employment). Private real investments are instrumental in that respect, and could be supported by a low rate of interest. As we know from macroeconomic theory, a public sector balance cannot be analysed in isolation. A specific target for the public sector budget has to be formulated with respect to the entire macroeconomic system. Otherwise, there is a risk of an inconsistent strategy, where the fulfilment of one specific target hinders other important macroeconomic goals. In this coherent macroeconomic perspective, it becomes obvious why a specific target for the public sector budget easily can represent one more constraint on effective demand, and hence an obstruction to achieve a full employment level of economic activity.[10]

Looking Ahead

The future is politically and economically uncertain. For this reason, it is beyond any doubt that the smallest of the ten new EU countries want to be full members of any EU institution as quickly as possible, and are willing to adopt the single currency. This is mainly a consequence of the past. These countries search for political security, which is found in the core of the EU institutions. Furthermore, these small open economies are so small that they cannot rock the EMU boat even if they will continue to be affected by macroeconomic imbalances.

But the EU institutions were originally designed to fit a small number of rather homogenous countries. At the time of writing, there are 25 countries members of the EU, and within a foreseeable future another eight countries might become members. Although these latter countries are all rather poor and less developed economies, they could, within ten years (or even less), conform to the Copenhagen criteria making EU membership possible. In that case, the diversity within the EU will have increased even further. It would then probably be more correct to speak, at least for a while, about disintegration rather than integration. This development would indeed raise the question of an EU with several speeds of integration and in different dimensions. In practice, this debate about how fast and how far the euro area can be enlarged has already started.

In the previous section, we argued that the macroeconomic stability of transition economies requires that effective demand should grow in tandem with potential output. This can be supported by an active *national* policy making based on the following principles:

- Direct fiscal policy towards full employment, in particular by matching the structural budget with the private sector's imbalance between savings and real investments.
- Prevent the rate of interest (and share prices) to drift too far away from the fundamentals (high employment and low inflation); when needed, reintroduce international capital controls until macroeconomic balance is established through an active monetary policy.
- Ensure a current account balance (or surplus) by a fixed, adjustable, and slightly undervalued exchange rate *à la* Bretton Woods.

Now, as long as new-consensus macroeconomics is the 'mainstream' economics within the EU, macroeconomic stability is identified, as we mentioned above, with a balanced (so-called sound) budget, strict monetary policy, and fixed exchange rates, without any consideration to employment and balance-of-payments problems.

If the EU transition economies decide quite quickly to become members of the EMU, they run the risk of being caught in a 'mainstream economics' trap. Indeed, they might initially gain from a lower real rate of interest and an unlimited access to foreign capital. This is a real temptation in the short run; but it represents a risk in the longer run, if the rate of inflation in these countries continues to stay above the EMU average level. Some European countries have in varying degrees experienced such a development, where the difference in price levels has accumulated to such an extent that the foreign competing sectors are hit hardly. There is no easy solution to this problem within the EMU. Without an extended EU budget and a much higher labour mobility across borders, it is difficult to imagine that national differences can be equalized within the foreseeable future.

CONCLUSION

Within the EU the arguments of new-consensus macroeconomics have hitherto dominated. In this respect, it is often argued that a monetary union with low inflation and balanced public budgets is a precondition for 'growth and stability'. Within the general equilibrium model it is easily shown that monetary control and a balanced budget are the best and most reliable instruments to secure growth, stability, and high employment.

The history of the EMU is somewhat different. Ever since it was designed in 1992 and implemented in 1999, economic growth has been unprecedentedly low and unemployment equally high in a number of countries. This development has, of course, questioned the relevance of the theoretical arguments behind the EMU. It is hardly an exaggeration to say that the predictions made by the new-consensus economists about the macroeconomic gains from the EMU have not yet materialized. A number of question marks with respect to the design of many European economic institutions have been set more and more frequently.

As an alternative, post-Keynesian macroeconomics emphasizes the constraints on effective demand as a major cause of this disappointing development. The design of the EMU process has a number of built-in deflationary biases. Furthermore, the new-consensus macroeconomics confuses macroeconomic targets with policy instruments. The public sector budget, the exchange rate, and the rate of interest are indeed instruments. Growth, inflation, and income distribution are the true targets. To make an instrument a target is counterproductive for economic policy making. As we have shown, the specific limit of the public sector budget became quickly an obstacle to macroeconomic stability. A fixed exchange rate can be useful as an instrument to break expectations of continued high inflation; but to make a monetary union a target of its own is an example of confusing aims with means to prosperity.

Further, to subdue the discretionary power of national fiscal policy by forcing all member states into a one-sized straightjacket of convergence criteria and fiscal control is one more example of misunderstood homogeneity. EU countries are rather different in structures and in political preferences. A common budget rule means in reality very different constraints on effective demand, which in the end might increase diversities within the EU and cause disintegration. This process will be enforced if the EU-10 countries prematurely join the EMU.

With regard to the EU-10 countries, a better macroeconomic policy would be to release them from the severe ERM2 requirement of a fixed exchange rate, recalling the history of the European Monetary System in the early 1990s. By contrast, an expansionary economic policy undertaken by the rich EMU countries, combined with substantial aid to the new members – like the 'Marshall Aid' – could much better facilitate the still needed structural adjustments. Such a 'helping-your-neighbour' policy would – as it did in the early 1950s – make effective demand higher and at the same time reduce the balance-of-payments constraint. Without doubt this extra foreign aid would increase economic growth in the EU-10 countries, which by itself could reduce public budget deficits, and makes the recipient countries spend more on imports, when the balance-of-payments constraint is relaxed.

In addition, it might be easier for the new EU member countries to reduce inflation rates, if they could participate at a later stage in the ERM2 at a *sustainable*, but still adjustable, exchange rate. For instance, the exchange rate arrangement could be quite similar to the Bretton Woods agreement, but with an expanded band of fluctuation, for instance ±15 per cent, where all countries (surplus as well as deficit countries) have the right and duty of adjusting the central rate whenever it is necessary according to some objective criteria.

Last, but not least, according to post-Keynesian macroeconomic theory the EU Treaty should be redrafted with regard to the role of the ECB. The macroeconomic reality does not conform to the abstract equilibrium model of new-consensus macroeconomics, which supports the construction behind the ECB. Post-Keynesians have shown empirically that there is no direct link between money supply (which is endogenously determined and cannot be controlled) and inflation. In fact, monetary policy can affect effective demand, real investments, and later on growth and employment. To ask the central bank to secure price stability is a contradiction in terms, because it has no instrument to control inflation really. In the real world, monetary policy (like fiscal and exchange rate policies) should be pursued as an integral part of a *national* policy of each individual EU country, which undertakes it in respect of the other member countries and of the EU as a whole.

NOTES

1. Davidson (2002a) gives a standard presentation of the post-Keynesian views on international economics.
2. The new consensus school considers its analytical framework of general equilibrium models based on microeconomic foundations and rational expectations as ideology-free. This is what it calls 'economics proper'. Therefore analytical deviations from this 'objective' model are caused by ideology or ignorance. This claim of ideology-free theory with regard to the construct of the EMU is challenged by a number of contributions in Moss (2004).
3. Employment in Germany increased from 37.2 million persons in 1997 to 38.9 million persons in 2001. See www.laborsta.ilo.org.
4. Davidson (2002b) elaborates on a proposal for a re-establishment of the Bretton Woods system in a modern design.
5. These countries have a population between 500,000 and 3 million inhabitants.
6. In March 2005, the EU Finance Ministers decided to pursue a less strict interpretation of the SGP in the future. In practice, this implies that fiscal policy in the future will not have to be tightened as much as originally required by the European Commission; but the upper limit of 3 per cent is still unchanged.
7. De Grauwe and Schnabl (2003) put forward a balanced view on political and economic considerations.
8. According to the EU enlargement plan, Rumania and Bulgaria will become members in January 2007.
9. At first, one may think that there are some similarities with the US economy; but the real difference is that the United States is the largest economy and the strongest political power in the world, which in any event remains very attractive for foreign investors.
10. This misunderstanding is now so well established that for instance the weekly magazine *The Economist* uses the phrase 'instability and stagnation pact' as a characteristic of the Stability and Growth Pact.

REFERENCES

Arestis, P. (1992), *The Post-Keynesian Approach to Economics: An Alternative Analysis of Economic Theory and Policy*, Aldershot, UK and Brookfield, USA: Edward Elgar.

Arestis, P. and M. Sawyer (1999), 'The deflationary consequences of the single currency', in M. Baimbridge, B. Burkitt and P. Whyman (eds), *The Impact of the Euro: Debating Britain's Future*, Basingstoke: Macmillan, 100–112.

Arestis, P. and M. Sawyer (2003), 'Macroeconomic policies of the EMU: theoretical underpinnings and challenges', *International Papers in Political Economy*, **10** (1), 1–54.

Bini Smaghi, L. (2004), 'What went wrong with the Stability and Growth Pact?', in P.B. Sørensen (ed.), *Monetary Union in Europe: Historical Perspectives and Prospects for the Future*, Copenhagen: DJØF Publishing, 167–85.

Danmarks Nationalbank (2004), *EUs udvidelse 2004*, 2. kvartal, 21–32.

Davidson, P. (1997), 'The *General Theory* in an open economy context', in G.C. Harcourt and P.A. Riach (eds), *A 'Second Edition' of The General Theory*, London and New York: Routledge, vol. 2, 102–30.

Davidson, P. (2002a), *Financial Markets, Money and the Real World*, Cheltenham,

UK and Northampton, MA, USA: Edward Elgar.

Davidson, P. (2002b), 'Fixed vs. flexible exchange rates, economic growth and international liquidity', paper presented at a conference at Downing College, Cambridge, April.

De Grauwe, P. (2005), *The Economics of Monetary Union*, Oxford: Oxford University Press, sixth edition.

De Grauwe, P. and G. Schnabl (2003), 'Exchange rate regimes and macroeconomic stability in Central and Eastern Europe', Katholieke Universiteit Leuven, Centre for Economic Studies, mimeo.

Frydman, R. and M. Goldberg (2004), 'Limiting exchange rate swings in a world of imperfect knowledge', in P.B. Sørensen (ed.), *Monetary Union in Europe: Historical Perspectives and Prospects for the Future*, Copenhagen: DJØF Publishing, 35–49.

Harvey, J.T. (1999), 'Exchange rates: volatility and misalignment in the post-Bretton Woods era', in J. Deprez and J.T. Harvey (eds), *Foundations of International Economics: Post-Keynesian Perspectives*, London and New York: Routledge, 200–11.

Jespersen, J. (2004), 'The Stability Pact: a macroeconomic straitjacket!', in J. Ljungberg (ed.), *The Price of the Euro*, Basingstoke: Palgrave Macmillan, 45–58.

McCombie, J.S.L. (2003), 'Balance-of-payments-constrained economic growth', in J.E. King (ed.), *The Elgar Companion to Post Keynesian Economics*, Cheltenham, UK and Northampton, MA, USA: Edward Elgar, 15–20.

Moss, B.H. (ed.) (2004), *Monetary Union in Crisis: The European Union as a Neo-Liberal Construction*, Basingstoke: Palgrave Macmillan.

Organisation for Economic Cooperation and Development (2004), *Economic Outlook*, Paris: Organisation for Economic Cooperation and Development, June, no. 75.

Organisation for Economic Cooperation and Development (2005), *Economic Outlook*, Paris: Organisation for Economic Cooperation and Development, June, no. 77.

Rochon, L.-P. and M. Vernengo (2000), 'Disentangling the confusion: exchange rate regimes, capital controls and the revenge of the rentiers', *Challenge*, November–December, 76–92.

Saint-Paul, G. (2004), 'Why are European countries diverging in their unemployment experience?', *Journal of Economic Perspectives*, **18** (4), 49–68.

Sørensen, P.B. and H.J. Whitta-Jacobsen (2004), *Introducing Advanced Macroeconomics: Growth and Business Cycles*, London and New York: McGraw-Hill Education.

Index